Changing Futures

The Influence of Reading Recovery in the United States

MARIBETH C. SCHMITT
Purdue University

BILLIE J. ASKEW
Texas Woman's University

IRENE C. FOUNTAS
Lesley University

CAROL A. LYONS
The Ohio State University

GAY SU PINNELL
The Ohio State University

Reading Recovery® Council
of North America

To Marie Clay,
who by "simply sailing in a new direction"
changed futures for countless children and teachers.

Reading Recovery Council of North America
400 W. Wilson Bridge Road, Suite 250
Worthington, OH 43085
www.readingrecovery.org

Library of Congress Control Number: 2005926278
ISBN 0-9763071-1-1

Technical editor: Debbie L. Bowman
Production and cover design: Vicki S. Fox

Printed in the United States of America on acid-free paper

TABLE OF CONTENTS

Changing Futures:
The Influence of Reading Recovery
in the United States

(continued)

INTRODUCTION

The real voyage of discovery consists not in seeking
new landscapes but in having new eyes.

— Marcel Proust —

Proust's words might describe our journeys over the last two decades. Through Reading Recovery, we learned to look at children's literacy development with new eyes and in completely new ways that were different from our previous learning and experience. Reading Recovery as a literacy intervention has made a difference for more than a million children in the United States and countless thousands more across three continents and five countries. All of this was possible because a New Zealand professor interested in children's literacy development wondered if things could be different for struggling learners if we looked at them with new eyes, as learners on individual paths of literacy learning with unique strengths and challenges. At that time, Marie Clay could not have imagined her work would influence teachers and researchers across the world for decades to come. This book provides a comprehensive description of Reading Recovery.

In *Changing Futures: The Influence of Reading Recovery in the United States*, we provide a history of Reading Recovery from the beginning when Marie Clay questioned what was possible for struggling learners. Also included are extensive explanations of the lesson framework, assessment and monitoring, professional development, and implementation issues within systems and schools.

The principles of learning that derive from the theoretical base for Reading Recovery precede a discussion regarding the necessity of early intervention as a preventative measure against failure. Programmatic evaluation procedures are clarified and the extensive research that documents the effectiveness of the intervention and the continued student progress is carefully presented.

It is necessary to emphasize that *Changing Futures* is a book about Reading Recovery in the United States. Various aspects of Reading Recovery are different in other countries and we wish not to confuse the readers. For example, often the terminology is different, the length of children's interventions varies according to school calendars and allows for carryover from year to year, and the administrative structures might be organized differently.

In addition, we have chosen not to repeat the name of the reconstruction of Reading Recovery in Spanish, Descubriendo la Lectura (DLL), every time we say Reading Recovery so that the text will read more smoothly. We remind the reader that the inclusion of DLL is implied whenever Reading Recovery is mentioned unless DLL needs to be included separately for clarity. Also, readers may notice redundancy of topics throughout the book, but be assured it is intentional so that each chapter can stand alone with optional references to other chapters. We felt this would allow readers to use selected chapters as comprehensive descriptions of a topic when needed.

We wish to thank the members of the Reading Recovery network of professionals and partners who contributed to our efforts to make this book possible, especially RRCNA Communications Director Dr. Marsha Studebaker. Her tireless efforts to track down information for us and to keep us on track were invaluable. Director of Advocacy Lucy Gettman provided information for the policy chapter and National Data Evaluation Center Director Francisco Gómez-Bellengé contributed to the chapter on programmatic evaluation of Reading Recovery. Many university trainers contributed information that was extremely helpful to the overall project, particularly the international trainers who provided information and feedback on the historical chapter.

In 2004 Marie Clay received the National Reading Conference Distinguished Scholar Lifetime Achievement Award. In her award address, "Simply by Sailing in a New Direction You Could Enlarge the World," Clay (2004) described her journey of discovery and learning:

> To leave no child behind in 1976, I thought I might try to sail in an unknown direction to get those children back to a normal trajectory. (p. 60)
>
> I have enjoyed sailing in new directions in the company of staunch supporters who have chosen to navigate the same route. (p. 66)

Without question the five of us have enjoyed being shipmates on the journey with Marie Clay. With our new eyes, we have seen futures change for children, teachers, and the broader educational community. And this Proustian voyage of discovery continues as we work collaboratively with colleagues inside and outside of Reading Recovery. We invite you to sail with us to make a difference in the futures of children. We hope *Changing Futures: The Influence of Reading Recovery in the United States* will inform your efforts.

CHAPTER 1

An Introduction
to Reading Recovery

One simply takes the child from where he is to somewhere else.

— Marie Clay —

Children who are having extreme difficulty learning to read and write deserve to have educators make every effort possible to ensure their success. Reading Recovery meets the challenge of such an effort. The early literacy intervention is designed to reduce the numbers of children in the low end of the distribution and the costs of these learners to the educational system. Serving as a safety net within a good instructional school literacy program, Reading Recovery is a part of a strong comprehensive approach for bringing all students to literacy.

Reading Recovery is a short-term early intervention designed to support classroom instruction for the lowest-achieving children in the first grade—those having difficulty learning to read and write. Children meet individually for 30 minutes daily with a specially trained teacher for an average of 12 to 20 weeks. During this relatively short-term instructional intervention, children make faster-than-average (i.e., accelerated) progress that permits them to catch up to their peers and continue to work on their own within an average group setting in the regular classroom program. Results indicate that Reading Recovery meets the challenge of closing the gap early, before a cycle of failure commences (Gómez-Bellengé, Rodgers, & Wang, 2004).

Reading Recovery, an exemplar of the model of prevention of reading failure described by Pianta (1990), represents a secondary prevention strategy for children who do not respond fully to a primary prevention strategy such as quality preschools and good classroom teaching. The effectiveness of Reading Recovery for struggling readers in the context of a comprehensive school approach to prevention is well-documented (see Allington & Walmsley, 1995; Crevola & Hill, 1998; Pikulski, 1994; Wasik & Slavin, 1993; and other chapters in this volume).

Several components contribute to Reading Recovery's effectiveness within a school system: the teaching of children, teacher professional development, evaluation and accountability, and implementation matters in schools and districts. These topics will be introduced in the following sections of this introductory chapter and more fully explained in later chapters of the book.

The Teaching of Children

Reading Recovery was designed to serve the lowest-achieving children in first grade because they are the least likely to be able to succeed in the classroom with whole-group or even small-group instruction. There are at least two rationales for taking only the lowest-achieving children in Reading Recovery. First, at entry to the program, the rate and level of progress cannot be reliably predicted for any child. Therefore, the most extreme cases are selected, and the program serves as a period of diagnostic teaching. Second, if the lowest achievers are not selected, the school will never clear the children with literacy difficulties from its rolls, and these children will return to haunt the program in subsequent years. To be in compliance with the standards and principles underlying Reading Recovery implementation, schools must serve the lowest children first.

The design of Reading Recovery also calls for it to be a one-to-one intervention: the teacher works from the individual child's knowledge and responses. When children are taught in a group, the teacher has to choose a compromise path, a next-appropriate teaching move for the group. To get results with the lowest achievers, the teacher must work with the particular (and very limited) response repertoire of a particular child using what that child knows as the context within which to introduce him or her to novel things. The goal of Reading Recovery is to prevent literacy problems and to serve as supplementary instruction that is not intended to supplant the literacy program of the classroom.

Highly skilled teachers provide the one-to-one instruction for these children who are at the most risk of failure. Through the Reading Recovery professional training program, these teachers develop an understanding of literacy processes and literacy acquisition. They learn how to observe children closely and how to decide when it is most effective to introduce new learning, as well as when and how to scaffold learning support. They are capable of providing individually designed lessons that follow each child's unique path to literacy learning. The lesson framework will be fully described in Chapter 7.

Reading Recovery lessons include explicit attention to the five essential components of reading instruction identified by the National Reading Panel and incorporated into Reading First of the No Child Left Behind Act: phonics, phonemic awareness, fluency, comprehension, and vocabulary. Each lesson includes reading, writing, and working with letters and sounds. Children develop phonemic awareness by learning to say words slowly and connect them in writing words for their generated story. They learn how to look at print and use the distinctive features of letters, to discover how words work including the use of relationships between letters and letter clusters and sounds, and how to problem-solve on novel text as the teacher uses what the child knows to build new understandings. The teacher demonstrates problem-solving strategies and creates instructional situations that allow children to take on strategies as a way to independently generate meaning from text.

A Reading Recovery lesson consists of

- reading familiar stories,
- reading a story that was read for the first time the day before while the teacher observes and records strategic processing for the purpose of cutting-edge teaching,
- working with words and letters using magnetic letters,
- composing and writing a message,
- assembling the message as a puzzle from its parts, and
- reading a new book that presents an appropriate challenge for the student.

With this specially designed instruction by a highly qualified teacher, the vast majority of children develop a self-extending system or a way to continue to get better at reading each time they read. In other words, children need to have independent problem-solving strategies for making all the information sources match as they read or generate meaningful texts, and the more opportunities they have to orchestrate the strategies, the better readers they become.

For children who participate in Reading Recovery lessons, there are two possible outcomes, both of them representing positive actions that benefit the children. The first is that the child no longer requires extra help and is able to make progress in reading and writing with good classroom instruction. This is referred to as having their program *discontinued*. The second possible outcome is that a recommendation is made for additional assessment. Appropriate school staff members collaborate to plan future learning opportunities for the child.

Even children who do not make the accelerated progress needed (i.e., they do not catch up with peers or meet criterion measures) make progress in Reading Recovery. Moreover, positive subsequent action is initiated to help such children continue to make progress. Educators learn much about the child through the Reading Recovery diagnostic processes and take informed steps to recommend future actions to support the child. Reading Recovery evaluation data show that the large majority of children served in the instructional intervention experience the first outcome; a smaller proportion are in the second category. Instead of waiting or allowing children to struggle, educators in Reading Recovery assume responsibility that something positive is going to happen for every child coming into the program. A secondary outcome of the process is that people work together to identify children who might be at risk and provide the necessary extra support at a critical time. There is recognition that everyone is responsible for every child.

Professional Development Model

If we can focus our energies on providing this generation of teachers with the kinds of knowledge and skills they need to help students succeed we will have made an enormous contribution to America's future. (Darling-Hammond, 1996, p. 194)

A recent large-scale study revealed that every additional dollar spent on raising teacher quality netted greater student achievement gains than did any other use of school resources (Darling-Hammond, 1996). Simply put, few educational programs offer a more powerful teacher education process than Reading Recovery with a full academic year of intensive training, where participants receive graduate-level university credit for their learning. This extensive training and ongoing professional development are hallmarks of Reading Recovery and contribute to its unprecedented success across the world.

According to Alvermann (1990), Reading Recovery training is best characterized as an inquiry-oriented model, where teachers construct their understandings via observation, reflection, and discussion using live case examples where they can build a base for teacher decision making. Reading Recovery training sessions involve extensive use of a one-way glass through which teachers watch each other work with children as they put their observations and analyses into words. In their conversations, they articulate their questions and dilemmas. The process challenges assumptions about children's learning; teachers think critically about the art of teaching. According to Clay (1997), they "need to become more flexible and tentative, to observe constantly and alter their assumptions in line with the behaviour they can observe as children work. They need to challenge their own thinking continually" (p. 63).

Rigorous and intensive training allows teachers to develop a repertoire of actions and decisions and then to adjust children's lessons to make the most of their knowledge base and strengths. Clay (1997) cites educator P. David Pearson's comments about the implication of teacher education in Reading Recovery:

Reading Recovery has managed to operationalize that vague notion that teachers ought to reflect on their own practice. That behind the glass play by play analysis and the collegial debriefing with the teacher after her teaching session represent some of the best teacher education I have witnessed in my 28 year history in the field. (p. 663)

The training model comprises a three-tiered structure of university training centers, teacher training sites, and schools to support training and implementation. Each level will be described below and more fully covered in Chapter 8.

Teacher Leader Training

The teacher leader training process begins with an intensive series of post-masters graduate-level courses at a university where a center has been established to support the training of teacher leaders. The training model involves

- a study of the teaching procedures for working with students across the course of a year,
- an in-depth study of the theoretical foundations upon which the procedures are based,
- comprehensive study of seminal and recent theories and research focusing on the reading and writing processes,
- training in the process of working with adult learners, and
- training in management and administrative services required to successfully implement and operate the program.

Following successful completion of the training year, teacher leaders begin to train teachers who will work with the lowest-achieving first-grade readers.

Teacher leaders continue to work with children as long as they are involved in their role as a way to enrich their understandings of how children learn and to contribute to their staff development roles. They "represent what may be a new role in education, the *practicing* professional teacher educator" (Lyons et al., 1993, p. 13).

Teacher leaders are selected for this role by a district or consortium of districts that are interested in establishing a teacher training site in the area or need to add or replace a teacher leader at an existing site.

Teacher Training

Training at the teacher level is also a yearlong commitment where teachers enroll in graduate-level courses taught by a certified teacher leader. They learn to administer the tasks published in *An Observation Survey of Early Literacy Achievement* (Clay, 2002) to identify children's strengths and knowledge and then, with their new perspective, how to work with children where they are in their development. Through clinical and peer-critiquing experiences that involve teaching observations behind a one-way glass, teachers learn to observe and describe student and teacher behaviors and develop skills in making moment-to-moment decisions to inform instruction.

It is important to note that although becoming a Reading Recovery teacher may be a professional decision made by individual teachers as part of their private career goals, Reading Recovery is a systemic intervention conducted as a schoolwide process, and Reading Recovery teachers are selected by appropriate personnel within a school site to serve in that role.

Trainers of Teacher Leaders

Literacy professors from more than 20 universities in North America oversee the professional development process as well as the implementation of Reading Recovery in the United States. These professors have completed a yearlong educational program to become trainers of teacher leaders at an approved university for training of trainers. According to Lyons et al. (1993), "Teaching the teacher-leader class requires a complex range of skills that include the teaching of children; the ability to present theoretical material; and the knowledge of Clay's theory and current research in language development, reading, writing, comprehension, spelling, and educational change" (p. 13).

The trainers "learn to work with children, be instructors of teachers and teacher leaders, and study the range of leadership roles needed to provide central support for the dynamic mechanisms of the project in their state or region" (p. 13). If they are involved in the clinical training of teacher leaders, they continue to teach children, which Lyons and her colleagues (1993) acknowledge is necessary to maintain a connection to the fundamental level of education in Reading Recovery.

Training at all levels continues after the initial year, with a built-in renewal system to update Reading Recovery educators on new ways to be effective in their work. A body of research indicates that Reading Recovery teacher training has a powerful and long-lasting impact on the teachers who participate. The skills and knowledge teachers develop in Reading Recovery contribute to their ongoing learning and result in an impact on children across time. There is also evidence that the communication between Reading Recovery teachers and classroom teachers supports literacy teaching in a school. In a study of change, classroom teachers cited the benefits of collaborating about individual children with a knowledgeable colleague (Blackburn, 1995). The investment in the professional skills of Reading Recovery teachers, then, appears to go beyond their work with individual children.

Evaluation and Accountability

Hallmarks of Reading Recovery in the United States are the established evaluation and accountability systems. Unparalleled in scale, participating schools have collected data on every single child served since 1984, when Reading Recovery was established in the United States. Results are reported to the National Data Evaluation Center (NDEC) located at The Ohio State University. The process is explained fully in Chapter 9. The national database has informed Reading Recovery research, made Reading Recovery accountable to schools and funding sources, and informed teaching and management decisions in schools and districts. Such rigorous data collection provides strong evidence of program effectiveness and affords ample documentation for decision making, which is integral to quality assurance of the program. The evaluation methodology is standardized nationally and follows accepted principles of evaluation research. Annual technical reports of Reading Recovery results in the United States are available through NDEC.

In addition, the collection of data on every child allows for an additional type of evaluation research: replication. The program replicates its effect at the level of individual subjects using systematic and simultaneous replication methodology. "Replication is important in all sciences because it is through replication that scientists verify research results" (Frymier, Barber, Gansneder, & Robertson, 1989). Reading Recovery replicates its effect at the level of individual subjects, and the same results are achieved again and again with different children, different teachers, and in different places.

Altogether, if a result is seen consistently across time and across locations, we can predict with some confidence that the results will occur. Repeatedly producing the same results with different students across different settings increases confidence in an intervention providing substantial evidence of the effectiveness of Reading Recovery tutoring. Since 1984, data have been reported to the NDEC on more than 1.4 million children with remarkably similar results year after year. Stakeholders, then, have substantive information about Reading Recovery program outcomes to use in decision making. What other widely disseminated programs can produce 20 or more years of data on every child served in the program to document results?

In addition to evaluation research as an accountability system, standards and guidelines for every aspect of the innovation, including professional development and implementation factors, have been developed by the leadership and set forth in *Standards and Guidelines of Reading Recovery in the United States* (2004). These standards and guidelines both inform and support the many professionals responsible for establishing and maintaining Reading Recovery sites across the United States. Reading Recovery professionals understand and apply the rationales underlying the standards and guidelines (see Chapter 9).

Reading Recovery's consistency and integrity are protected by a trademark granted by founder Marie M. Clay to The Ohio State University in the United States. Permission to use the trademark is granted royalty-free and is contingent upon compliance with the published standards and guidelines.

Implementation Issues

In education, true innovation is difficult to achieve. Too often, innovations appear to come and go with little lasting impact. Any time an innovation is adopted, it inevitably means there must be adjustments in the system. In the case of Reading

Recovery, for example, educators had to adjust to a number of different routines and procedures by providing for

- one-to-one teaching time and space,
- a yearlong initial training period as well as ongoing training of teachers,
- a special facility so that observation of lessons could take place, and
- transportation of children for lessons behind the one-way glass.

All of these requirements meant changes in the usual way of doing things.

It is true that most innovations fail; that is, they have no lasting effect. When innovations are introduced into a system, one of three things is likely to happen:

1. Because of the difficulties involved in change, the educational innovation is adopted but is rejected before a true test of its worthiness is made.
2. The innovation is adopted in a half-hearted manner so that the characteristics that provided the benefit are watered down or eliminated altogether.
3. The innovation is adopted but after a short time is itself changed so that the system is accommodated.

When one thinks of the possibilities listed above, it is easy to see why innovations vary so widely from place to place or have no lasting power at all.

Assuring that Reading Recovery remains a successful, high-quality innovation is no different than working toward that goal with any other intervention. Achieving positive results for Reading Recovery students depends not only on instruction, but also upon a school environment that supports efficient operations. Smart administrators protect their investment by assuring a high-quality implementation of Reading Recovery in their context.

Consideration must be given to the processes involved in opening up the existing system to accommodate and support this innovation. First, it is important to lay a strong foundation for success by fully understanding the innovation and considering what it will accomplish as a service that concentrates on first grade, as in what Reading Recovery is and is not in Table 1.1.

Then it is important to have a specific plan for implementing Reading Recovery over time. The benefits will be evident immediately as children make accelerated progress even when teachers are in their training year. However, long-term planning is required to realize the full potential and to institutionalize the innovation. When there are enough Reading Recovery teachers to serve all the lowest-performing first graders, schools find that the tail end of the distribution curve is removed so that nearly all children can achieve through good classroom instruction.

Overall, well-planned implementation is critical to program success and includes such factors as those described below and more fully covered in Chapter 12.

Shared Ownership

In order to sustain an innovation, basic understandings regarding the purposes, rationales, and processes of the innovation must be shared. In addition to shared understandings, ownership must be felt by the stakeholders who collaborate to provide the structures for successful implementation within the system. All stakeholders must be perceived to have a responsibility for the success of each child served.

Level of Coverage

Each school or system must determine the number of children needing the service. A school or system has reached full coverage or full implementation when there is sufficient Reading Recovery teacher time to serve all children defined as needing the service in the school or in the system. Systems move to achieve full-

Table 1.1 What Reading Recovery Is and Is Not	
WHAT READING RECOVERY *IS*	**WHAT READING RECOVERY *IS NOT***
• one-to-one individual teaching	• group or classroom instruction
• provided by a specially trained, certified teacher	• delivered by volunteers or paraprofessionals
• ongoing professional development for teachers	• a program you buy to put in place for teachers
• adopted as a school initiative by the school staff	• one person's mandated program
• supplementary to good classroom teaching	• the only reading instruction a child receives and also not a substitute for good classroom teaching
• for lowest-achieving first-grade readers only	• a comprehensive program to improve literacy achievement in all grades
• data-driven teaching to continuously monitor children's progress	• a program that labels children through extended testing for disabilities
• a short-term early intervention that prevents further difficulties in literacy	• a long-term service for children
• a long-term school commitment for lowest-achieving first graders	• a quick fix

coverage over several years. It is only at the stage of full coverage that a dramatic decrease in the number of children with literacy difficulties can be realized.

Partial implementation is a temporary condition and a period that reveals all the implementation difficulties. It is a time for persistence and a focus on individual success stories. As schools move toward full coverage, many problems—such as determining how to meet the needs of the children who need Reading Recovery but cannot receive the service—disappear. Flexible staffing plans support full implementation. For example, schools with a significant number of trained Reading Recovery teachers have the capacity to serve all needy children within a flexible staffing framework.

Informed Administration

As with any school or system commitment, the role of the administrator is critical. In Reading Recovery, the system-level administrators and the school-level administrators must be knowledgeable and collaborative in working with all stakeholders on behalf of the children needing the intervention service.

Continuous Attention to Quality in Training and Teaching

As stated earlier, Reading Recovery is an investment in teachers and teacher training. Selection of the highest-quality teacher leaders and teachers is essential for a successful program. Initial training at both levels must be strong. An important feature of Reading Recovery is the ongoing nature of training through ongoing professional development. The quality of the professional development sessions will also impact the success of the program.

A high-quality implementation demands the full attention of the teacher leader. Administrators are cautioned to refrain from stretching the roles of the Reading Recovery teacher leaders and teachers beyond their training expertise and beyond their ability to continue to perform their primary role successfully. When this happens, program results may suffer.

Sustained Focus on the Goal of Reading Recovery and its Attainment

All stakeholders must retain the focus of Reading Recovery: to reduce dramatically the number of children unable to work within average levels within their classrooms. There is a temptation to focus on other worthy goals that may interfere with the primary goal of supporting successful performance of children.

Examination of Data to Uncover and Solve Problems

Each school and each system involved in Reading Recovery will benefit from a careful examination of student outcomes. This exploration will document the program's effectiveness as well as identify problem areas in implementation that need to be addressed.

Implementation is important in any venture. "The failure to institutionalize an innovation and build it into the normal structures and practices of the organization underlies the disappearance of many reforms" (Fullan & Miles, 1992, p. 748). "In too many cases, where ideas deserve consideration, the processes through which they were implemented were self-defeating " (Sarason, 1991, p. 99).

In Reading Recovery, factors related to establishing a new program in a school and district context are not ignored. Although implementation issues are still being examined and refined, a structured process exists to assist local educators in implementing a consistent, high-quality program.

A Collaborative Mission: Literacy Opportunities for All Children

Bringing all children to literacy in the first years of schooling is not an easy task. It requires collaboration among professional educators with respect to good classroom teaching and safety nets for children who need additional literacy support. Reading Recovery professionals are interested in working with educators and researchers who share the mission of acting in the interests of children to alter their paths of progress and change their futures.

The safety net known as Reading Recovery represents a partnership—a concentrated, continuous, united effort in which teachers, administrators, parents, and policy makers work together to change the status of low-achieving children in literacy. In an ongoing process of educational redesign, Reading Recovery partners continue to evaluate the program by collecting data on every child served, analyzing program strengths, and making recommendations for improvement.

In his book on redesigning education, Nobel Prize-winning physicist and educational reformer Kenneth G. Wilson (Wilson & Daviss, 1994) uses Reading Recovery as a model for the process. He comments: "Reading Recovery offers United States education its first real demonstration of the power of a process combining research, development (including ongoing teacher education), marketing, and technical support in an orchestrated system of change" (p. 76). He suggests that in three ways, Reading Recovery can encourage the process of educational redesign:

1. It proves that a well-designed educational program can be replicated among teachers and schools across a wide array of locations and cultures and still yield uniformly superior results.

2. It indicates that investing money and effort in educational design can earn dramatic rewards—if it is made in a properly researched and designed program that offers thorough teacher training and support.

3. It shows that when educators find a program that meets these two criteria and proves that it can earn a good result, schools are willing to make its adoption a budget priority.

According to Wilson and Daviss (1994), Reading Recovery is the best evidence yet of the direct link between good design and educational excellence.

All educators acknowledge that change is hard work. Anything that tackles the complex problems of today's literacy education is going to be difficult. It means that the educational community must work together to solve problems in a constructive way, collaborating across groups and with all stakeholders to build broad ownership in a shared goal of literacy opportunities for all children. Reading Recovery professionals welcome the challenge to make these literacy opportunities a reality by building partnerships with all who share this goal. This book represents an effort to encourage those already involved and to invite others to join in the partnership in any way they can to assure literacy for all children.

CHAPTER 2

United States Reading Recovery
in a Rich Historical
and International Context

Clay's comments regarding the central tenets of Reading Recovery may very well reflect the reason for its growth and endurance across time and place:

> Central tenets of Reading Recovery have been tentativeness, flexibility, and problem-solving. These qualities have surfaced in the ways in which the teaching addresses individual patterns of strengths and weakness in children, and in how the teachers are training to design lesson series for in-dividual children, and again in the solutions people have found for implementing Reading Recovery. Somehow Reading Recovery professionals have learned how to hold fast to principles, practices and rationales while at the same time allowing for variability in the educational practices and beliefs, and change over time in society. (Clay, 2001, p. 298)

Although the focus of this book is on the influence of Reading Recovery in U.S. education systems, its rich historical and international contexts contribute to its quality as a force in literacy learning and instruction across the world.

The history of Reading Recovery reveals an account of a modest beginning (focused research observations of one teacher "in a lean-to behind an old house in Wynyard Street" [Clay, 1997, p. 658]), to extensive growth, compelling research, and unprecedented success as both an early literacy intervention for children and a professional development model for teachers that reaches across the world. Its story involves the dedication of countless individuals whose vision, dedication, and laudable efforts have effected systemic change in schools and districts, demonstrating that an early literacy intervention can foster literacy success for children (Doyle, 2000).

It is also a story of successful partnerships forged across international boundaries and academic settings by collaborators—researchers and practitioners—who share the same mission. The strength of these partnerships lends credence to the integrity and endurance of Reading Recovery in any setting (Doyle, 2000). The historical description in this chapter highlights the development of an international network of professionals whose contributions have made Reading Recovery historically stronger and more enduring for the future, providing a strong foundation for a systemic model of literacy teaching and learning.

Implementation of Reading Recovery Across the World

Marie Clay's interest in early literacy began when she was a lecturer and doctoral student at the University of Auckland, New Zealand. She asked the question, "Can we see the process of learning to read going off-course close to the onset of instruction?" Her doctoral dissertation, "Emergent Reading Behaviours" (1966), examined how all children were learning to read and write in their first year of instruction. Because she studied and recorded the entire span of change for children at all levels of progress, she began to understand the teaching necessary for low-achieving children. At that time, she could not have imagined that her work would inspire teachers across the world for decades to come.

In the mid-1970s, after becoming the first female professor and head of the Department of Education at the University of Auckland, she embarked on observational research that led to the development of Reading Recovery. For a full year, she observed and recorded how one teacher worked individually with harder-to-teach children. In the second year, she recruited a team of other teachers, supervising teachers, reading advisers, and senior university students who taught children individually and worked to identify appropriate instructional strategies for specific situations. As they observed lessons, the team discussed teacher-child interactions; after each lesson, observers asked the teacher to explain why a particular technique or book was selected. During these discussions, the teacher's implicit assumptions had to be explained and justified verbally rather than remaining simply intuitive hunches. Clay explained, "A large number of techniques were piloted, observed, discussed, argued over, related to theory, analyzed, written up, modified and tried out in various ways, and most important, many were discarded" (Clay, 1993, p. 61).

This work with 6-year-old children revealed that they had diverse problems with print, but they also had diverse strengths and skills. Building on these strengths, teachers discovered they could design individual instruction to accelerate learning and change the paths of progress for these children. Marie Clay (1997) wrote of this time, "By the end of 1977 we had a well-documented miracle full of surprises" (p. 658).

After the development phase Reading Recovery was field-tested in five diverse Auckland schools in 1978, where teachers used the teaching procedures with children who were falling behind their classmates in their second year of instruction. Teachers learned to observe children's strengths and to design individual lessons to optimize instruction and rapidly expand their abilities. By the end of the year, the majority of low-performing students had been brought into the average band of their class. An in-service course in 1979 provided training to new teachers from 48 Auckland schools. Results for the second year of implementation in school settings revealed the same rate of success in bringing low-performing students up to the average band of their class. Follow-up studies in 1981 of the children taught in 1978 confirmed that those students had continued to make good progress relative to their classmates (Clay, 1993).

As a result of strong success in Auckland schools, the intervention continued to expand. Reading Recovery was implemented nationally in 1983 with the support of the Ministry of Education. In 1984, Clay also established a national data collection and monitoring procedure for the Ministry. National monitoring of the delivery and outcomes of Reading Recovery is now reported annually by the Ministry of Education. In 2003 Reading Recovery was operating in 1,389 schools, accounting for 67% of New Zealand state and state-integrated schools, and any 6-year-old who needs help can be selected from 78% of the age group.

To support the teacher training program, a government-funded tutor training and coordination program was established in 1983 (now part of the Faculty of Education, University of Auckland). Approximately 7,000 Reading Recovery teachers have been trained by Reading Recovery tutors since teacher training began in 1979, with 133 tutors and 25 trainers trained for New Zealand and many overseas education systems.

Although the intervention started in New Zealand, by 1990 Reading Recovery had emigrated to Australia, the United States, Canada, and the United Kingdom as explained below.

Australia: The First Replication

In the *Handbook of Research on Teaching Literacy Through the Communicative and Visual Arts* (Flood, Heath, & Lapp, 1997), Marie Clay describes the early quest to consider whether Reading Recovery could be replicated in another country in "International Perspectives on the Reading Recovery Program":

> Education is usually not considered to be exportable as education systems are organized and managed differently with different political agendas and a superior result from a program on home ground did not justify the optimism about replication in another education system. (Clay, 1997, p. 659)

Clay's presentation on Reading Recovery at the Darwin Reading Conference of Australian Reading Association spurred implementations in Victoria and the Australian Capital Territory. Clay felt it was important for the program to be implemented without her presence to document its replicability across systems, and it was studied from the point of view of acceptance by teachers, school staff, and parents by Peter Geekie (1992) with Brian Cambourne. The first trainer was trained in Auckland and returned to Bendigo in 1984. Three training programs were then initiated in Victoria at the Bendigo College of Advanced Education, at the La Trobe University, and at Melbourne University.

Reading Recovery has since spread to all but one of the Australian states and territories. The sites are primarily structured within state and non-state education authorities in terms of funding sources and responsibility for the integrity of the implementation of the program. Each state is required to maintain standards and guidelines that are similar throughout the country. Training and professional development align with New Zealand models of Reading Recovery, and trademark issues are currently being discussed. Eight trainers across Australia have supported approximately 200 tutors and 9,000 teachers who have delivered Reading Recovery across the country.

Clay notes that much was learned from the replication of Reading Recovery in Australia with respect to such issues as age at entry to school, expectations for emphasis during the first year of school, variations of curriculum and materials, and assessment procedures. And the apparent answer to whether Reading Recovery was exportable was "yes" because the Australian implementation remains strong to this day.

Not long after the start in Australia, the United States was expressing interest, as described in the next section.

The United States: Celebrating 20 Years of Success

Gay Su Pinnell, Charlotte Huck, and Martha L. King from The Ohio State University spent time in Auckland observing and speaking with teachers and researchers regarding aspects of teaching and implementation before becoming determined to replicate Reading Recovery with integrity in the city schools of Columbus, Ohio. Marie Clay and Barbara Watson arrived in Columbus in the fall of 1984 to begin teaching one university faculty trainer, three teacher leaders, and 13 teachers at the university. In January 1985 the first Columbus children began Reading Recovery lessons; books were leveled for the first time; and the first U.S. book list was created. It was not long before Reading Recovery spread beyond the city borders to the state of Ohio (1985) and then to other states (1986) as educators recognized its extraordinary success with struggling learners.

The Ohio State University Reading Recovery Training Center maintains the National Data Evaluation Center for Reading Recovery research data and has responsibility for the trademark in the United States, which was granted royalty-free by Marie Clay for the purpose of maintaining the integrity of the original design of the model. For Reading Recovery to spread beyond Ohio, it was necessary for other universities to assume the same leadership role in a region as Ohio State had done. So Ohio State professors worked with university faculty to establish university training centers that now form the infrastructure of support for Reading Recovery regionally.

In 1987 the National Diffusion Network (USDE) selected Reading Recovery as a demonstration project and provided funds to make the program available outside of Ohio. In 1989 Ohio State received a $750,000 grant from the John D. and Katherine T. McArthur Foundation for Reading Recovery research that established empirically the effectiveness of Reading Recovery over other teaching strategies and group configurations. The seminal study on Reading Recovery (Pinnell, Lyons, DeFord, Bryk, & Seltzer, 1994) was designed and monitored by a panel of nationally known experts selected by the foundation to support the integrity of the outcomes. The panel included such esteemed researchers as Rebecca Barr, Isabel Beck, Gerald Bracey, Shirley Brice-Heath, Robert Slavin, Dorothy Strickland, and Richard Venezky. Jeanne Chall and Jana Mason served as outside advisors. The data were independently analyzed by Anthony Bryk and Michael Seltzer of the University of Chicago, who also provided consultation on the design. The study serves as scientific evidence that Reading Recovery is an effective and research-based approach to early literacy intervention.

In addition to The Ohio State University, the following universities have served at varying times as university training centers during Reading Recovery's first 20 years in the United States (1985–2005):

California State University at Fresno
California State University at San Bernardino
Clemson University
Emporia State University
Jackson State University
Lesley University
National-Louis University
New York University
Oakland University
St. Mary's College
Purdue University
San Diego State University
Shippensburg University of Pennsylvania
Southeast Missouri State at Cape Girardeau
Texas Woman's University
University of Arizona
University of Arkansas at Little Rock
University of Alabama at Birmingham
University of Connecticut
University of Kentucky

University of Illinois
University of Iowa
University of Maine
University of Nebraska–Kearney
University of North Carolina–Wilmington
University of South Dakota
University of Wisconsin
Western Michigan University
West Virginia Graduate College

As of 2004, 1.4 million children in the United States have participated in Reading Recovery since the beginning year in Columbus, Ohio, and tens of thousands of teachers have enriched their skills beyond their imagination, meeting the needs of children in ways they thought were not possible.

United States Department of Defense Dependents Schools

The United States Department of Defense operates a preschool-12 school system that educates children of American military and civilian personnel assigned overseas by the U.S. government. In the late 1980s, the director of the Department of Defense Dependents Schools (DoDDS) in Arlington, Virginia asked Jim Eckel, systemwide reading coordinator, to investigate Reading Recovery for the overseas schools. After careful review of the program, Jim convinced DoDDS officials of the program's value and the importance of establishing ongoing support with Ohio State faculty. In Europe, five teacher leaders work in seven different countries supporting Reading Recovery teachers. DoDDS-Europe is geographically the largest Reading Recovery site in the world, reaching from Iceland in the north to Sicily in the south. In the Pacific, one teacher leader supported 10 schools located in Japan, Korea, and Guam from the training site in Okinawa.

Descubriendo la Lectura

The development of Descubriendo la Lectura began during the 1988–1989 academic year when teachers who were in Reading Recovery training in Tucson, Arizona, became interested in exploring how the teaching could be adapted for Spanish-speaking children whose initial literacy instruction is being delivered in Spanish. In 1989 the Collaborative for Reading Recovery in Spanish was formally established and Descubriendo la Lectura educators began the work of reconstructing the literacy tasks found in *An Observation Survey of Early Literacy Achievement* (Clay, 2002). Validity and reliability were established in 1991 with Spanish-speaking children from Arizona, Illinois, and Texas (Escamilla, 1992).

With Marie Clay's guidance, Descubriendo la Lectura educators not only produced the bilingual text *Instrumento de Observación de los Logros de la Lecto-Escrit-*

ura Inicial (Escamilla, Andrade, Basurto, Ruiz, & Clay, 1996), which is the reconstruction of *An Observation Survey of Early Literacy Achievement* in Spanish, but also applicable sections of *Reading Recovery: A Guidebook for Teachers in Training* (Clay, 1993). Research has confirmed that Descubriendo la Lectura produces results similar to those of Reading Recovery in English (Escamilla, 1994).

Teachers making the shift from one language to another work under the tutelage of a teacher leader or trainer with expertise in both Reading Recovery and Descubriendo la Lectura for a sustained period of time. Therefore, teachers trained in Reading Recovery or in Descubriendo la Lectura participate in an additional year of training to implement the program in another language. The university training course known as *bridging* prepares teachers who have been initially trained in Reading Recovery to teach in Descubriendo la Lectura (and vice versa).

Descubriendo la Lectura has served students in Arizona, California, Colorado, Illinois, Massachusetts, New Jersey, New York, Rhode Island, Texas, and Washington. In 1999, the White House Initiative on Educational Excellence for Hispanic Americans recognized Descubriendo la Lectura as a program that is effective for Latino youth.

Canada Extends North American Implementation

In 1988 school administrators from the Scarborough Board of Education in Ontario attended the National Reading Recovery Conference in Columbus, Ohio. They became very interested in implementing Reading Recovery in their board. As a result, they hired a teacher leader who was trained at The Ohio State University, and the first class of teachers was trained in Scarborough, Ontario, in 1988–1989. The implementation of Reading Recovery began in Nova Scotia the following year.

By 1992, it was evident that the expansion of Reading Recovery across Canada would require the training of teacher leaders locally. In 1992, a partnership between the Scarborough Board of Education and the Faculty of Education/University of Toronto resulted in the establishment of the Canadian Institute of Reading Recovery (CIRR). CIRR is a nonprofit organization which received the authorization of Marie Clay to register the term Reading Recovery as a trademark in Canada. CIRR is operated by a volunteer board, and its purpose is to support the work of the Reading Recovery professionals in Canada. The institute made it possible to send trainers to New Zealand to prepare for training teacher leaders in Canada.

Prior to the establishment of CIRR, training for Canadian teacher leaders was conducted at either the National Reading Recovery Centre in Auckland, New Zealand, or The Ohio State University in Columbus, Ohio. In 1993–1994, the first course for teacher leaders began at the Canadian Institute of Reading Recovery. To facilitate the training of teacher leaders in other regions of Canada, the

Western Canadian Institute of Reading Recovery opened in Winnipeg, Manitoba, in 1995, and most recently an institute opened at Mount St. Vincent University in Halifax, Nova Scotia. Over the past decade, eight Reading Recovery university trainers have been certified.

Reading Recovery is now implemented in nine provinces and the Yukon Territory. Provincial funding is provided in Manitoba, Prince Edward Island, Nova Scotia, and the Yukon Territory. In 1995–1996, the Canadian trainers, with the support of CIRR, created a national Reading Recovery database. The purpose was to describe the Canadian implementation and to report the program growth and outcomes for students. More than 76,000 children have received Reading Recovery in Canada since the beginning of national data collection in 1995–1996.

Intervention Préventive en Lecture-Écriture

In 1995, a plan for the redevelopment of Reading Recovery in French was conceived in collaboration with Marie Clay. It was determined that the first phase would be the adaptation of *An Observation Survey of Early Literacy Achievement*, resulting in the writing of *Le sondage d'oservation en lecture-écriture* (Clay, 2003b). The Nova Scotia Department of Education conducted the first translation. However, it soon became apparent that there was a need to undertake additional adaptations in order to reflect the differences between English and French. With the initial adaptation completed, developers of the French reconstruction conducted validation and norming research. These studies were carried out in 2000–2001 under the auspices of the Canadian Institute of Reading Recovery/Institut Canadien d'Intervention Préventive en Lecture-Écriture.

The first implementation of Reading Recovery in French was conducted in Canada because the nation has two official languages, English and French. Although the majority of the French population in Canada is located in Québec, there are French communities in every Canadian province. Reading Recovery was offered in a French school board for the first time in 2000–2001 in the province of Nova Scotia. The Conseil Scolaire Acadien Provincial (CSAP) conducted the first pilot of Reading Recovery in French. The following year, 2001–2002, CSAP was implementing the program in its other schools, and three additional teacher leaders were in training to implement Reading Recovery in French in their own school board. In 2002–2003, Intervention Préventive en Lecture-Écriture was offered to two school boards in Ontario, and in 2004 it was implemented in a third province, New Brunswick.

United Kingdom: Reading Recovery Travels to a New Continent

Reading Recovery was first introduced to teachers in England in 1990 by a Surrey head teacher who had trained as a teacher leader in New Zealand. In 1991, the Institute of Education at the University of London, in close association with Marie Clay and supported by the Paul Hamlyn Foundation, initiated tutor and trainer training courses. Reading Recovery is now widespread in England and has also established training bases in Jersey, Wales, Scotland, and Northern Ireland, where it is an integral part of the Northern Ireland Literacy Strategy. It has also spread beyond the United Kingdom to neighbors in the Republic of Ireland and Denmark, where they anticipate considerable expansion within different educational systems. The intervention is being redeveloped into Danish for implementation in Denmark, and *An Observation Survey of Early Literacy Achievement* is being redeveloped as a research instrument in Irish, Spanish, and Slovak for use by teachers in Ireland, Spain, and Slovakia.

A national network advisory group, consisting of teacher leaders representing every geographical area of the United Kingdom and Ireland as well as National Coordination Team trainers from the United Kingdom and Ireland, exists to support communication among teacher leaders and between teacher leaders and trainers. This group provides a forum for discussion of issues arising within Reading Recovery and the various education authorities and education library boards across the United Kingdom and Ireland. In 1993 a system of annual national monitoring and reporting was established which has informed the implementation and raised awareness of the potential of Reading Recovery to achieve change both locally and nationally.

Approximately 5,000 children are served annually across the entire implementation, and the teacher leaders support around 600 teachers in any one year. Funding for the program varies across the different sites, but the British government has consistently supported coordination.

Trainer Leadership Groups

Leadership structures have been created to direct Reading Recovery professionals and stakeholders throughout the world. They include the International Reading Recovery Trainers Organization, the Australia and New Zealand Trainer Team, the European Trainer Group, and the North American Trainers Group, all of which are described in the following sections.

International Reading Recovery Trainers Organization

To assure that Reading Recovery would continue well into the future with the same high quality and integrity of the early years, as well as to support continued development in response to research, an international leadership structure was created. This leadership group called the International Reading Recovery Trainers Organization (IRRTO), with an executive board of equal representation from each country, provides a system for decision making with committees orchestrating issues regarding research and development, training of trainers, funding, communications, and systems design. The group, which includes trainers from all university training centers across the world, meets every 18 months.

The IRRTO Executive Board has been created to direct the operations of IRRTO and Reading Recovery internationally. The IRRTO Executive Board is comprised of five elected members with representation from each country, and a nonvoting chair.

The IRRTO Executive Board is responsible for monitoring the implementation and future development of Reading Recovery internationally and setting policy related to the monitoring and upholding the Reading Recovery trademarks; future expansion of Reading Recovery throughout the world; and the translation of Reading Recovery procedures, practices, and materials in other languages. The IRRTO Executive Board meets once a year.

In early stages of establishing the decision-making organization, the international university trainers and Marie Clay generated the rationale for the global network, including these important factors:

- Reading Recovery provides a model for educational innovation across international boundaries.

- Dynamic growth and change in Reading Recovery draws on international theory, research, and practice broadly and within Reading Recovery.

- Reading Recovery is equally effective in varying national contexts.

- Ideas are shared among international partners and help clarify practices and broaden theory.

The planning group established the vision of the organization: "to maximize the availability of Reading Recovery for any children who need early literacy intervention in any country." IRRTO is committed to maintaining the quality, upholding the integrity, improving the efficiency and effectiveness, and supporting change and growth in Reading Recovery through international collaboration, research, and resource development.

IRRTO coordinates an International Reading Recovery Institute every 3 years in different countries, thus far including Australia, Canada, New Zealand, and the United States. The institutes have included internationally renowned researchers and scholars as speakers whose work can inform teaching, implementation, and research in Reading Recovery. Early work of the organization indicates there is a strong leadership structure that can assure Reading Recovery will continue to be a powerful, dynamic, and developing educational entity in literacy instruction around the world.

Australia and New Zealand Trainer Team

In 1996 Reading Recovery trainers in Australia and New Zealand formed a professional leadership network. The network provides a forum to discuss issues of mutual interest and a vehicle for continuing professional development aimed at supporting and strengthening the implementation of Reading Recovery in the region. The group comprises trainers from New Zealand and the three Australian states with statewide Reading Recovery implementations (Queensland, New South Wales, and Victoria). Annual meetings are held to discuss recent publications and research, observe and discuss teaching, update each other on regional and national events, and discuss issues of common concern related to all aspects of training. The inaugural meeting was held in Sydney in 1996, with subsequent meetings held on a rotational basis in the four trainer sites. The team has been fortunate to have Marie Clay attend in most years. On occasion, trainers training in New Zealand and visiting trainers from other parts of the world have also attended.

European Trainer Group

In Europe, trainer leadership for Reading Recovery comprises two levels. First there is the European Trainer Group (ETG), which serves as an overarching support group for all trainers in Europe. Second, both the United Kingdom and Republic of Ireland National Coordination Teams and the Danish trainer and national coordinator are located within the structure of ETG.

The European Centre for Education in Reading Recovery is located at the University of London Institute of Education. When the first trainers were prepared for the United Kingdom at the institute in 1992, a Centre for National Coordination was established at the site. Since then, the National Coordination Team members have continued to work as a closely knit team to support quality implementation. They provide leadership, training, and ongoing professional education for teacher leaders. They liaise with national and local government bodies to ensure the continuing effectiveness of the implementation in their jurisdiction, and they provide advisory services to authorities who are newly implementing Reading Recovery.

The National Coordination Team trainers undertake quality assurance and research activity, as well as provide oversight of Reading Recovery for the whole of the United Kingdom, extending into the Republic of Ireland since 1999. In 2001, the centre was recognized as the European Centre for the Training of Trainers, and ETG expanded to include the trainer for Denmark in 2002.

North American Trainers Group

Although a leadership group existed since there were multiple university training centers, across the years, the trainers of teacher leaders from all Reading Recovery university training centers in the United States and Canada formalized an organizational structure. The North American Trainers Group (NATG) was created to serve a variety of purposes, but primarily to generate and monitor standards and guidelines that assure the operation of Reading Recovery in a standard way with high quality and integrity. The members of the organization uphold the integrity of Reading Recovery by providing leadership and high-quality continuous learning for the educators who comprise the network of professionals involved in the mission of dramatically increasing the numbers of children who learn to read and write. They engage in strategic planning for continued success in meeting the needs of children and teachers, and they plan and conduct research that informs the profession.

The NATG governing structure includes an executive committee comprised of president, past president, vice president, secretary, treasurer, and two at-large members. There are three major working committees: Teaching and Training, Implementation, and Research. The NATG oversees Reading Recovery in all matters related to these three areas, but works in concert with the Reading Recovery Council of North America, the Canadian Institute of Reading Recovery, and the National Data Evaluation Center at The Ohio State University in specific matters. NATG is not connected to any particular university but is supported by the Reading Recovery Council of North America in carrying out many tasks and functions.

Reading Recovery Council of North America

The Reading Recovery Council of North America (RRCNA) was initially created to assist the trainers of teacher leaders from the various universities in the United States and Canada in supporting all stakeholders in achieving the mission of Reading Recovery. A formative meeting for the council occurred in Texas in 1993 when a small group of representatives from the university training centers gathered to create a vision for how Reading Recovery could best be supported and expanded. Each participant at the meeting wrote a personal check to start the organization. The ideas developed at that meeting reflect the core of today's RRCNA:

- the **vision** that children will be proficient readers and writers by the end of first grade
- the **mission** to ensure access to Reading Recovery for every child who needs its support
- the **purpose** statement to sustain the integrity of Reading Recovery and to expand its implementation by increasing the number of individuals who understand, support, and collaborate to achieve the mission.

Over the next 2 years, a structure was developed to include the current five member categories: teachers, teacher leaders, trainers, site coordinators, and partners. The RRCNA Board of Directors includes members from each of these five categories plus officers and representatives of other specific groups: Descubriendo la Lectura, the Canadian Institute of Reading Recovery, The Ohio State University as trademark holders, and the deans of university training centers.

Council members receive a variety of benefits, including publications and ongoing professional development at national conferences, institutes, and academies. The council promotes Reading Recovery on behalf of the members through high-quality education and extensive federal and state advocacy efforts and works to maintain the integrity and quality of Reading Recovery. The university trainers from NATG support many of the council's activities in a mutually beneficial relationship, such as writing for the publications, organizing and conducting professional development and conference sessions, and designing and carrying out a research agenda. The council has worked with several foundations to support its missions, including such groups as the Verizon Foundation and Ronald McDonald House.

Conclusion

In summary, Marie Clay's initial interest in how struggling learners get off-track early inspired educators to see the world differently as well. Her influence developed in an exponential fashion that resulted in the growth of an international network of collaborators who have made their mark on literacy learning and teaching across the world. Because of their commitment, many children have gone down a path that would have been inaccessible without Reading Recovery and the dedication of the professionals who created it and helped it prosper. This collaborative network continues to work to change futures for the young children who find literacy learning difficult.

CHAPTER 3

Early Intervention
to Prevent Reading Failure

Learning to read is essential to success in school and important for social and economic advancement in our society. The majority of first-grade children learn to read quickly, easily, and efficiently in almost any classroom, with almost any instructional emphasis (Clay, 1993). Nonetheless, a small percentage of first-grade children, including children from all races, socioeconomic levels, and social classes, have significant difficulties learning to read. Typically, these children have been in school for several years before they are identified to receive compensatory education. Once placed in remedial or compensatory programs, it is highly likely the children will remain in these programs for extended periods of time (Allington & Walmsley, 1995). An unfortunate characteristic of remedial programs is the limited success they have had in resolving the difficulties of children who have failed to learn to read in the classroom (Johnston & Allington, 1991).

Recently, however, there has been much interest among educators in implementing early intervention programs. This is probably due to reports of the success of early intervention in reducing the number of children who are placed in remedial or compensatory education programs (Pikulski, 1994; Walmsley & Allington, 1995; Wasik & Slavin, 1993). In addition there has been an increasing acceptance and awareness of the emergent view of literacy acquisition (Teale & Sulzby, 1986) and a focus on good first teaching for all children in the primary grades (Fountas & Pinnell, 1996). There has also been a substantial increase in federal funding available for early identification and education of children experiencing difficulty in the first few years of schooling (Allington & Walmsley, 1995).

In 1996, the U.S. Departments of Education and Health and Human Services asked the National Academy of Sciences to establish a committee to investigate the effectiveness of early intervention as a way to prevent reading difficulties in later years. The decision to establish the committee was prompted by concern for an increasing number of children failing to learn how to read well enough to meet the rising demands for higher literacy in today's technological society. After extensive research and review, the Committee on the Prevention of Reading Difficulties in Young Children recommended that educators view early intervention as a way to prevent reading difficulties (Snow, Burns, & Griffin, 1998). Despite this recommendation, some educators continue to argue that early intervention is too costly and may not be worth the investment.

In this chapter, we present some compelling reasons to intervene early with children who are experiencing reading difficulties and to prevent these difficulties from happening in the first place. We begin by examining the concept of prevention and its relationship to reading failure. We then discuss the importance of early intervention as a preventative approach to reading failure. We conclude with a discussion of Reading Recovery's concept of early intervention.

Prevention of Reading Failure

Most people would agree that compared with intervention after a problem has occurred, prevention is not only easier, it is probably less expensive and better for the child's well-being and educational future. In retrospective studies of school dropouts, for example, Fitzsimmons, Cheever, Leonard, and Macunovich (1969) found that signs of learning and reading problems were apparent early in the school lives of these students. Fifty percent of the dropouts were identifiable in second grade, and 75% were identifiable by fourth grade.

Additional research has revealed a significantly higher school dropout rate for students who could not read and were retained in the elementary grades (Roderick, 1994). Further research evidence "uniformly demonstrates that retention increases the chance that a student will leave school; in fact it's an even stronger predictor of dropping out than is socioeconomic status" (Kohn, 2004, p. 574). In their synthesis of research on early reading development, the Committee on the Prevention of Reading Difficulties in Young Children concluded that it is easier and better for children to prevent reading problems in the first place than it is to retain or attempt to remediate children in the later grades (Snow et al., 1998).

Prevention of reading problems also makes sense financially. Special remedial provisions add considerably to educational costs every year the child receives supplemental services. The per-pupil cost for children placed in various pull-out programs or referred to resource-room services, as well as the per-pupil cost for their classroom seat, add up (Allington & Walmsley, 1995). Furthermore, studies investigating compensatory and remedial reading programs reveal that remediation is not only costly but also ineffective (Allington & Walmsley, 1995; Johnston & Allington, 1991; Kennedy, Birman, & Demaline, 1986).

If the effects of early intervention are of a long-term nature, then the costs of the intervention might be covered in reductions in long-term compensatory education and special education placements (McGill-Franzen, 1994). Additionally, if these effects are essentially permanent in preventing reading failure, then the cost of the intervention might be a wise investment in terms of reducing the costs associated with social problems such as school dropouts, unemployment, delinquency, and welfare.

In addition to financial consideration, early reading failure can be a powerful force in shaping children's perceptions of themselves. Children's negative views of their learning potential and self-worth sometimes persist, even in the face of eventual success (Coles, 1987, 1998). The emotional consequences of reading failure, and in some cases the cognitive and motivation consequences, can be avoided only if reading failure is addressed early on or prevented entirely (Lyons, 2003).

Prevention is critical if children are to avoid the self-devaluation resulting from reading failure (Levine, 2002). Some authors argue that we now know enough to prevent most cases of reading failure and thus have a moral obligation to act on that knowledge, regardless of cost (Slavin, Madden, Karweit, Livermon, & Dolan, 1990). Wasik and Slavin (1993) argue further that we have "an ethical and perhaps legal responsibility" (p. 198) to prevent reading failure. Providing every child the opportunity for success in learning to read and write should be designated as an area of highest priority in the United States.

Definitions of Prevention

According to Webster's New World Dictionary (1988) *prevention* means "to keep from happening by some prior action." Dictionary definitions of prevention describe it as an action to avoid occurrence of a disease or disability in large populations. The classic public health definition of prevention is a three-part definition with special relevance to preventive approaches in education (Caplan, 1964; Pianta, 1990).

1. *Primary prevention* actions are taken prior to the onset of a disease to intercept its causation or to modify its course of action. In medicine one would get an inoculation, for example, to prevent polio. Primary prevention is thus concerned with "reducing the number of new cases (incidence) of an identified condition or problem in the population" (Snow et al., 1998, p. 16).

   A primary prevention for literacy failure is good kindergarten and Grade 1 classroom instruction. Snow et al. (1998) argue that good first teaching is crucial for reducing the number of children who experience difficulty learning to read. They also recommend that competent, well-trained, certified teachers who will help every child, including those who are experiencing some difficulties, are hired to teach reading in the primary grades.

2. *Secondary prevention* approaches in medicine include early diagnosis and treatment for the specific disorder. The earlier a disease is diagnosed and the sooner treatment is started, the more likely the progression of the disease will be stopped and hopefully eradicated.

Secondary prevention is concerned with "reducing the number of exist-ing cases (prevalence) of an identified condition or problem in the pop-ulation" (Snow et al., 1998, p. 16). Early diagnosis of potential reading problems will help children at higher risk of developing reading difficul-ties before any serious long-term deficit has emerged. Secondary inter-vention involves early diagnosis and extra help for children experiencing reading difficulties and for whom classroom instruction is not enough. Reading Recovery is a secondary prevention.

3. *Tertiary prevention* involves rehabilitation efforts to reduce the residual effects of an illness or disorder. Tertiary prevention is concerned with "reducing the complications associated with an identified problem or condition" (Snow et al., 1998, p. 16). Children who have made inade-quate progress after the secondary prevention are provided additional diagnosis and specially designed long-term supplemental instruction. Special education or remedial classes from a reading specialist is a terti-ary prevention.

Barriers to Implementing a Preventative Literacy Intervention

There is generally support among concerned citizens and policymakers that pre-venting disease is critical to the health and welfare of children. For example, pedi-atricians routinely immunize infants to prevent them from contracting polio, diphtheria, measles, tuberculosis, and whooping cough. The U.S. Congress ap-propriates millions of dollars annually to immunize those most likely to contract a disease or illness (infants, young children, and the elderly).

There are, however, several barriers to implementing a preventative program to reading failure. First, traditional research methods are generally inadequate for demonstrating the results of the prevention (Clay, 2003a). The need for control groups in a typical paradigm raises ethical questions and issues because such con-trol conditions imply the withholding of services or the manipulation of individuals.

Second, the need for time to demonstrate results adds to the difficulties re-searchers face in documenting what has not happened in a preventative program. It is difficult to make a case for early intervention to prevent subsequent learning difficulties. Yet once a child experiences learning difficulties, it becomes obvious that the child would have benefited from early intervention (Coles, 1998; Vel-lutino & Scanlon, 2002).

A third barrier is a lack of broad-based support among administrators and pol-icymakers for implementing preventative programs. In many school districts, cur-rent legislation for remedial or special education services gives strong legal and financial encouragement to local school districts to implement programs for failing children only after they have failed. This position is taken despite compelling research that preventing early reading failure is cost-effective in the long run (Askew, Kaye, et al., 2002; Hummel-Rossi & Ashdown, 2002; Pinnell et al., 1994; Wasik & Slavin, 1993).

A fourth barrier is a general lack of understanding among administrators, classroom teachers, and support teachers about how to design and implement preventative literacy programs. One of the most complex challenges confronting educators today may be the development of collaborative relationships among school personnel to create a comprehensive, school-based literacy plan to meet the changing literacy needs of every child, including those who are struggling to learn, in the elementary school building (see Chapter 12).

Organizing for the Prevention of Early Reading Failure

Most classroom teachers believe that they are preventing reading failure. In order to launch a preventative approach to reading failure, however, administrators and school personnel must organize for prevention. Clay (1991) provides the following guidance for implementing preventative literacy programs in first grade.

- Administrators should consider the importance of the first year of classroom instruction for helping children construct an effective literacy processing system. First-grade classroom teachers need to be able to analyze students' reading and writing behaviors to determine if they have begun to construct an effective or ineffective literacy processing system. Classroom teachers must be carefully selected.

- First-grade classes must be small so that teachers are able to interact with beginning readers and writers, noting their confusions and supporting their tentative attempts. If class size is too large, teachers will not be able to closely observe the reading and writing progress of each child.

- First-grade reading progress should be carefully monitored by sensitive observation of the literacy progress of children as it changes over time. Time for close observation must be made available. Classroom teachers should be taught how to observe and interpret children's reading and writing behaviors, and they should be encouraged to develop ways of using the information collected.

- As each child reaches a benchmark, for example 3–5 months of instruction, progress should be checked through individual assessments. If the child is making satisfactory progress, a detailed analysis of the reading and writing processing skills are not necessary. If, however, the benchmark assessment reveals inadequate progress, supplemental help in addition to regular classroom reading and writing instruction will be necessary.

- A well-trained, flexible, and experienced teacher who understands the reading and writing processes at the acquisition stage and is also well-versed in teaching low-progress children must be available for more intensive and sustained teaching of the children making the lowest progress in first grade.

When school systems are organized in these ways, a preventative approach to reading and writing problems is possible. Only a few children (usually the lowest 20% of the first-grade class) will need a secondary prevention program to supplement good first-grade classroom teaching.

Early Intervention: A Preventative Approach to Reading Failure

During the last two decades there has been an emphasis in early interventions to reduce the incidence of literacy problems among the lowest-achieving children in first grade and provide supplemental individual help for children to catch up to their peers by the end of first grade (Clay, 1998). In times past, it was not considered the critical principle that it is today. Previously it was believed that some young children were simply not ready to learn how to read, and given more time they would mature and become ready to learn. It was also assumed that once slow starters became ready to learn, they would progress rapidly and eventually read as well as children who started reading much earlier. Educators who held the maturation (reading readiness) point of view did nothing but wait until children were ready to learn.

This conventional wisdom has not been borne out by research (Gaffney, 1994; Hiebert & Taylor, 1994; Juel, 1988). While it is true that children begin reading at different ages and at different times in the year, if delays appear to be outside the time when the majority of children learn to read, simply waiting for children to catch up is not effective (Clay, 2001, 2003a; Johnston & Allington, 1991).

Numerous studies have reported that early intervention is necessary to reduce the number of children who cannot read and write in the primary grades. In a study of one-to-one tutoring programs designed to prevent early reading failure, Wasik and Slavin (1993) concluded that early intervention, preferably in the first grade, may provide a reliable means of abolishing illiteracy among young children who are at risk for long-term school failure. Vellutino et al. (1996) studied first-grade children who were struggling to learn how to read and found that early, individualized, and intensive intervention was effective in reducing reading difficulties. In their book on effective early literacy interventions, Hiebert and Taylor (1994) concluded that "early literacy interventions with a focus on accelerated learning and on authentic reading and writing tasks can prevent many first grade children from failing to learn to read" (p. 3).

Rationale for Early Intervention

There are three key reasons that educators should consider early intervention to reduce the number of children who fail to learn how to read and write in the primary grades. First, considering how much progress the average reader makes in reading during the first grade, it is easy to see how there are great differences between lowest achievers and children who are learning to read and write successfully. Individualized instruction to suit struggling children's strengths and pace in learning must be designed to accelerate their learning (see Chapter 6). The longer we wait, the more difficult it will be for them to catch up to their peers. An early intervention program is essential to catch children before they fail and before they fall so far behind their peers they cannot profit from classroom instruction.

Second, if we do not significantly reduce the number of children struggling to read and write in the early years of schooling, it becomes more and more detrimental to the emotional and social development of the child. All children have fear. Teachers can easily understand some of these fears (fear of injections, hospitals, the dentist), while others are harder to comprehend (fear of failure, reading aloud in class, making a mistake). Helping children deal with the anxiety-producing situations is a complex process. Some children's fear of reading failure is intense enough to require expert consultation (Coles, 1998). However, research offers teachers helpful suggestions to assist low-progress readers in coping with their fears and regulating their level of fear and anxiety (Lyons, 2003). Because early reading success is so important to later reading success and because early reading failure is likely to haunt a young child for many years (Stanovich, 1986), early literacy intervention to help lower-than-expected achievers in reading to catch up with able-reading peers is essential.

Finally, reducing the number of children who need long-term remedial and special education classes is a wise financial decision for the education system. Researchers investigating early intervention (Clay, 1993, 2001; Hiebert & Taylor, 1994; Vellutino et al., 1996) have advocated for an early intervention model of assistance before referral to long-term remediation or retention is even considered. Allington and McGill-Franzen (1995) argue that we must work to eliminate retention and referral to long-term remediation and hold on to some of the money that will be realized in savings. Then we will be able to fund early intervention programs that will accelerate literacy development for struggling readers and make it clear that they can become literate along with their peers.

Reading Recovery's Concept of Early Intervention

Prevention is a central concept of Reading Recovery. A preponderance of evidence indicates that preventing reading difficulties is the best course of action to take with struggling children in terms of both their academic and social-psychological effects (Snow et al., 1998). Key to the success of Reading Recovery is a well-trained teacher working intensively every day with a struggling learner one to one (see Chapter 6). According to Marie Clay (2001):

> What has much to do with success in early interventions is a well-trained special teacher, given the opportunity to design a programme to suit each child and taking each child by a somewhat different path to the desired outcome of satisfactory work in a classroom, documenting the progress made daily. (p. 256)

Reading Recovery's concept of early intervention is based on five unique principles about children's learning and teaching. These principles are woven "into a theory of how children learn, how teachers can teach, and how a sound delivery system can be mounted" (Clay, 2001, p. 256; see Chapter 4). Underlying each principle is a sense of urgency and expectation that each Reading Recovery teacher will effectively work to change how particular children learn so they continue to learn by reading and writing independently.

1. Individual Differences in Learning
There is a tremendous range of individual differences in what children have learned about reading and writing when they enter kindergarten and first grade. Whatever the origins of these differences, they have a large learned component (Clay, 2001). Even with excellent classroom instruction, a small percentage of children are going to struggle to learn to read and write. What children know about literacy when they enter school is not about competency or their ability to learn; it is about the opportunities they have had to learn about reading and writing by participating in literate experiences prior to entering school.

2. Early Detection of Reading Difficulties
You can see the doors to effective literacy learning beginning to close for some children during kindergarten and at the beginning of first grade (Clay, 1998). The tasks published in *An Observation Survey of Early Literacy Achievement* (Clay, 2002) help to identify the learning needs of children most in need of additional support. The lowest-performing first-grade students must receive additional help as soon as possible be-

cause they have the most to learn and may need a longer time to catch up to their peers.

3. *Intervention at the Beginning of First Grade*

Some educators think children beginning to struggle need more time and we should wait to provide supplemental help. Reading Recovery educators' response to this argument is that the longer children's development is allowed to lag behind their peers, the more difficult it becomes to accelerate their learning and the less likely it is that these children will ever develop their full capacity to read and write. By waiting for low-progress children to mature when it is experience that is lacking, we deprive them of opportunities to learn.

4. *Intensive and Individual Instruction*

Reading Recovery instruction is based on detailed, ongoing observations of the child as a reader and writer over time. Therefore, the teacher works from the child's strengths and does not waste time teaching the child something already known, which suggests that the quantity, quality, and intensity of literacy instruction needed for every child to become literate will differ. Furthermore, struggling children need explicit, individual, intensive instruction early to meet their individual learning needs and pace of learning.

5. *Accelerative Learning*

We need to ensure accelerated learning so that the lowest achievers catch up to their peers. Acceleration of instruction means we offer children larger amounts of more intense teaching in order to enhance the pace of literacy development. The lowest children will have to learn at an accelerative rate because their classmates are continuing to make progress. Reading Recovery is designed to bring each child as rapidly as possible to a level in the class where that child can sustain gains with regular classroom literacy instruction.

Supportive Evaluations of Reading Recovery

Reading Recovery professionals in the United States have documented over 20 years of evaluation research showing that by intervening early, Reading Recovery not only prevents further reading difficulties but helps to close the achievement gap between the lowest-achieving first-grade children and their peers before the gap becomes too large to bridge (see Chapter 9). Reviews conducted by researchers independent of Reading Recovery professionals have also commented positively about the conceptual basis of the early intervention and the effectiveness of the program. Shanahan and Neuman (1997) report:

> No study has so successfully influenced remedial reading instruction as the Reading Recovery program....In a series of studies conducted over a 5-year period, Clay examined the effects of her innovative one-on-one tutorial program to intervene early in reading failure. Up to then, remediation was usually delayed until students were in the fourth grade, as it was assumed that they might catch up on their own. Clay intervened, often successfully, after only one year of instruction. Unlike traditional remedial programs, Clay emphasized instruction in the context of oral reading, observation as a key assessment technique, high quality teacher education as a fundamental part of the intervention, and individual instruction that would raise student achievement to the average level of class performance. (p. 207)

In an independent evaluation of the effects of Reading Recovery, Shanahan and Barr (1995) say that Reading Recovery does what it was intended to do; that is, bring the learning of the lowest-achieving students up to that of the average-achieving peers. They further contend that Reading Recovery is a robust program in terms of consequences for student learning and replicability across sites. They also credit Reading Recovery with being a significant force in shaping the way early literacy development is viewed nationally and internationally.

Conclusion

Most children will learn to read and write in first grade when there is a good curriculum for literacy learning and good first teaching. For the small percentage of first-grade students who are having difficulty and are being left behind by fast-learning classmates, Reading Recovery can bring the child's progress back into the average band of achievement in 12 to 20 weeks of individualized instruction.

Reading Recovery is designed to be an essential part of a school's comprehensive literacy plan. It is a safety net for children who are struggling to learn to read and write in first grade. Struggling readers are provided individual intensive instruction so they catch up to their classmates and continue to learn satisfactorily, supported by the classroom teacher in classroom literacy programs.

Schools that do not have a safety net for the lowest achievers at the end of first grade have five options. One option is to retain the child. Educators who support retention believe that if the pace of instruction is slowed down and low-progress children have a second chance in first grade, they might learn to read. There is "probably no other single educational practice with such a consistently negative educational impact on students" (Allington & McGill-Franzen, 1995, p. 45).

A second option is to promote the child and hope that he or she will learn to read in the second grade. Research shows, however, that children who enter second grade below grade level will continue to fall further and further behind their peers (Stanovich, 1986).

A third option is to classify the child learning disabled and place him or her in special education. Once children are classified as learning disabled, few attain academic achievement comparable to their peers. Children classified as learning disabled fall further and further behind their peers after participating in special education programs (Walmsley & Allington, 1995).

A fourth option, usually offered during the school year, is to place the child in a small-group compensatory (Title I) program. Although children in compensatory programs routinely receive reading services, there is little documentation as to whether the children learned to read or how well. The nature of the instruction, materials, and instructional time spent per student varies. There is little expectation that children receiving compensatory education will ever catch up to their peers (McGill-Franzen, 1994). Some of these children are retained, socially promoted, or placed in special education programs at the end of the year.

The fifth option is to eliminate the literacy problem altogether or at least reduce the problem as soon as it is identified in an intensive short-term one-to-one intervention. Reading Recovery offers this solution. Reading Recovery is the only early intervention program that has 20 years of data on every child served to document its effectiveness.

Reading Recovery, with its strong preventative perspective and stellar teacher training, has one clear goal: "to dramatically reduce the number of learners who have extreme difficulty with literacy learning and the cost of these learners to educational systems" (Clay, 1998, p. 210). While it offers a solution to reducing the growing number of children struggling to learn to read and write, Reading Recovery cannot work alone. The focus and pace of classroom literacy instruction can "reinforce or impede the progress children are making during the intervention (Reading Recovery) and following it" (Shanahan & Barr, 1995, p. 992).

Reading Recovery has been described as an insurance policy taken out by a school district against the risk of having children with literacy problems in the upper primary and middle-school grades (Clay, 1998). Reading Recovery evaluation data and follow-up studies (Askew, Fountas, Lyons, Pinnell, & Schmitt, 1998; see Chapters 9 and 10) provide convincing evidence that the insurance policy has paid for itself many times.

CHAPTER 4

The Theoretical Base
for Reading Recovery

Our knowledge base underlying reading and literacy learning for children at risk of failure has expanded dramatically over the past 20 years. Since the initial description and research results of Reading Recovery (Clay, 1979; Pinnell, 1989) there has been a growing interest in early identification of children who are at risk of reading failure and in providing these children with early intervention to ameliorate such difficulties before they become compounded. Today, early identification and intervention for children who fall significantly below their peers in reading is widely accepted by policymakers, educators, and researchers throughout the United States.

Reading Recovery has consistently proven its ability to bring the lowest-achieving first-grade students up to the level of their peers. For the last 20 years in the United States, ongoing evaluation through the collection of data on every child who enters and leaves Reading Recovery has shown that the same results are achieved time and time again with different children, different languages, different teachers, and in different geographic locations (see Chapter 9). Researchers evaluating the effects of early intervention programs have commented on the effectiveness of Reading Recovery.

- "The effects of Reading Recovery are impressive at the end of the implementation year and the effects are maintained for at least 2 years" (Wasik & Slavin, 1993, p. 187).

- "When you compare the success rate of Reading Recovery with other programs that keep children for years and never get them reading on grade level, Reading Recovery is a bargain" (Cunningham & Allington, 1994, p. 255).

- "Reading Recovery is one of the very few instructional support programs to have demonstrated long-term effects on children's reading abilities" (Allington & Walsmley, 1995, p. 253).

- "It (Reading Recovery) has proven to be a robust program, both in terms of its consequences for student learning and its replicability across sites. Further, it has become a significant force in shaping the way we view literacy learning development" (Shanahan & Barr, 1995, p. 992).

- "Evidence firmly supports the conclusion that Reading Recovery does bring the learning of many children up to that of their average-achieving peers. Thus, in answer to the question, 'Does reading recovery work?' we must respond in the affirmative" (Shanahan & Barr, 1995, p. 989).

- "Reading Recovery proves that a well-designed educational program can be replicated among teachers and schools across a wide array of locations and cultures and still yield uniformly superior results" (Wilson & Daviss, 1994, p. 76).

The Reading Recovery initial yearlong course of study and ongoing professional development of teachers is also widely acclaimed. In an independent study of 10 promising intervention programs for low-achieving students, Herman and Stringfield (1997) commented on the strength of the Reading Recovery staff development model:

> The intensity and the methods utilized by Reading Recovery in training and the insistence on high level reading recovery performance provided an almost singularly attractive model for future staff development efforts, regardless of the program type. As schools systematize and create more opportunities for serious staff development, the thoroughness of the Reading Recovery model seems to be well worth emulating. (p. 86)

Why is this individual intervention program so highly regarded?

There are three interrelated answers to this question. First, a strong theoretical and research base underlies its initial development and implementation. Second, Reading Recovery teachers are enrolled in a yearlong course of study to develop theoretical understandings of the reading and writing processes from which to teach. Finally, all Reading Recovery professionals (teachers, teacher leaders, and university trainers) are provided ongoing professional development to keep their knowledge base dynamic and current and to further develop their expertise in teaching the hardest-to-teach children. Continuing education ensures the quality of lessons for each child and promotes success across all schools that implement Reading Recovery. *In every way—the teaching of children, the initial training, and the ongoing professional development of teachers—Reading Recovery has shown its robust theory.*

In this chapter we explore the theoretical grounding of Reading Recovery. We examine Reading Recovery's program for children and training of teachers that make it so effective. We begin by summarizing Clay's early research that led to the development of Reading Recovery. We then examine the theoretical foundations of Reading Recovery and discuss seven coherent principles of learning based on Clay's theory. In the final section of the chapter, we describe four assumptions that underlie Reading Recovery instruction and the training of Reading Recovery professionals. We conclude with a summary and discussion of the impact Clay's research and theory of literacy learning and early intervention have had on teaching and teacher education worldwide.

Clay's Early Research Leading to the Development of Reading Recovery

Marie Clay's interest in early literacy began in 1963 when she was a lecturer in developmental psychology and doctoral student at the University of Auckland, New Zealand. From the beginning of her career, she was interested in how to help struggling readers. In her dissertation study, "Emergent Reading Behaviour," Clay (1966) asked the question, "Can we see the process of learning to read going off course close to the onset of instruction?" She conducted weekly observations of 100 5-year-old children from their fifth to sixth birthdays and recorded in minute detail the different ways they constructed complex literacy processing systems to read and write. She examined and interpreted a full range of behaviors related to high-, average-, and low-performing children. As a result of examining and recording an entire span of change of many children at all levels of progress, Clay found

- children become literate at varied points in time throughout the year
- there is more than one route to learning how to read and write

Through these observational studies, Clay learned what high-, average-, and low-progress readers attend to as they learn to read and write. She also began to understand what low-progress children needed to learn how to do in order to become more proficient.

By 1972, Marie Clay was able to describe, for the use of teachers, some of the observation techniques that were developed to capture the changes in literacy learning during the first year of instruction (see Chapter 5). The classroom teachers found the procedures and observation tools useful in selecting children who needed additional help, but wanted specific guidance for teaching these lowest-performing children. In response to the teachers' requests, Clay launched a second research study to help teachers learn how to effectively teach children who were not learning how to read and write during their first year of classroom instruction.

The Development of Reading Recovery

In 1976, Marie Clay embarked on a 2-year observation study that led to the development of Reading Recovery. This time her research question became, "Can we use the collective expertise of good teachers to develop and describe some teaching procedures that can be used with failing children in schools?" (Clay, 1979, p. 1). For a full year, Clay observed and recorded how one teacher worked individually with hard-to-teach children. After a year of detailed observation and record keeping, she recruited a team of six specialist teachers to determine which teaching activities worked best in which situations. The research team met each week. One teacher taught a low-progress child behind a one-way glass while the rest of the team talked about what was occurring. These lessons were authentic experiences for teacher learning.

As they observed, the team tried to understand the immediate effects of the teacher's decision on the child's response and subsequent learning. They discussed what the child had difficulty learning and how the teacher responded. They discussed why a teacher response was effective or ineffective and provided specific evidence to back up their observations. They related what they were observing to their own teaching, and in the process they gained deeper insights and understandings about effective teaching techniques to help struggling readers become literate.

After each lesson, observers shared what they had observed and asked the teacher to explain why a particular technique or book was chosen. During these discussions the teacher's implicit assumptions and decision-making processes were revealed and explained verbally rather than remaining intuitive hunches. The observers and teacher discussed the child's difficulties and related their collective knowledge of theory about learning and becoming literate to the practical experience. They discussed procedures and techniques that worked and did not work, and they hypothesized why this may be the case. They discovered the decision-making and teaching techniques good teachers used with slow readers and why they were more or less effective. The discussion while viewing a lesson was so useful in helping these teachers learn how to describe, analyze, and understand the reading and writing processes as children become literate that it became a technological requirement for training Reading Recovery teachers throughout the world.

The research team's work with 6-year-old children who were unable to make satisfactory progress in their classrooms revealed the following:

- Children have diverse problems with print and diverse strengths and skills.

- By building on children's strengths, teachers could design individual instruction to accelerate learning.

- In order for the lowest-achieving children to be brought into the average band of their class, one-to-one instruction is necessary (see Chapter 6).

By the end of 1977, Clay and the research team had developed a well-documented set of Reading Recovery teaching procedures to help the lowest-achieving children learn how to read and write. These teaching procedures were field tested in five diverse Auckland, New Zealand, schools in 1978–1979. The field trials in

New Zealand laid the groundwork for what has become standard training for Reading Recovery teachers. Studies of the initial yearlong course in Reading Recovery (see Chapter 8) indicate that opportunities to observe and discuss demonstration lessons behind the one-way glass with a supportive group of peers is necessary to help teachers develop a theory of literacy learning that informs practice. Clay's theory of literacy learning in continuous text (Clay, 1966, 1991, 2001) has become a foundation for subsequent research and evaluation designs, including Reading Recovery.

The Theoretical Foundation of the Reading Recovery Program for Children

Most theoretical models of reading (see Holmes, 1960; Rumelhart, 1994; Singer, 1994) begin their description about acquisition from the point where children have already created links between language and print and visual perception and print; they have caught on to the directional rules of print and have learned to work in primitive ways with it (Clay, 2001). These models gave little attention to the early formative period of becoming literate when children enter formal schooling. Clay's research is unique because it focuses on the formative years of literacy learning.

From her original dissertation studies (Clay, 1966) and follow-up studies describing young children's emergent literacy patterns of behaviors (Clay, 1979, 1991, 2001), Clay developed a theory of literacy learning that made a considerable contribution to the field. The origins of Reading Recovery are grounded and guided by seven key theoretical principles that emerged from Clay's theory and will be discussed separately.

1. Reading is a complex problem-solving process.

2. Children construct their own understandings.

3. Children come to literacy with varying knowledge.

4. Reading and writing are reciprocal and interrelated processes.

5. Learning to read involves a process of reading and writing continuous text.

6. Learning to read involves a continuous process of changes over time.

7. Children take different paths to literacy learning.

Reading Is a Complex Problem-Solving Process

To be successful, readers must extract information from many sources in text, cross-checking one source with another until they find the one best fit. The beginning reader has to learn what kinds of information exist in texts and to what to attend in order to extract that information (Clay, 1991, 2001). The following list of behaviors reveals some of the complex problem solving children must learn how to do well:

- get meaning from text
- discover how their oral language relates to the text
- work out how their syntactic structures are relevant to reading the text
- learn that existing phonological awareness of a spoken language can be used to read
- find out how visual sources of information facilitate processing letters, letter clusters, words, phrases, and various print conventions (e.g., punctuation, spacing, left-to-right directionality)
- discover how books work and texts vary, and that the way they are introduced to the readers helps them
- discover how book language is different from oral language

Research reports of preschool children reading reveal that they pick up different kinds of information in sequence (Ferrerio & Teberovsky, 1982). For example, they might attend to the first letter, then glance at the picture on the page, look at the word again, reread the line, and make up a sentence that goes with the picture. Gradually emergent readers attend to more than one kind of information to solve words and phrases, such as pictures, story, letters, words, or language structure. For example, they may use a range of information—visual, phonological, syntactic, from printed text—and relate these one to the other to solve a problem to understand the message of the text. Clay (2001) writes:

> Quite early children can be observed to check one kind of information with another and when two sources of information produce competing alternatives the reader often notices that something is not right. For familiar words on easy text the processing becomes rapid and it appears to arise simultaneously from several features at once. Young children mix slow sequential processing on 'harder words' with faster processing on 'easy words.' (p. 125)

As beginning readers start to work with different kinds of information, their problem solving changes and processing becomes more labored, observable, and sequential. They make perceptual and cognitive decisions like those described by Bruner (1957) who argued cognitive and perceptual processing share a common decision-making process.

Clay (2001) provides a description of the young reader's perceptual and cognitive decision-making activities to construct meaning:

- the conscious search for, and analysis of, different types of information in print,
- the necessary monitoring and error detection processes,
- together with highly practiced and fast perceptual responding. (p. 106)

Beginning readers adjust their problem-solving processes to the complexity and demands of the text. For example, when reading easy or familiar text a young reader's processing is quick and fluent. As the text becomes more challenging, their processing slows down and they become less fluent. Beginning readers also self-monitor, problem-solve using various sources of information, choose among alternative responses, and self-correct. Clay (2001) points out that "self-monitoring and self-correcting appear early in the first attempts at text reading, and they persist as good indicators of change in inner-control in oral reading for two or three years" (p. 126).

Since first described in 1966, Clay's theory of literacy learning has taken into account the critical role phonological awareness and letter-sound information play in learning to read and write. However "knowing the sounds of letters and letter clusters is essential but not sufficient for successful reading of texts" (Clay, 2001, p. 98). Reading is a complex process in which the child must develop "control systems to manage the different types of information and to manage the assembly of working systems needed to get the problem-solving done" (Clay, 2001, p. 128). Young children's perceptual/cognitive processing begins as primitive, simple working systems in the brain that become more complex as information in texts becomes increasingly more difficult.

Children Construct Their Own Understandings

Studies of children's thinking (Duckworth, 1996; Piaget, 1973) and language acquisition (Halliday, 1975) reveal that children construct and act on their own theories of how things work and change their theories slowly if their experiences contradict that existing theory. For example, toddlers may call every man they meet daddy until they realize that their daddy has specific features that distinguish him from every other man they know.

Just as toddlers construct language to gain meaning through conversations with others, so too does the young reader construct some message-getting activities to gain meaning from text. Initially they construct very simple working systems that pull together necessary semantic, syntactic, and graphophonemic information from text in simple ways. But as opportunities to read and write accumulate over time, the learner becomes able to quickly and momentarily construct more complex working systems that might solve the problem.

As text difficulty increases, children initiate and actively consolidate their learning and construct new ways to solve problems. They become aware of new items of knowledge and sources of information to use to analyze unknown words while reading and writing. As children construct new ways of problem solving and checking on themselves, new strategic behaviors emerge. Clay (2001) writes:

> In a complex model of interacting competencies in reading and writing the reader can potentially draw from all his or her current understandings, and all his or her language competencies, and visual information, and phonological information, and knowledge of print conventions, in ways which *extend both the searching and linking processes as well as the item knowledge repertoires.* (p. 224)

The learner is constructing neurological networks for efficiently reading and writing texts. This independent learning is a *system in use*, the processing carried out by the brain for reading and writing to occur, which Clay (2001) describes as a self-extending system. The child is the constructor of this working system.

Children Come to Literacy With Varying Knowledge

Clay's theory of literacy acquisition recognizes the fact that children come to literacy knowledge in very different ways. They enter school having learned many different things in different ways, in different cultures, and in different contexts. The explanations for difficulties in acquiring literacy are also diverse, arising from differences in language development and experiences with books and print. Despite these differences, every child entering school has strengths.

First and foremost, school entrants have acquired the ability to use language to make themselves understood and to understand what others are saying. They already control linguistic processing strategies in oral language. Some children as young as 2½ years old can make themselves understood. In the following example, Michael is trying to tell his mother that he spilled his cup of milk on the floor.

Michael milk…

Michael floor…

Sippy cup floor…

Michael milk sippy cup on floor.

This child has brought together different kinds of information learned from his experience, different syntactic or phrase structures, different mental activities, and different word choices to put his thoughts into words. He is assembling a working system using different invisible knowledge sources (phonological, structural, and semantic [meaning]) that will be useful when he reads and writes.

Researchers investigating the beginnings of literacy (Cazden, 1988; Clay, 1966, 2001; Teale & Sulzby, 1986) agree that learning to read and write is a continuation of the process of language learning that is already well established in speech. Reading and writing are thus ways of constructing and conveying meaning with written language that build on ways young children learn to construct and convey meaning through talk.

Researchers studying language development (Cazden, 1988; Halliday, 1975; Wells, 1981) and early literacy development (Clay, 1966, 2001) have found that conversation with others, especially adults, plays a critical role in enabling children to read and write. Learning to talk and early literacy (reading and writing) development do not simply happen; rather, they are part of a social process, embedded in children's early childhood experiences (e.g., hearing and sharing stories, dramatizing stories, reacting to stories, painting and coloring pictures, writing their names, writing stories). Furthermore, these preschool experiences are enriched, extended, and supported by conversations with others. Heath (1983) notes that whether and how preschool children make connections between talking, playing, drawing, reading, and writing depends on the following:

- what is available and valued in their homes and culture;

- how the people in their environment use reading and writing in their own lives; and

- how these people initiate, support, and respond to children's early attempts to read and write.

Many children have listened to and discussed thousands of stories before they begin formal schooling. They have also had many opportunities to read, respond to, and write their own messages. Family members and others have provided literacy lessons every day in response to their early attempts to read and write—experiences necessary to help them benefit from more formal schooling.

Some children, however, have not had rich preschool literacy experiences. Nobody has read to them or helped them write their names. There are no books or writing paper in the home. While they can express themselves using language, they have not had opportunities to react to a story and express themselves in writing. No one served as a model, providing reading and writing materials, demonstrating their use, offering assistance and encouragement as the child attempted to read and write. Children's limited literacy experiences may not provide a strong framework for the instruction they will receive in school. Learning to read and write will be more difficult for the child with few literacy experiences.

Differences in school entrants' achievements arise from different exposure to literacy opportunities, not from brain deficits. Children whose opportunities for literacy learning have been limited before they come to school will have to do that learning in school. Clay (1991) writes:

> An emphasis on individual differences in preschool children's experiences (stemming largely from their different ways of exploring their environments) signals the need for schools to plan and provide for activities in the first year of school which allow all children to widen the range of their preschool experiences, wherever they are starting from. Success in school will be fostered by a program that goes to where each individual child is in his or her exploration of literacy and provides appropriate experiences for building that existing knowledge. Each child should be introduced to the school's program at some level with which he or she can engage. (p. 44)

Reading and Writing Are Reciprocal and Interrelated Processes

Reading and writing are reciprocal and interrelated processes that affect one another, whether we plan for it or not (Clay, 2001). Writing can foster reading competence and reading can foster writing competence if the learner becomes aware of the reciprocal nature of these acts (Clay, 1998).

A rich network of processing connections is constructed by children who are taught to read and write texts of many kinds. Clay (1998) makes a case for such reciprocity of learning and the use of common sources of information in both reading and writing, citing the following advantages:

1. *Writing fosters slow analysis.* Writing is the slowest of the language activities, which allows the writer to develop phonemic awareness, focuses attention on the detail of print, and helps the learner to observe organizational and sequential features of printed language. "This could be critical experience at a time when learners are constructing fundamental and fast visual perception processes for reorganizing print forms" (Clay, 1998, p. 138).

2. *Writing highlights letter forms, letter sequences, and letter clusters.* Writing helps the child learn how to analyze print at the letter level and analyze letters at the feature level. It also helps the learner group letters into sequences and clusters in order to get the message down before it is forgotten. Control over a cluster of letters frees attention to concentrate on the meaning and structure of the next sentence the child is trying to write.

3. *Writing helps the learner switch between different knowledge sources.* The writer composes the sentence in his or her head and writes a word letter by letter to make a word; word by word to make a phrase; phrase by

phrase to make a sentence, paragraph, and story. The writer learns how to use any feature within the language hierarchy (e.g., sounds, letter, word, sentence), which fosters the visual perception skills required to read.

4. *Cognitive advantages can be predicted.* Learning how to link letters, words, and sentences as well as compare, contrast, and self-correct in writing is necessary for monitoring performance. The same cognitive processes lead to self-corrections in reading.

Writers have to know how to do certain things with language that overlap with things that readers have to know how to do. In both activities, children draw on the same cognitive/processing networks. For example, in writing children compose language by attending to every feature of every letter in correct sequence and to words in the text just as they do in reading. When children learn to read and write concurrently, these activities help them to attend analytically to the oral language they already use. They learn to make links between speaking, reading, and writing as they try to write their earliest messages and then read them.

Learning to Read Involves a Process of Reading and Writing Continuous Text

Learning to read involves a process of reading and writing continuous text. Effective processing is supported by and related to textual factors. Gradient of difficulty and text selection support an individual child's building of a processing system; children make a series of sequential decisions based on a simple text. What they know and do depends on their current understandings and problem-solving strategies and how they choose to process a particular text. Over time, young children construct a vast range of complex processing activities finely tuned for reading and writing continuous text.

Clay's theory about emergent readers—who work across continuous text and construct meaning and who work on the syntactic structures of sentences while building relationships between letters and words—suggests a theory of comprehension (Clay, 2001). Although Clay suggests that we reserve the terms *comprehension* and *understanding* for some overarching processes, she argues that the word-by-word decision making marks out a path towards comprehension which can be observed in both reading and writing. In the following example, Lyons (2003, p. 34) illustrates the word-by-word decision making of a young reader as the child monitors reading, takes a closer look at the unknown word, and after making several attempts to make the unknown word look like the word in the text, self-corrects—all while attending to language structure and meaning of the sentence.

Text:	*Child's comments:*

fix

On Monday Willy helped me fold the clothes.   "It can't be fix. No *x*."

f-i-n-d

On Monday Willy helped me fold the clothes.   "There's no *o*."

fold

On Monday Willy helped me fold the clothes.   "Yea, that makes sense and the word looks like *fold*."

Clay argues that comprehension is involved in all reading and writing of continuous text, even a one-sentence message such as the one described above. Clay (2001) explains this child's processing as follows:

> Sequential decision-making depends on tentative understanding of the message so far, while allowing the language user to change direction en route. Early effective reading and writing of continuous text places high demands on understanding groupings of words in the messages read and written so far. (pp. 106–107)

Jones and Smith-Burke (1999) point out that Clay's theory of literacy acquisition is about learning to read and write more than it is about methods for teaching literacy. Clay (1993) suggests that her theory of reading is based on a general theory of learning that assumes:

> …a theory of reading continuous texts cannot arise from a theory of word reading because it involves the integration of many behaviours not studied in a theory of reading words. (It must, of course, explain the role of word reading and letter recognition within the theory of reading continuous text.) (p. 7)

Learning to Read Involves a Continuous Process of Changing Over Time

An Observation Survey of Early Literacy Achievement (Clay, 2002) provides a basis for identifying and describing what a particular child has learned about reading and writing and how the child works on texts (see Chapter 5). As children begin to learn how to read, they attend to a few aspects of texts (e.g., letters, letter clusters, words, pictures, language structure, meaning of the story). Gradually their learning expands in each of these areas, and they begin to develop ways of working on the interrelationships of these areas. Tasks that required close attention at first gradually require less and less focused attention; this continues to change, requiring less and less attention as the child becomes more and more proficient. For example, initially the young reader reads the text slowly, checking each word closely to see if it looks right. After several weeks, the child becomes more proficient and fluent, quickly scanning the printed words while reading the text. There is a change over time not only in what the child knows, but in the child's neural processing (Clay, 1993).

Learning to read involves a continuous process of changing over time as new processes are acquired and expanded. As readers become competent, the strategies they use to problem-solve adapt to solve new problems. This repertoire of problem-solving strategies expands and develops to solve new problems and novel features of text that children encounter as texts become more difficult.

Children Take Different Paths to Literacy Learning

No sequenced course of study or literacy program will meet every child's needs. There is no set series of activities or mapped sequence through which all children should or can pass. It is the body of knowledge in the heads of teachers that guides their instruction and interactions with children. "Whether this knowledge helps or hinders children's literacy growth and development depends on the tentativeness and reflective practice of the teachers" (Clay, 1998, pp. 95–96).

> If my program can take different Johnnies and Janes by different paths to similar outcomes, I may be addressing individual differences and cultural differences....I can interact with each learner at that learner's specific level of ability, as literacy tasks come under the child's control, woven in unknowable patterns into complex processing, which will produce ever-expanding control over literacy tasks. (Clay, 1998, p. 95)

Close observation of a child talking and attempting to read and write will help teachers to infer the nature of their underlying learning processes. In observing and listening, and trying to understand what the child understands, they are working from the child's perspective (Clay, 1998). Only then will teachers be able to provide learning opportunities that empower children to do what they can do and help them engage in activities through which they can learn something new every day. Then children with few literacy opportunities in preschool will be able to catch up to their classmates and participate fully in classroom activities. And despite these variations in literacy knowledge and skill at the beginning of school, after 2 or 3 years of schooling they become successful readers and writers. They just took different paths to common outcomes. But their futures have changed. Clay (1998) writes:

> If children are to achieve common outcomes after two or three years in school it will be necessary to recognize that they enter school having

learned different things in different ways in different cultures and communities. I assure that what one already knows is important in determining what one will come to know and, if teachers believe that, they would search for what each new entrant to school, or any slow-to-get-started learner, already knows about how one can learn. (p. 1)

In the following section we will discuss Reading Recovery, the intervention that is grounded and framed by these seven key principles of literacy learning.

Theoretical Assumptions That Underlie Reading Recovery Instruction and the Training of Reading Recovery Teachers

The Reading Recovery course of study does not separate theory building and training from practice. Teachers-in-training are provided many experiences to develop a solid theoretical understanding of how children learn to read and write from which to work. They learn how to use what they are learning while teaching struggling readers. They also learn how to make their developing theories about reading and writing explicit by observing one member of their group teaching a child through a one-way glass and simultaneously analyzing and discussing the interactions of teacher and student (see Chapter 8).

Clay (1997) cites David Pearson's comment about the implications of teacher education in Reading Recovery:

Reading Recovery has managed to operationalize that vague notion that teachers ought to reflect on their own practice. That behind the glass play by play analysis and the collegial debriefing with the teacher after her teaching session represent some of the best teacher education I have witnessed in my 28 year history in the field. (p. 663)

As previously discussed, Clay's theoretical model of literacy processing, which includes seven principles of literacy learning, emerged after research observations of successful children learning how to read and write. This model arose for and alongside an intervention for children critically in need of special instruction to build an effective literacy processing system. To understand how the lowest-performing first-grade children can make accelerative progress and reach average reading levels in their respective Grade 1 classrooms, one needs to examine four assumptions that underlie Reading Recovery instruction and the training of Reading Recovery teachers:

1. Reading and writing are learned behaviors.

2. Systematic observation informs teaching.

3. Building on children's strengths makes it easy for them to learn.

4. Accelerative learning is critical to success.

Reading and Writing Are Learned Behaviors

Many things that are critical for successful achievement in reading and writing—such as oral language (coordinating oral utterances with the language printed in a book), visual perception (attending to the details of letter formation), and motor behaviors (hand movements to support left-to-right directional scanning of the eyes)—are learned. Children entering school with more or less learning in each of these areas can be helped to round out their foundational learning at the same time as they begin to read and write. It is pointless to waste valuable time waiting for children who have not learned these foundational skills to mature or become ready to learn (Clay, 2001).

Whatever their origin, reading and writing difficulties have a large learned component. If low-progress children's learning difficulties are not discovered or left untreated, they will fall behind their classmates and possibly experience a lifetime of failure. That is why early intervention as a preventative of subsequent difficulties is necessary (see Chapter 3).

Systematic Observation Informs Teaching

Reading Recovery instruction is based on a detailed observation of the child as a reader and writer with particular attention to what the child can do. Close systematic observation is necessary in order to determine children's level of competence, foundational knowledge and skills, and what they need to learn how to do next to develop an effective processing system.

Reading Recovery teachers watch for new things children attend to, notice, talk about, and point out in the texts they read and write. The observant teacher selects texts for particular children to read that require them to use their current working systems and problem-solving strategies. Reading Recovery teachers also gradually take children up a gradient of text difficulty, asking them to lift their level of functioning to attempt to read and write more complex text.

Systematic observation is critical to determining if the task must be altered to make it more or less difficult. Reading Recovery teachers do not simplify the complexity if that complexity is the target of new learning. They share the task with the child and demonstrate the problem-solving process (Clay, 2001). Reading Recovery teachers support "the development of literacy processing by astute selection of tasks, judicious sharing of tasks, and by varying the time, difficulty, content, interest and method of instruction, and type and amount of conversation within the shared lesson activities" (Clay, 2001, p. 225).

No child goes through the same sequence of instruction. No two children read the same number and kinds of books. Children read different books at different levels of difficulty and achieve very different, unique writing vocabularies (Askew & Frasier, 1999). What works for one child does not work for another. Only through close and systematic observation and focused explicit teaching tailored to meet the idiosyncratic needs of each child will struggling readers become successful.

Building on Children's Strengths Makes It Easy for Them to Learn

All children enter school with stores of knowledge and ways of processing information from the world and from language. The beginning reader is where he or she is and can be nowhere else. Therefore instruction must go to where a particular learner is and take him or her somewhere else. No two Reading Recovery children have the same lesson because no two children have had the same literacy opportunities or experiences. They have different strengths, and observant teachers know the strengths of each child.

Literacy instruction can build upon a child's prior knowledge and experiences. Every day, Reading Recovery teachers observe children closely as they read and write, analyze their current understandings (evident in how they respond to texts), and build on their strengths to teach them something new. Building on children's strengths makes it easier for them to learn, and it is the more efficient and effective way to accelerate learning.

The Reading Recovery teacher does not waste time teaching something children already know and can do; the teacher builds their confidence by supporting and confirming their knowledge and skill. The teacher also makes maximum use of the existing response repertoire of each child, and thus every child's lessons are different.

Accelerative Learning Is Critical to Success

Children who make slow progress learning to read and write in first grade are dropping further and further behind their classmates every day. It stands to reason that in order for them to become average readers, for a period of time they must make faster progress than their classmates. Acceleration refers to this rate of progress.

In order for accelerative progress to occur, one-to-one instruction is necessary (see Chapter 6). Additionally, the one-to-one instruction must start with the child's strengths and proceed according to what he or she is able to discover about reading and writing. Reading Recovery teachers' decision making is the critical factor in helping children make accelerative progress. The teacher must follow the child's lead.

The child is the constructor of knowledge. Therefore the teacher must foster and support active and constructive problem solving, self-monitoring, and self-correction from the first lesson, helping learners understand that they must take over the expansion of their own competencies. Acceleration depends upon how well the teacher selects the clearest, easiest, most memorable examples with which to establish a new response or skill (Clay, 1993).

As children are constructing a processing system, Reading Recovery teachers focus on how the brain gets and uses information rather than accuracy, and they temporarily value responses that are partially correct. Acceleration is achieved as children take over the learning process and work independently, discovering new things for themselves in the Reading Recovery lesson and the classroom. Reading Recovery teachers set the level of task difficulty to ensure high rates of correct responding and appropriate challenge so children learn from their own attempts to read and write and go beyond their current knowledge. Clay (1993) argues, "it is the learner who accelerates because some things, which no longer need his attention are done more easily, freeing him to attend to new things. When this happens at an ever-increasing rate, acceleration of learning occurs" (p. 9).

Summary and Conclusion

Marie Clay's pioneering research and thinking over the last 40 years has influenced educational practice throughout the world. We close this chapter by discussing four contributions that have had a major impact on theory, research, and practice.

First, Clay's research in the 1960s, investigating how both effective and ineffective readers attempt to read and write, led her to the realization that young children construct their literacy knowledge gradually. Furthermore, learning to read is not about every child mastering a set of literacy skills at the same time. It is about young children actively constructing their own unique understandings of how to read and write over time. Today her theory of literacy learning and her conceptual explanation of this early literacy learning phase is widely accepted by literacy educators (e.g., Cunningham & Allington, 1994; Teale & Sulzby, 1986).

Second, Clay's intensive, detailed observations of emergent literacy behaviors revealed that children enter formal schooling with varying understandings about reading and writing. Some children have had many opportunities to engage in literacy activities while others have had few experiences. Consequently, they are behind their classmates from the start.

Her longitudinal research also revealed that it is difficult to predict precisely which young children will have the most difficulty learning to read and write. Therefore, prevention efforts must reach every struggling first-grade child. Today the concept of early intervention to prevent reading difficulties is widely accepted by national leaders and researchers (Snow et al., 1998).

Third, Clay's early research focused on the critical role observation plays in assessing children's literacy learning. This notion led her to develop observation tools to assist classroom teachers in detecting children who were experiencing difficulties early on in the school year. The tasks published in *An Observation Survey of Early Literacy Achievement* (Clay, 2002) have been widely accepted as an effective tool in helping classroom teachers assess literacy progress. It has been translated into Spanish and French and is used throughout the world to assess young readers' early literacy development (see Chapter 5).

And finally, Clay's early research convinced her that (a) the lowest-achieving children had varying degrees of difficulty learning to read and write, but that all can be helped with one-to-one instruction; (b) prescriptive programs do not produce the necessary results with the most difficult children; and (c) the principles for teaching the most-difficult-to-teach children are essentially the same as for those of other first-grade children, only there is less room for error in teacher decision making.

The Reading Recovery lesson framework and instructional procedures (see Chapter 7) were developed by Clay as she worked with a group of experienced, effective specialist teachers analyzing their own teaching of struggling readers to determine the most effective ways to teach the lowest-progress children. Simply using the Reading Recovery framework and engaging in recommended instructional techniques does not guarantee that every child who receives the intervention will learn to read as well as his or her peers. Teacher decision making is critical.

Reading Recovery teachers must learn how to observe and adjust instruction to meet the idiosyncratic strengths and needs of the child. Since no two children exhibit the same behaviors, they must begin teaching the child at whatever point that child has reached as an emergent reader. They must also make astute decisions based on their knowledge of the theoretical principles and practices described in this chapter. Teachers develop their skills by participating in the intensive, high-quality professional training described in Chapter 8.

We conclude this chapter by recognizing that for all those fruitful years, the results of Clay's exemplary research—her inquiring mind and her commitment to struggling learners—have paid off. Today researchers, educators, and legislators have turned their attention to prevention rather than remediation of reading difficulties (Snow et al., 1998; Vellutino & Scanlon, 2002). Additionally, Reading Recovery has proven to be more effective and efficient at preventing and correcting reading problems for low-achieving students (Wilson & Daviss, 1994).

Her colleagues and peers have recognized Marie Clay's research and achievements in the fields of developmental psychology, school psychology, and literacy education. In 1978, she was awarded the International Citation of Merit at the International Reading Association World Congress on Reading. In 1979, she received the David H. Russell Award from the National Council of Teachers of English for "the depth and scope of her scholarship and the impact which it has made on the education of young children." She was inducted into the Reading

Hall of Fame in 1982. In 1993, she was a co-recipient with Gay Su Pinnell of the Charles A. Dana Foundation Award for Pioneering Achievements in Health and Education. In 2003, the National Reading Conference, which includes national and international literacy researchers, selected her to receive the Distinguished Scholar Lifetime Achievement Award for her lifetime contribution to the field of literacy theory, research, and practice. Marie Clay has also been awarded two Fulbright Scholarships and five honorary doctorates from four U.S. universities and the University of London. An endowed chair in Reading Recovery and Early Literacy has been established in Marie Clay's name in the College of Education at The Ohio State University.

Gaffney and Askew (1999) have captured the essence of her lifetime achievements in *Stirring the Waters: The Influence of Marie Clay*:

> A major contribution of Marie Clay's has been to change the conversation about what is possible for individual learners when the teaching permits different routes to be taken to desired outcomes. This conversation is now embedded in diverse international educational systems. Our thinking has been stretched in ways that make some former assumptions about the lowest-achieving children intolerable. We now live inside a new agreement about what is possible...an agreement, a paradigm that did not previously exist and that will shape future actions and conversations. (p. xii)

CHAPTER 5

Observing, Assessing, Selecting, and Monitoring Children in Reading Recovery

Educators have traditionally relied on systematic testing of outcomes rather than systematic observation of learning (Clay, 2002), yet young children's early literacy behaviors are difficult to assess. Standardized measurement tools for use with children as they are beginning to learn to read and write are unreliable, and the scores do not adequately inform teaching. Although norm-referenced tests may yield valid comparisons of mean scores derived from groups of students who are already reading, they are not sensitive to variability in emerging readers and are not useful as baseline measures for assessing change over time in individual learners.

To address measurement needs of young children, we need an alternative view of assessment that focuses on observation. Marie Clay uses the term *unusual lens* to refer to "any observational or research methodology which gathers detailed data on changes in the literacy behaviors of young children as they learn to read and write continuous text over a period of time" (Clay, 2001, p. 42). The unusual lens focuses on detailed observation and analysis of young children's behaviors as they construct effective processing systems early in their literacy acquisition.

> Planned observations can capture evidence of early progress. All science is based on systematic observation of phenomena under known conditions....In the past it was not easy to convince teachers that observing individual children at work was a legitimate part of literacy teaching and assessment. Today, despite some lingering mistrust, direct observation in research about young learners is not only acceptable but has a complementary role to play alongside other research and assessment approaches. (Clay, 2002, p. 4)

In this chapter, we (a) explore observation and assessment as they relate to measuring where children are in the complex process of learning to be literate, (b) describe the standard set of tasks used in Reading Recovery for assessment and selection of children for participation in Reading Recovery instruction, (c) explain the monitoring tools teachers use to support their observations, and finally, (d) consider how observation leads to theory building and action on the part of teachers.

Assessment tools and the interpretations of them are directly linked with one's theory of literacy acquisition. Clay's theory of literacy processing (see Chapter 4) is the foundation for her observational tasks. Jones and Smith-Burke (1999) cited five key ideas within Clay's theory that are particularly relevant to her assessment tools and her evaluation design for practical application:

- learning to read and write on continuous text
- observing change over time as learning and development move forward
- acknowledging the reciprocal relationship of reading and writing
- taking different paths to common outcomes in literacy learning
- building a learning system that continually extends control of literacy processes

The measurement of early literacy is a complex issue and requires a commitment to careful and systematic observation. Observation is one way of gathering information as teachers work with children. When paired with carefully crafted tools, the power of both observation and tools is increased. Also, observational data must be reliable to be acceptable as evidence. The tasks published in *An Observation Survey of Early Literacy Achievement* (Clay, 2002) and running records of text reading have been shown to be reliable tools for measuring literacy behaviors as children perform tasks on letters, words, and texts. These will be explained separately in the next section.

An Observation Survey of Early Literacy Achievement

An Observation Survey of Early Literacy Achievement (Clay, 2002) was developed to meet the unique need to assess emergent literacy in young children. In the 1960s there were few studies of literacy acquisition or credible theories of literacy development using close observation over time during the first year of school. Marie Clay was committed to rationality and scientific methodology; the research designs she used and the standard measures she developed followed rigorous standards of research. Since the 1960s, Clay has engaged in more than 40 years of in-depth research and analysis of evidence to construct her theory and to validate measures that describe the range of differences and change over time among the lowest-achieving students (Clay, 2001). These studies, discussed in *Observing Young Readers* (Clay, 1982), extend or verify elements of her theory.

The Observation Survey has been reconstructed and validated in other languages. The Spanish version, published in *Instrumento de Observación de los Logros de la Lecto-Escritura Inicial* (Escamilla et al., 1996), is used by Descubriendo la Lectura teachers in the United States with children whose initial literacy instruction is in Spanish. French Canadians use *Le sondage d'observation en lecture-ecriture* (Clay, 2003b) with children who are learning to read and write in French.

The six tasks of the Observation Survey are used for assessment in Reading Recovery, but more importantly, they have been widely used with the 5- to 7-year-old age group across many countries. Users of the Observation Survey include classroom teachers, teachers working individually with children having temporary difficulties with literacy learning, administrators who want accounts of individual progress of children across time, and researchers probing how young children learn about literacy.

The Observation Survey incorporates both open and closed assessment tasks that allow for observation of emerging, tentative behaviors to detect the variability of individual paths to literacy achievement. "Powerful statistical analyses have shown that these procedures, which permit more detailed recording of individual responses than a normative test nevertheless have proved to be sound measurement devices" (Clay, 1982, p. 6).

The Observation Survey adheres to characteristics of good measurement instruments: standard tasks, standard ways of administering the tasks, ways of knowing about reliability of observations, and real-world tasks that establish validity of the observation. These controlled observation tasks have been widely used in literacy research. According to Clay (2002), they:

> can feed data into analyses of researchers, and best of all, they can provide evidence of learning on repeated measurements of tasks the child is actually undertaking in the classroom. In every way the information that is gathered in systematic observation reduces our uncertainties and improves our instruction. (p. 3)

In Table 5.1, we describe the tasks of the Observation Survey and explain the purpose of each.

Clay (2002) has provided extensive evidence to support the validity and reliability of both the Observation Survey and the Spanish Observation Survey. Detailed information is available in Appendix 1 of the 2002 edition of *An Observation Survey of Early Literacy Achievement* (see pp. 159–162). The discussion of validity estimates in the book includes information on

- content validity,
- face validity,
- curriculum validity,
- concurrent validity,
- predictive validity,
- construct validity, and
- convergent validity.

Updated New Zealand norms are located on pages 148–158 of Appendix 1 in the 2002 edition of *An Observation Survey of Early Literacy Achievement* (Clay,

Table 5.1 An Observation Survey of Early Literacy Achievement

Tasks published in *An Observation Survey of Early Literacy Achievement* are described below. Measures in Spanish vary only in the number of items for some tasks.

LETTER IDENTIFICATION

Purpose
To determine which letters the child knows and the preferred mode of identification

Task
Children are asked to identify 54 characters, the upper- and lower-case standard letters as well as the print forms of *a* and *g*.

WORD TEST

Purpose
To determine if the child is building a personal resource of reading vocabulary

Task
Children are asked to read a list of frequently occurring words in text. Three alternative lists are available for testing and retesting.

CONCEPTS ABOUT PRINT

Purpose
To determine what the child has learned about the way spoken language is represented in print

Task
The examiner reads a short book and invites the child to perform a variety of tasks such as indicating where to start reading on the page. Four versions are available. This task reflects important concepts to be acquired by children in the beginning stages of learning to read.

WRITING VOCABULARY

Purpose
To determine if the child is building a personal resource of words that are known and can be written in every detail

Task
Children are asked to write all of the words they can within a maximum 10-minute time period. Within guidelines for testing, examiners are permitted to prompt possible words as needed.

HEARING AND RECORDING SOUNDS IN WORDS

Purpose
To assess phonemic awareness by determining how well the child represents the sounds of words in letters and clusters of letters in graphic form

Task
The examiner reads a short sentence or two and asks the child to write the words. Children's scores represent every sound recorded accurately in this assessment of phonemic and orthographic awareness.

TEXT READING

Purpose
To determine an appropriate level of text difficulty and to record, using a running record, what the child does when reading continuous text

Task
Children are asked to read a series of increasingly more difficult texts. The tester provides a minimal, scripted introduction and records reading behaviors, such as rereading, using a running record. The texts used for Reading Recovery testing in the United States are not used in instruction, nor were they created for Reading Recovery. They were drawn from established basal systems and have, over the years, been shown to be a stable measure of reading performance. Texts represent escalating gradients of difficulty.

2002). U.S. norms are reported on pages 168–169; however, U.S. norms were updated in 2004 and are now available (www.ndec.us/). Johnson and Young-Hubbard (2003) conducted an evaluation of Observation Survey norms, reliability of scores, and the validity of decisions based on the instrument results and published an informative report in *The Journal of Reading Recovery*.

Reliability of scores depends on the standard administration of the Observation Survey. In Reading Recovery, teachers receive extensive training in the systematic, objective procedures specified for the administration, scoring, and analysis of this instrument.

The six tasks of the Observation Survey can be justified by theories of measurement, and they take other theories into account as well (e.g., from the psychology of learning, developmental psychology, studies of individual differences, and theories about social factors and the influences of contexts on learning). Observation Survey tasks are derived from a theory of how young children come to master the complex tasks of reading and writing continuous texts (Clay, 1991, 2001, 2002). Observation allows us to watch children as they work on print-monitoring their behaviors, searching for information, confirming notions, and solving problems. When children are encouraged to read and write texts, systematic observations are needed to inform the teaching process, the parents, and the administrators (Clay, 2002).

Many of the tasks in the Observation Survey are similar to tasks in other widely used standardized and norm-referenced tests such as informal reading inventories, word tests, and tests of phonemic awareness. But most of those tests assess parts of a complex process. Because the Observation Survey is administered when literacy learning is just beginning, a broad range of observations is needed to assess the diversity in children's learning. In addition to capturing observations of children's reading and writing on continuous texts, the Observation Survey includes tasks that contribute to reading and writing performance such as letter identification, concepts about print, knowledge of phonemic awareness, and word knowledge. The entire set of tasks is needed to describe a young child's emerging literacy abilities (Jones & Smith-Burke, 1999).

Reading Recovery appropriately uses the Observation Survey in pretreatment and posttreatment of children's progress (see Chapter 9). In an evaluation of the Observation Survey, a researcher and a practitioner concluded that "the Observation Survey supports teachers in systematically assessing early literacy achievement and making decisions about the progress of emergent readers" (Johnson & Young-Hubbard, 2003, p. 48).

Running Records as Part of the Observation Survey in Reading Recovery

Running records are used as part of the Observation Survey to assess text reading. The Text Reading Measure used within Reading Recovery in the United States uses texts from the ScottForesman Reading Systems Special Practice Books. To standardize the administration of the Text Reading Measure, brief introductions were produced and a standard format of administration was established. In a 1987–1988 study, The Ohio State University researchers piloted texts and procedures (Lyons, Pinnell, McCarrier, Young, & DeFord, 1988). Changes were made and a larger-scale sampling was completed to test these materials against a previously used testing program. There was .85 reliability between the original testing levels and the new ScottForesman levels when children were assessed using both sets of equivalent tests.

In 1990–1991, a random sample of 155 urban kindergarten and first-grade children were sampled using the Diagnostic Survey tasks (Clay, 1985) and the Reading Recovery text reading materials. An analysis of the text reading materials was completed on the first graders in the study (n=96) to determine the reliability of the scale using a Rasch rating scale analysis (Wright, Linacre, & Schultz, 1989). This analysis showed that the text reading scale had a reliability of .83 (person) and .98 (item). When the Text Reading Measure was combined with the other two tasks (a measure of print concepts and phonemic representation), the power of the assessment increased. It verified that while the Text Reading Measure does not provide an equal interval scale, the item difficulty scale itself across these three measures is robust and highly reliable (scale formula r=.99).

Reading Recovery analyses of text reading levels provide descriptive data of behavior on a scale of relative difficulty, and they provide data about change over time. These analyses are appropriate assessment and measurement techniques commonly used in the educational measurement field to validate such observation data as ordinal information, time series samples, and more. These techniques to transform observations into measures date back to the early 20th century (Thorndike, 1904; Thurstone, 1925; Wright & Linacre, 1989) and have since been perfected by advanced statistical procedures (Rasch, 1960).

Identification and Selection of Children for Reading Recovery

As a prereferral intervention, Reading Recovery is provided to the lowest-achieving children who

- are in Grade 1 for the first time,

- are experiencing the most difficulty learning to read and write in the classroom literacy program, and

- are not receiving other supplementary literacy interventions.

The first children who enter Reading Recovery are those with the most extreme difficulties. Students selected for Descubriendo la Lectura must also be receiving literacy teaching in Spanish throughout the first grade. English-language learners who are receiving literacy instruction in English are eligible for Reading Recovery if they meet selection criteria.

A team of teachers in a school select the lowest performers based on low literacy achievement relative to classmates. Classroom teachers nominate their poorest performers, and other teachers check the selection with the standard assessment tasks with established measures of reliability and validity described in previous sections of this chapter. The Observation Survey or Instrumento de Observación is administered early in the school year to first graders identified as having literacy difficulties.

These standard measurement tasks provide a profile of literacy repertoires that is used to select children for Reading Recovery, to make exit decisions, and to examine change over time at the end of the school year. Stanines have been developed for three points in time.

To ensure reliability in administration, scoring, and interpreting the results of the Observation Survey, extensive training is provided to teachers. In the United States, the equivalent of a week of assessment training is required before Reading Recovery teachers use the systematic and objective procedures required for student selection. Educators can be confident of the selection process because of the established reliability and validity of the instrument, the rigorous training of those who will administer it, and the informed input of a team of school professionals. Children admitted to the individual teaching setting are those who have not made good progress in literacy tasks in classrooms.

The design of Reading Recovery requires that the lowest-achieving children are the first to be placed in the available teaching slots. The selection process is guided by the teacher leader who has particular expertise in assisting teachers in the analysis of data and the selection of children and is supported by a school team. As teaching slots become available during the year, the Observation Survey is administered again to determine which children will move into those slots.

There are at least three rationales for taking the lowest-achieving children in Reading Recovery. First, when a child enters Reading Recovery, it is difficult to predict the level and rate of progress (Clay, 1993, pp. 86–94; Clay & Tuck, 1991). Though sometimes educators argue to select the children who may benefit most from the intervention and show higher scores, research data demonstrate that the lowest-scoring children can succeed in Reading Recovery (see Chapter 9). An analysis of the achievement of 2,037 first-grade children who entered Reading Recovery at the start of the school year confirms this conclusion. Students with the lowest scores on all but one or two measures (lowest 5%) had their series of lessons discontinued at the same percentage as the others in the lowest 20% achievement group who entered Reading Recovery (Gómez-Bellengé & Thompson, 2002). Also, there is no evidence that children who enter with the highest scores take less time in the program.

Second, the lowest-achieving children are the least able to wait for the intervention because they are not benefiting as much from the classroom literacy program. Left to wait, they will fall further behind.

Third, if the lowest achievers are not selected for Reading Recovery, the school will not eliminate the children with literacy difficulties from the school rosters. The lowest-achieving first-grade children will continue to have difficulty with literacy learning in subsequent years. In other words, the school will not benefit from the power of the intervention in reducing the incidence of literacy difficulty.

A set of standards and guidelines, as published in *Standards and Guidelines of Reading Recovery in the United States* (2004), guides the operation of Reading Recovery. The standards specify that the first children who enter Reading Recovery must be the extreme cases. This practice protects the integrity of selection and minimizes the risk of selecting children who may not need the intervention. Clay (1990) accepts as inevitable that in any prevention strategy some children could be selected for whom it is unnecessary. Early intervention programs involve predictions about future risk of educational failure and involve making judgments about how much risk a system is prepared to make. Reading Recovery reduces the possibility of selection errors by choosing the lowest children using standard and reliable measurements. Any site that does not enter the lowest children first is in violation of the standards and may not use the name Reading Recovery to identify the intervention.

Reading Recovery Selection Reflects an Inclusive Process

Selection of children for Reading Recovery is based on the following rationale provided by Marie Clay and reported in each edition of the *Standards and Guidelines of Reading Recovery in the United States (2004)*:

> Reading Recovery is designed for children who are the lowest achievers in the class/age group. What is used is an inclusive definition. Principals have sometimes argued to exclude this or that category of children or to save places for children who might seem to 'benefit the most,' but that is not using the full power of the program. It has been one of the surprises of Reading Recovery that all kinds of children with all kinds of difficulties can be included, can learn, and can reach average-band performance for their class in both reading and writing achievement. Exceptions are not made for children of lower intelligence, for second language children, for children with low language skills, for children with poor motor coordination, for children who seem immature, for children who score poorly on readiness measures, or for children who have been categorized by someone else as learning disabled. (p. 8)

Some of the children served in Reading Recovery are learning English as an additional language. If they are able to understand the tasks of the Observation Survey and are the lowest-achieving in the cohort, they are eligible for Reading Recovery. A series of individual lessons is ideal for children who are expanding their language and literacy skills at the same time because it builds on individual strengths and addresses the unique needs of each learner. Research evidence demonstrates that children for whom English is a second language profit greatly from Reading Recovery (Neal & Kelly, 1999). A school team with the consultation of the teacher leader may decide that a child is not able to understand the tasks of the assessment and may wait for a period of time to give the child an opportunity to experience the rich classroom language program prior to entry. Then they watch the child closely to determine an appropriate time for entry into Reading Recovery when a teaching slot becomes available.

Children are not penalized for previous absences in school, and a high absence pattern does not prevent the child from entering the intervention; however, it is particularly important to take preventative measures when a child enters Reading Recovery. At the point of entry, caregivers are educated about the importance of daily attendance and enlisted in the problem-solving process. Close contact with the caregivers may be needed to help the children have a successful experience. If high patterns of absence persist, the teacher leader will be helpful in the problem-solving process.

Monitoring Tools Used to Support Observation in Reading Recovery

All teachers make assumptions about children as they observe their behaviors; some assumptions are valid and useful, while others may be misleading. Clay (1982) explains the difficulties:

> It is easy to arrive at false assumptions about a process as complex as learning to read. Firstly, we are likely to average a vast amount of evidence in order to arrive at a program decision. Secondly, we may do this on the basis of superficial or highly selected observations. Thirdly, our assumption may be the result of an oversimplified, logical analysis of the task which bears little relationship to the ways in which individual children learn. (p. xi)

Teachers, therefore, need ways of checking their assumptions. This is especially important with children who are finding literacy learning difficult. With records of children's reading and writing behaviors, teachers can check their assumptions. In addition to an analysis of tasks on the Observation Survey, Reading Recovery teachers regularly and systematically use daily running records, daily lesson records, writing books, weekly records of book level, and weekly records of writing vocabulary to check their assumptions about change over time in each child's processing behaviors in both reading and writing.

Daily Running Records

Running records of text reading, taken at selected intervals, provide ongoing assessment information to the teacher (Clay, 2002; Fountas & Pinnell, 1996; Johnston, 1997, 2000). Clay (2000) suggests three important reasons to use running records with young readers:

1. to guide teaching by using recorded behaviors to make appropriate teaching decisions on the spot or at a later time,

2. to assess text difficulty to ensure appropriate level of difficulty and a suitable level of challenge, and

3. to capture progress of learners as they meet the challenges of increasingly difficult tasks.

For each child in Reading Recovery, teachers take a daily running record of yesterday's new book. After the reading, the teacher checks the record for any processing problems and potential learning points. The teacher uses this record to analyze behaviors used and neglected as well as to guide teaching decisions. These records are also a check on progress and a factor in selecting appropriate text levels for each child.

Interpretations of running records in Reading Recovery are based on a literacy processing theory that progress depends on increasing complexity in a child's processing. The child learns to work with several kinds of information and to read more difficult texts. The running record provides evidence of change over time in the child's processing behaviors (Clay, 2002).

Daily Lesson Records

Reading Recovery teachers keep a written record of each lesson with each child, detailing teacher moves and child responses. Evidence of behaviors during the reading of familiar and new texts is recorded. Observational notes also include information about the child's progress in knowledge of letters and how words work. Teachers record their observations of how children construct written stories and how they respond when putting the cut-up story back into whole text. Teachers also make comments about their teaching and their next moves for this child. These daily lesson records are also analyzed to examine change over time in all aspects of the child's literacy learning.

Writing Books

Each day in Reading Recovery, the child composes and writes a sentence or a short story. The writing book itself is a valuable resource for the teacher in monitoring change over time. The working space at the top allows the child and teacher to interact in problem solving and constructive collaboration. This working page provides a record of most of the teacher-child interactions during the writing of the story (Clay, 1993). From the writing book, the Reading Recovery teacher can also observe change over time in the complexity of messages as well as shifts in legibility and the use of space and size of print.

Weekly Records of Book Level

Reading Recovery teachers take running records daily. A graph of book-level progress is plotted from one running record each week. In addition to text levels, the graph indicates whether texts were at or above an instructional level or were too difficult. The graph gives the teacher and others involved in the child's education a graphic representation of progress on book-level reading.

Weekly Records of Writing Vocabulary

Reading Recovery teachers also keep a weekly record of new words a child can write without assistance. These words are recorded on a chart that allows the teacher to monitor growth in writing vocabulary and to hold the child accountable for words the child can write independently. The teacher also takes stock to see if the child's repertoire includes high-frequency words and words with high utility for future learning.

Observation Leads to Theory Building

"An interesting change occurs in teachers who observe closely. They begin to question educational assumptions" (Clay, 1982, p. 3). Skilled observers, then, build literacy theories and have ways to check against those theories. The following quote from Clay's work highlights the powerful impact that careful observation can have on teachers:

> Teachers can become astute observers of reading and writing behaviours and skilled at producing responses which advance the child's learning. In doing this they become more articulate about child behaviours, and what they may mean (Clay, 1987). Observing reading behaviour informs a teacher's intuitive understanding of cognitive processes and her teaching improves. *She has a way of gathering data during teaching and she has a way of keeping her explanations of her teaching in line with what her pupils actu-*

ally do. So every teacher builds a kind of 'personal theory' of what the surface behaviours in reading imply about the underlying cognitive processes. (Clay, 1991, p. 232)

For Reading Recovery teachers, the observation of reading and writing behaviors guides what they do, and this systematic collection of data increases the quality of their teaching. Teachers begin to look for better explanations of how children are producing those behaviors; they have a means of refining their personal theories of what it is to learn to read and write.

The teacher has a general theory in her head about children's responding. This is a theory she should check against what she is able to observe and infer from the individual child's responding, and which she should be prepared to change if the two are in conflict. (Clay, 1991, p. 233)

So, observation and assessment in Reading Recovery yield benefits for children and for teachers. Teachers grow in their understandings of literacy processes and are empowered to continue to refine their thinking and their teaching. This is a powerful bonus at a time when educators recognize the importance of assessment and monitoring in successful teaching. The benefits for children involve a successful start in their schooling which can change their paths of progress in very positive directions.

CHAPTER 6

One-To-One Teaching:
The Research and the Benefits

The one-to-one instructional setting is not a new concept in education (Clay, 2003a; Invernizzi, 2001; Wasik & Slavin, 1993). Examples include the historical role of the governess and the success of rural schools where one teacher teaches one or two children across several grade levels. Private tutors and reading clinics provide tutoring service to the privileged who can pay the price. Within schools, teachers often work with individual children as time permits during or outside the school day. Schools often offer one-to-one coaching in music, sports, second-language learning, speech and language therapy, and special education. Consider other one-to-one options in any district's offerings. Why would we resist a short-term one-to-one intervention for the most vulnerable literacy learners at the onset of schooling? A child with a full series of Reading Recovery lessons (12 to 20 weeks of daily 30-minute lessons) receives 30 to 50 hours teaching time—a small price to pay.

Individual instruction sounds like an expensive approach but has proved to be economical for two reasons (see Chapter 11). First, children move through Reading Recovery in a short period of time, usually between 12 to 20 weeks, and their places are taken immediately by other children. Second, after exiting the program, most children can move forward with the average children in their classes, with few needing additional help (Clay, 1993). There is a savings in costs for special education, compensatory education, and retention in grade level. Decision makers must view cost in a visionary perspective—making an early investment to realize later savings. And savings go beyond those measured by dollars; the cost of saving children from a future of illiteracy is incalculable.

The current emphasis to have all children reading and writing by third or fourth grade often ignores some important issues (Clay, 1998):

• the complexity of literacy learning,
• the varied histories of schooling that individuals have (caused by factors like societal differences and mobility),
• the limitations that all of us have with some aspects of learning, and
• the inability of the educational delivery systems of education to meet the learning needs of many learners. (p. 195)

The higher we set the hurdles, the more efforts and resources we will need to accommodate diversity in learners while trying to bring children with difficulties into the average range of performance (Clay, 1998). It will take timely individual teaching to accommodate the differences among these learners.

The following issues guide the discussion in this chapter:

1. Evidence for the value of group interventions for children with reading difficulties is not convincing (Hurry, 2000; Slavin, Karweit, & Madden, 1989).

2. Children with literacy difficulties have already demonstrated that group instruction in classrooms is not sufficient.

3. Children demonstrate a wide range of responses to classroom instruction in Grade 1. Clay refers to awkward responses as the unusual, unexpected, inept, and apparently unconnected responses produced by the lowest achievers that challenge classroom teachers. A short series of individually designed lessons is needed to respond to the wide range of awkward responses that can occur (Clay, 2003a).

4. Low achievers bring unique and limited strengths and diverse needs to the literacy learning process. For them to become active and constructive learners, teachers must focus on what they can do and build on that foundation. It will take individually designed and individually delivered instruction for these learners to achieve accelerated progress and benefit from classroom instruction. They take different paths to achieve the same outcome.

In this chapter, we first offer a brief summary of research on one-to-one teaching. We then discuss benefits of one-to-one teaching to children, to teachers, and to schools and systems. The chapter concludes with a discussion of the complexity of issues involved in one-to-one teaching and a plea for individual teaching rather than group instruction for a small number of first graders with extreme difficulties in literacy learning.

Research Support for One-To-One Teaching

Research supports one-to-one tutoring and indicates that it may be essential for children who are at high risk (Bloom, 1984; Snow et al., 1998; Vellutino et al., 1996; Wasik & Slavin, 1993). The U.S. Department of Education's Institute of Education Sciences identified "one-on-one tutoring by qualified tutors for at-risk readers in grades 1-3" (Institute of Education Sciences, 2003, p. iii) as meeting research's gold standard for establishing what works. The gold standard represents outcomes that have been found to be effective in randomized controlled trials.

Bloom (1984) highlighted the effectiveness of one-to-one tutoring. In a series of experimental design studies, two University of Chicago doctoral students (Anania, 1982, 1983; Burke, 1984) compared three conditions of instruction: (a) conventional, (b) mastery learning which added feedback and corrective procedures to the conventional teaching, and (c) tutoring. They found striking differences in the final achievement measures among the three conditions. The average student in the tutoring condition was about two standard deviations above the average of the control class, and the average student in the mastery learning condition was about one standard deviation above the average of the control class students. They reported that the variation of students' achievement also changed. Only the highest 20% of the students under conventional instruction attained the level of summative achievement of 90% of the tutorial students and 70% of the mastery learning children.

Bloom concluded that the tutoring process demonstrates that most students have the potential to reach a high level of learning. His research focus then became a search for ways to achieve this high level of learning in other more realistic settings. He suggested that more than group instruction had to be considered, namely, ways of improving students' learning processes, curriculum and instructional materials, and the home environmental support of students' school learning.

Bloom's work was generally with children in later grades and in classrooms with a broad range of achievement. Although not studying early interventions, his work may have even more relevance for the benefits of tutoring children with the highest need at a point when tutoring time can be dramatically reduced. The one-to-one setting in Reading Recovery can be viewed as practical and realistic because it is short-term and restricted to a small number of children with extreme difficulties in literacy learning.

Wasik and Slavin (1993) studied the effectiveness of five tutorial programs from two perspectives: empirical and pragmatic. They reviewed quantitative and qualitative research on Reading Recovery, Success for All, Prevention of Learning Disabilities, Wallach Tutoring Program, and Programmed Tutorial Reading. After reviewing 16 studies, Wasik and Slavin offered the following conclusion:

> It appears from the research reviewed in this article that one-to-one tutoring is a potentially effective means of preventing student reading failure. As such, preventive tutoring deserves an important place in discussions of reform in compensatory, remedial, and special education. If we know how to ensure that students will learn to read in the early grades, we have an ethical and perhaps legal responsibility to see that they do so. Preventive tutoring can be an alternative for providing a reliable means of abolishing illiteracy among young children who are at risk for school failure. (p. 198)

Wasik and Slavin also concluded that one-to-one tutoring is effective when the programs represent comprehensive models of reading and complete instructional interventions, when content and instructional delivery are considered, and when certified teachers rather than paraprofessionals are involved.

Vellutino and his colleagues (1996) studied first graders who were given daily tutoring as a first intervention to aid in distinguishing between reading difficulties caused by cognitive deficits and those caused by experiential deficits. They found that early and intensive individual tutoring, in most cases, is a more effective intervention procedure than small-group instruction. They argued:

> To render a diagnosis of specific reading disability in the absence of early and labor-intensive remedial reading that has been tailored to the child's individual needs is, at best a hazardous and dubious enterprise, given all of the stereotypes attached to this diagnosis. (p. 632)

The Committee on the Prevention of Reading Difficulties in Young Children was charged with the study of the effectiveness of interventions for young children at risk of having problems learning to read (Snow et al., 1998). The committee emphasized quality instruction and appropriate curriculum as the primary route to preventing most reading difficulties. Yet they acknowledged that additional efforts would be needed for young children, including supplementary tutoring provided by skilled professionals. They further emphasized the need for this type of intervention to be provided in first grade.

Research Support for One-To-One Teaching in Reading Recovery

Solid scientific evidence supports the effectiveness of Reading Recovery's one-to-one tutoring model versus small-group instruction for the lowest-performing first graders (Dorn & Allen, 1995; Harrison, 2002; Pinnell et al., 1994). Three studies demonstrating the power of one-to-one teaching in Reading Recovery are summarized below.

A MacArthur Foundation–funded study (Pinnell et al., 1994) provides support for one-to-one instruction.

This well-designed, large-scale experimental field study (40 schools) was designed in response to challenges about the delivery system of Reading Recovery. It was systematically compared with (a) another one-to-one intervention, (b) a one-to-one intervention with teachers who had limited training in Reading Recovery, and (c) group instruction based on Reading Recovery principles with trained Reading Recovery teachers. The lowest children (N=324) in the 40 schools were randomly assigned within schools to one of the four treatments or a control group.

Measures included those used in Reading Recovery as well as widely used reading tests (Gates-MacGinitie Reading Test and Woodcock Reading Mastery). The study employed a formal experimental design that used split plots to control effects that may result from differing cultures among school districts or individual schools. The difficulty of small standard errors in analysis of data at the student level was addressed by using the Hierarchical Linear Model (Bryk & Raudenbush, 1992) for data analysis.

Researchers at the University of Chicago independently analyzed the data. In addition, a renowned national panel of researchers not involved in Reading Recovery and appointed by the MacArthur Foundation provided oversight for analyzing the results.

Results were definitive. Reading Recovery subjects performed significantly better than any other treatment and the control group on all measures. Essential differences were related to the combination of individual instruction, the lesson framework, and teacher training.

An Arkansas study (Dorn & Allen, 1995) supports one-to-one instruction.

Dorn and Allen reported the simultaneous implementation of Reading Recovery and a specially designed small-group model. Extensive staff development was provided to Reading Recovery teachers who taught Reading Recovery (30-minute sessions) for part of the day and small groups (45-minute sessions) for part of the day.

The lowest children were served first in Reading Recovery; others were placed in groups of five. When a child exited Reading Recovery, the lowest child in a small group or the lowest from a classroom was placed in Reading Recovery. Priority was given to the individual tutoring for children who needed it most.

Data for 231 children were analyzed: 95 received Reading Recovery tutoring only, 93 received group services only, and 43 children received a combination of group service and Reading Recovery. Of the children receiving Reading Recovery only (initially the lowest children in the study), 76% had their series of lessons discontinued. Of the children receiving group service only, 30% reached successful levels of reading achievement. These children were initially higher than the Reading Recovery group in reading performance. Dorn and Allen concluded that Reading Recovery was the most effective program for the lowest-achieving children who must have individually tailored lessons.

A second Arkansas study (Harrison, 2002) replicates earlier findings.

A second Arkansas study examined issues related to one-to-one tutoring and small group instruction. The progress of 307 children in four instructional arrangements was examined: (a) Reading Recovery only, (b) small group only, (c) small group prior to Reading Recovery, and (d) Reading Recovery prior to small-group instruction. The lowest-achieving children were served by Reading Recovery as their first intervention. Harrison reached the following conclusions:

1. The lowest-achieving children need a one-to-one tutorial—the first-cut diagnosis for readers with the most confusions.

2. A small number of children need additional support through small-group instruction after Reading Recovery.

3. For some children, participation in a small group prior to Reading Recovery influenced the length of their Reading Recovery programs. However, these were not the lowest achievers.

4. Small-group instruction is more beneficial for children who need less supplemental help.

5. Children served in small groups alone (those initially higher than the children served in Reading Recovery) tend to be in that instructional setting for longer periods of time, usually all of the first-grade year.

Responding to Research Challenging One-To-One Teaching

Some educators are tempted to support small-group rather than one-to-one instruction for this vulnerable group of first graders. And although a recent meta-analysis (Elbaum, Vaughn, Hughes, & Moody, 2000) found large and significant effect sizes for Reading Recovery as a tutoring program, the authors suggested that small-group instruction may be as effective as one-to-one teaching. Their recommendations may be misleading, however, because support for small groups was based on studies that were not comparable across variables such as grade level, level of teacher training, foci of instruction, and outcome measures.

As evidence that Reading Recovery as a one-to-one tutorial had no advantage over small groups, Elbaum et al. (2000) cited two studies—one master's thesis and one doctoral dissertation. In one study, there were four Reading Recovery children in the sample, and they were taught by a teacher at the beginning of her yearlong Reading Recovery training. In the other study, the teachers for the Reading Recovery children (n=4) were special education teachers with no Reading Recovery training. Therefore, evidence provided in this study does not convincingly challenge the documented support for one-to-one teaching with young children at high risk of literacy failure. In fact, Elbaum and colleagues conclude:

In sum, the findings of this meta-analysis support the argument that well-designed, reliably implemented, one-to-one interventions can make a significant contribution to improved reading outcomes for many students whose poor reading skills place them at risk for reading failure. (p. 617)

An unpublished doctoral dissertation that claimed support for small groups must also be interpreted cautiously (Iversen, 1997). The one-to-one intervention in this study was far from standard Reading Recovery, yet it was called Reading Recovery. There were differences in the training model, the procedures for selecting children, teaching procedures, and issues of implementation and evaluation practices.

These studies remind us that we must be cautious about studies that compare Reading Recovery with group interventions. We must ask questions about the group intervention such as those listed below:

- Is the design and delivery of the intervention adequately described?
- Are the samples or populations clearly defined? Are groups comparable to Reading Recovery samples? Is the sample large enough to ensure confidence?
- What are the entry scores for the children in the groups?
- What is the duration—lesson time and length of intervention?
- Are the measures and analyses appropriate?
- Are conclusions based on data presented?

We must also ask key questions about interventions that identify themselves as Reading Recovery:

- Is the Reading Recovery intervention delivered as designed, including service to the lowest children first?
- What is the quality and the age of the implementation?
- What is the level of Reading Recovery coverage in the schools?
- How long have the teachers been teaching in Reading Recovery?
- What is the level of administrative support and the quality of classroom support?

Benefits to Children's Learning

For young learners with literacy confusions, one-to-one tutoring is essential. Consider the differences among first graders. They come with very different kinds of experiences and they bring to the task a variety of ways to respond. Also consider the complexity of the process of learning to read and write. For schools to meet the special needs of all children, programs must "first meet the individuals at their personal learning points and bring them slowly but surely to common ground so they can learn in class and small group activities" (Clay, 1991, p. 68). The most effective and efficient way to bring children who are struggling with literacy learning in first grade to common ground is one-to-one teaching.

One-to-one teaching in Reading Recovery benefits each child by ensuring that

- instruction is at an appropriate level and is built on the child's current strengths.
- expectations and challenges are appropriate.
- pace of instruction is appropriate.
- the child's attention is focused on literacy tasks.
- the child is an active and constructive learner.
- time is designated daily for reading and writing continuous text with skilled guidance.
- language and communication skills are enhanced.
- the child receives immediate feedback and explicit guidance.
- there is an opportunity for accelerated learning and a quicker successful return to mainstream literacy instruction.
- children receive emotional support that fosters learning—support that enhances attitudes, motivation, confidence, and trust.

Benefits to Teachers

An interesting perspective on one-to-one teaching was provided by a mathematics professor (Lederhouse, 2003). She observed primary students as they attempted to solve mathematical problems, noting that one-to-one evaluations revealed verbal abilities, organizational patterns, and levels of engagement. Only through the one-to-one interactions could she see the processes through which individual students deduced their correct and partially correct responses. She concluded that only through close individual observations can we see how a student arrives at a solution, revealing far more about the effectiveness of instructional methods than the number of correct answers on a test. Certainly, Reading Recovery teachers recognize the many benefits of one-to-one teaching as they work with each child every day.

Why is a switch to individual instruction so powerful in its effect? It allows for a revolutionary change in teaching, devising lessons which work out from what the child can already do, and not from the teacher's pre-selected programme sequence. When two or three children are taught in a group the teacher cannot make this change; she has to choose a compromise path, a new move for 'the group.' To get results with the lowest achievers the teacher must work with the particular (and very limited) response repertoire of a particular child using what he knows as the context within which to introduce him to novel things. (Clay, 1993, p. 8)

The individual tutoring in Reading Recovery enables the teacher to tailor each lesson to the unique needs of each struggling reader. This individual tutoring is efficient because the teacher does not waste time on what the child already knows. The Reading Recovery framework is qualitatively different for each child because the teacher makes decisions based on individual needs within each lesson component. The teacher is always pushing the boundaries of the learning of the particular child. The explicit and intensive instruction would be weakened if teacher time was divided among several other children.

One-to-one teaching in Reading Recovery benefits teachers by ensuring that

- they are able to closely observe and monitor literacy behaviors of individuals.

- they can make maximum use of the existing response repertoire of each child.

- they can support each child "by astute selection of tasks, judicious sharing of tasks, and by varying the time, difficulty, content, interest and method of instruction, and type and amount of conversation within the standard lesson activities" (Clay, 2001, p. 225).

- they can pinpoint confusions and intervene in a timely fashion.

- they can hold each child accountable for what he or she can do, thus fostering active problem solving, self-monitoring, and self-correction from the first lesson.

- their teaching is free from interfering variables of group dynamics.

- their knowledge of teacher-child interactions can help in their other professional role.

Benefits to Schools and Systems

The assertion of superior cost-effectiveness of small-group instruction goes against years of research documenting the failure of small-group remedial instruction to close the achievement gap (Allington, 2001; Allington & Cunningham, 2002;

Shephard, 1991). Yet in a world of shrinking resources, it is tempting to move toward serving more children. But we cannot be satisfied with service without assurance concerning student outcomes.

The service mentality in American education sometimes goes awry. There are educators who claim with pride how many at-risk children they have served, but they fail to report the outcomes. We cannot be satisfied with a vague notion of progress. The consequences are too great. We must demand rigorous outcomes for successful performance in regular classroom instruction as well as in interventions.

If one-to-one teaching yields positive outcomes for children, it is worth the investment. For the most vulnerable children at the onset of literacy learning, we argue that one-to-one teaching provides a switching station for some children, taking them to a kind of survival status in which they can benefit from class and small-group instruction. The investment not only pays off for the child, but for the school and the larger context of the society.

One-to-one teaching in Reading Recovery benefits schools and systems in several ways:

- The tutorial session with a highly qualified teacher ensures the basic goal of education—to teach each child at his or her current level of proficiency.

- This level of teaching dramatically increases the probability of meeting the challenges of federal and state initiatives.

- Children are able to benefit from classroom teaching after a minimum time in the intervention.

- Classroom teachers benefit from children who are able to fully participate in the classroom.

- The skills of highly trained Reading Recovery teachers influence their other instructional roles and their interactions with teachers.

- Schools have a demonstration that low-achieving children can learn, changing perceptions and expectations.

- Funds that would most likely be needed for retention, special education, and long-term remedial efforts can be dramatically reduced.

- The comprehensive literacy plan for the school or system will include an early and intensive safety net for the most vulnerable first graders.

- The enhanced self-esteem and self-efficacy of initially low-achieving children who are learning to read and write is a payoff to teachers, administrators, parents, and the greater community.

Groups Versus One-To-One Teaching

Reading Recovery provides a demonstration of what can be accomplished when teaching is designed to capitalize upon individual strengths—working one to one.

> There is a categorical difference between the kinds of teaching and learning interactions that can occur in individual instruction and the kinds of teaching that can occur in group and class settings. We will have to differentiate our theories rather than treat the two categories as if they were one. It is acceptable to believe that in learning to play golf and learning to play the cello, individual tuition will be more productive than group tuition, and I believe that following surgery, individual intensive care suited to my critical condition will be the treatment of choice for a short period of time even when the level of care provided in the general wards of hospitals is superb! (Clay, 2003a, p. 303)

As soon as a teacher must work with more than one child at a time, the lesson can no longer precisely address the needs of the child. Management of behavior is also likely to become an issue. Even in small groups formed to be homogeneous, differences among the children will emerge almost immediately (Hurry, 2000).

Certainly small-group instruction is a viable practice in classrooms and in many educational settings. But we have evidence that for a small number of young children who are the most vulnerable, one-to-one teaching is essential. In Chapter 12, we propose a framework for preventing reading failure and for creating a comprehensive literacy plan for schools. These plans would institutionalize the flexible use of a variety of instructional settings—whole group, small group, and individual—to meet the needs of all children.

Is One-To-One Enough?

We know that not all one-to-one interventions and not all small-group programs yield positive outcomes for all children. Therefore, consideration of complex factors contributing to success in both delivery systems merits attention. It is not simply a question of one-to-one versus small-group instruction. Hurry (2000) argues that while one-to-one tuition is important, the curriculum content and pedagogy are also important. Similarly, Pinnell et al. (1994) identified three factors required for successful intervention: (a) one-to-one teaching, (b) a lesson framework with appropriate literacy experiences, and (c) long-term teacher training.

In addition to the one-to-one nature of tutorials, Wasik and Slavin (1993) noted three patterns in successful tutorials: (a) a comprehensive model of reading (such as in Reading Recovery), (b) content and form of instructional delivery, and (c) certified teachers instead of paraprofessionals. Similarly, Invernizzi (2001) offers three attributes related to the effectiveness of one-to-one tutoring: (a) the structure and content of the lesson; (b) the consistency, frequency, and duration of the lesson; and (c) the knowledge, skill, and guidance of the tutor. She suggests there is a trade-off among these attributes that can lead to positive or negative outcomes for children. Reading Recovery addresses each attribute, strengthening its capacity for effectiveness in schools.

As educators, we know that the teaching of reading and writing is a complex issue, even when the children have no difficulties (Snow et al., 1998). Teaching children with reading and writing difficulties requires additional expertise. The instructional setting will need to be modified for a short period of time in order to meet the unique needs of these children. Because we know what to do to prevent literacy failure in the early grades, we are obligated to provide the human resources to do what it takes.

CHAPTER 7

Teaching Children:
The Reading Recovery Lesson Framework

The Reading Recovery lesson addresses the complexity of literacy learning, helping individuals in different ways perform complex literacy activities so they move up a steep gradient of difficulty with success during individually designed and individually delivered lessons. What Reading Recovery teachers do cannot be achieved in small-group or classroom instruction because they make adjustments for each individual, moment by moment, taking into account whatever shifts a particular student needs to make (Clay, 2005). A Reading Recovery teacher

- finds each learner's starting point,
- observes how the child works on easy tasks when things go well,
- responds to the child's initiatives,
- interacts with the learner's thinking,
- observes how this child works on novel things,
- applauds what is correct in a partially correct response, and
- identifies strengths as firm ground on which to build. (Clay, 2005)

In this chapter we describe the lesson framework, include the rationale for each activity, highlight the role of the teacher who designs the lesson series for each individual, and briefly describe materials used to facilitate the child's learning.

The Lesson Framework

Each required segment of the Reading Recovery framework is an activity within which the teacher creates learning opportunities for a particular individual at a particular moment in time. In every 30-minute lesson, a Reading Recovery child

- reads familiar books;
- rereads yesterday's new book;
- does a few minutes of work with magnetic letters, identifying letters, breaking up words, and constructing words;
- composes and writes a message;
- reassembles that message as a puzzle from its parts;

- is introduced to a new reading book; and

- reads that new book for the first time.

Many people are puzzled by the set of activities that comprise a Reading Recovery lesson, but the tasks are all designed to elicit, demand, and support a broad range of strategic behaviors needed to problem-solve in a variety of ways in both reading and writing (Clay, 2001). Each lesson activity is described below with rationales for inclusion in a Reading Recovery lesson. The following descriptions are based on information included in Chapter 6 of *Change Over Time in Children's Literacy Achievement* (Clay, 2001).

Rereading Familiar Texts

At the beginning of each lesson the child reads several books that have been read in previous lessons. Familiar rereading affords opportunities for the child to practice the orchestration of all the complex range of behaviors he or she must use in reading on easy texts that still challenge the child to do some reading work, engage with print, and learn more about the written code. The teacher observes and redirects the child's attention in ways that support processing behaviors. Clay (2001) notes that reading familiar books provides benefits to the learner such as

- increasing the volume of reading;

- consolidating learning that is not yet secure;

- reading in a well-paced way;

- putting all the processes together;

- using both print and language to guide reading;

- discovering new things about print;

- making effective decisions and self-correcting errors; and

- solving problems independently.

Reading Yesterday's New Book

The child independently reads a book that was introduced and read for the first time the previous day. The teacher observes carefully, taking a running record that documents significant behaviors that indicate both learning and learning needs. (See Chapter 5 for an explanation of running records.) After the reading, the teacher checks the record for any processing problems and for other potential learning points. This activity offers a number of benefits to the learner, including opportunities to

- problem-solve continuous text independently; and
- monitor, search for information, choose, confirm or revise, and make appropriate links to what he or she knows well.

Letter Identification, Breaking Words Apart, and Words in Isolation

The child manipulates magnetic letters to extend the range of known letters and words. Fast visual discrimination is encouraged as the child identifies letters and breaks words apart in different ways. Soon the learning shifts to the construction of new words from known ones. The activity is designed to provide the child with opportunities to

- attend to detail in print;
- attend to phonemes, patterns, clusters, syllables, and words;
- construct words;
- attend to the order of letters left to right; and
- use what is known to get to something new.

Composing and Writing a Message

The child composes a brief message and then writes it word by word, rereading as necessary. Embedded within this activity is a detailed analysis of the sequences of sounds in words, attention to visual details and letter formation, the building of a writing vocabulary, and the use of analogy to construct new words. The child has multiple opportunities to

- hear and record sounds in words, operating on phonological or spelling knowledge;
- learn how text is constructed orally and how it is compiled from letters and words;
- build a writing vocabulary of known words that can be written quickly;
- use what is known to get to new learning;
- reread messages to keep the cycle going; and
- learn about the function of letters, clusters, and words in texts.

Reassembling the Cut-Up Story

The teacher quickly writes the child's message on a sentence strip and cuts it apart as the child reads it. The process of putting the message back together requires the child to search for the particular words in sequence. This task provides opportunities for the child to

- search for and use visual information, noticing the details of words;
- reconstruct his or her own messages while practicing fluent, phrased reading; and
- self-monitor, check, and self-correct.

Introducing a New Book

The teacher selects a new book that has been thoughtfully chosen to "suit the child's level of processing and to present new challenges, tempting the child to lift his or her processing to another level" (Clay, 2001, p. 230). The teacher introduces the text carefully, helping the child become familiar with the meaning of the whole text, recalling some essential background knowledge, highlighting language that may be difficult, and letting the child echo this language. During the book introduction, the child learns to

- orient him or herself to a new text;
- access knowledge using context, print information, and self-questioning; and
- approach a variety of text types and genres flexibly.

Reading a New Book

After the teacher's book introduction, the child reads the new text with teacher support. The aim is to provide opportunities for the child to bring all he or she knows to novel text and to support tentative efforts. The child is encouraged to read as much as possible independently and to problem-solve the new features of this text using current strategic behaviors, with help from the teacher through prompting and confirming. Many opportunities for new learning are available to the learner during this activity:

- using emerging strategies on new text;
- consolidating some strategies;
- learning new strategies;
- linking and making connections;
- going beyond the information given;
- solving problems independently;
- reading and understanding a new text;

- revisiting known vocabulary in novel texts; and

- reading, anticipating, monitoring and self-correcting, guided by information from different sources.

Tailoring Lessons to Individual Needs as They Change Over Time

Learners are coming to complex learning from different directions. What occurs in each part of the lesson is determined by what the individual learner needs at that time. The difficulty and challenge increases for the child until the tasks are as advanced as those completed by most of the children in the classroom. The Reading Recovery teacher designs each task to provide scope for an individual learner to act and to move forward (Clay, 2005).

Reading Recovery lessons are individually designed by teachers who have participated in training over and above their classroom expertise. These teachers must be knowledgeable about a wide range of alternatives for working with the limited response repertoires of the children. *The individually designed lessons allow the child's rate of learning to occur faster than that of his or her classmates, leading to the accelerated progress needed to catch up with peers.*

Reading Recovery teaching derived from a theoretical model, grounded in field research on how children become literate (Clay, 1966). It was developed to provide an intervention for "children critically in need of special scaffolding to build a literacy processing system" (Clay, 2001, p. 225). The features of the instruction clearly call for intensive teaching:

- The teacher would make maximum use of the existing response repertoire of each child, and hence every child's lessons would be different.

- The teacher would support the development of literacy processing by astute selection of tasks, judicious sharing of tasks, and by varying the time, difficulty, content, interest and method of instruction, and type and amount of conversation within the standard lesson activities.

- The teacher would foster and support active constructive problem-solving, self-monitoring and self-correction from the first lesson, helping learners to understand that they must take over the expansion of their own competencies. To do this the teacher would focus on process variables (how to get and use information) rather than on mere correctness and habitual responses, and would temporarily value responses that were partially correct for whatever they contributed towards correctness.

- The teacher would set the level of task difficulty to ensure high rates of correct responding plus appropriate challenge so that the active processing system could learn from its own attempts to go beyond current knowledge. (Clay, 2001, p. 225)

Clay (2003a) made an interesting claim:

> Reading Recovery produces similar outcomes in three languages, which is surprising considering how much research effort is currently being spent on describing how learning to read differs in different languages.…Yet while we do know *what* children learn in Reading Recovery (the outcomes), *how* they achieve a multitude of changes in a short series of thirty-minute lessons has yet to be traced in detail in research studies. Despite our best attempts to capture, analyze, and explain to parents, teachers, politicians, and administrators how Reading Recovery children learn, too much of what is happening remains complex. (p. 298)

Attempts have been made over the last decade to uncover student-teacher interactions that are characteristic of Reading Recovery. Some examples are summarized in Table 7.1. These studies demonstrate the power of teaching in Reading Recovery. It is clear that complex teaching interactions lead to student learning.

Materials That Support Reading Recovery Teaching

The primary materials used in a Reading Recovery lesson include a large quantity and variety of carefully selected little books for rereading and for new reading, a blank book and sentence strips for writing and working on written stories, and magnetic letters for work with letters and words. These materials are briefly explained below.

The Texts

Each day and for each child, the teacher selects a new title from a Reading Recovery book list of hundreds of books arranged along a gradient of difficulty. The book collection for Reading Recovery teachers is carefully constructed to assure a high-quality assortment of selections and a range of content and language styles to use with different children. A variety of text types and genres comprise the collection that represents books from many publishers. The child will have multiple opportunities to reread these texts across lessons. Since Reading Recovery children read several books and write daily, the teacher has numerous opportunities to observe how the child is working with print and can design a series of lessons that enable the child to build effective reading and writing processes. The quality of the teacher-child interaction with the texts is the critical issue related to gains in the child's control in reading and writing continuous text.

Table 7.1 Research on Student-Teacher Interactions

STUDY/SOURCE	METHOD	BASIC FINDINGS/CONCLUSONS
B. J. Askew The Effect of Multiple Readings on the Behaviors of Children and Teachers in an Early Intervention Program *Reading and Writing Quarterly: Overcoming Learning Difficulties*	Analyzed taped interactions between children and teachers across four readings of the same text.	The study revealed that children's problem solving, error detection, and self-correction behaviors change as texts become more familiar. Fluent reading increased and teacher intervention decreased. The findings support the inclusion of rereading texts.
B. J. Askew & D. Frasier Early Writing: An Exploration of Literacy Opportunities *Literacy Teaching and Learning: An International Journal of Early Reading and Writing*	Studied the opportunities low-progress first-grade children had in learning to use strategies while writing a brief message during the writing component of Reading Recovery. Subjects were 82 children from eight states. Documents examined were writing books, vocabulary charts, records of text reading, and teachers' lesson records. Three strategies were investigated: writing known words, analyzing words by hearing and recording sounds, and using analogy to write new words.	Their analyses provided evidence that low-progress children acquire a considerable amount of knowledge about words, about letters and letter clusters and their sounds, and about the orthography of the language. This learning takes place in a relatively short period of time during individual tutoring.
D. E. DeFord Early Writing: Teachers and Children in Reading Recovery *Literacy, Teaching and Learning: An International Journal of Early Literacy*	Focusing on the writing component, examined differences among students (n=12) and teachers (n=8), half of whom represented higher and lower outcomes of program tutoring. Analyzed videotaped lessons, student writing books, pre- and posttest measures, and lesson records over time.	The study suggested that higher outcomes were related to teachers' supporting efforts at independent problem solving and making decisions about how to use tools such as hearing and recording sounds in words as well as use of word analogies across the child's program. Independent phonological analysis, generating new words from known examples, and fluent writing facilitated rapid progress. The researcher concluded that writing is especially helpful early in the child's program.
L. Dorn A Vygotskian Perspective on Literacy Acquisition: Talk and Action in the Child's Construction of Literate Awareness *Literacy, Teaching and Learning: An International Journal of Early Literacy*	Conducted case studies of one teacher and two African-American male students; data included audio and video recordings as well as observation and artifacts from lessons. Examined the types of conversations that occurred between the teacher and child during the first 2 weeks of the tutoring program, a time when the teacher is prepared to help the child fluently use the body of knowl-	The researcher's analyses confirmed that teachers used a variety of talk to facilitate children's literacy growth. This included responding to the child's demonstrations of literacy, activating the child's prior knowledge, describing the child's accomplishments. The study confirmed the central role of observation in Reading Recovery teaching and documented transitions from teacher regulation to child regulation in literacy events.

Table 7.1 continued

STUDY/SOURCE	METHOD	BASIC FINDINGS/CONCLUSONS
L. Dorn *continued*	edge and skill that the child already has as a foundation for accelerated learning.	
C. B. Elliott Pedagogical Reasoning: Understanding Teacher Decision Making in a Cognitive Apprenticeship Setting *Literacy, Teaching and Learning: An International Journal of Early Literacy*	Employed a qualitative case study approach to examine decision making by one effective Reading Recovery teacher.	The study revealed that the teacher's knowledge was built upon multiple sources of information: knowledge of the child (specific knowledge of current skills), pedagogical content knowledge (understanding of role as teacher), and knowledge of content (understandings specific to literacy and how literacy is learned). The research concluded that responsive teaching is not one of apply-ing a particular teaching move to a par-ticular response but of constantly syn-thesizing and analyzing relative to the individual child.
D. Frasier A Study of Strategy Use by Two Emergent Readers in a One-To-One Tutorial Setting Unpublished doctoral dissertation, The Ohio State University	Compared use of strategies by two readers and also examined the teacher's prompting for strategy use. One child made accelerated progress in Reading Recovery, while the other made much slower progress in learning.	This study indicated that while both readers made progress in learning and evidenced the development of strategies, the two differed in several ways. The high-progress student had more initial control of oral language and more readi-ly noticed and used visual information in print. The slow-progress student required more prompting from the teacher to take on every new behavior.
S. Fullerton Achieving Motivation: Guiding Edward's Journey to Literacy *Literacy Teaching and Learning: An International Journal of Early Reading and Writing* (Reprinted in S. Forbes & C. Briggs [Eds.], *Research in Reading Recovery, Volume Two*)	Studied one teacher's retro-spective account of a teacher working with a child.	The study provided insight into ways a teacher may scaffold for changes in motivational and cognitive processing. This documentation yielded evidence that Reading Recovery relationships are complex and involve emotion.
E. L. Kaye Variety, Complexity, and Change in Reading Behaviors of Second-Grade Students Unpublished doctoral dissertation, Texas Woman's University	Explored variety, complexity, and change in second graders' reading behaviors across one academic year. Analysis of more than 2,500 text reading behaviors revealed six major behavior categories (substitution, solv-ing, repetition, omission, insertion, and other). Findings highlighted readers'	This study revealed second-grade stu-dents' flexible control of a broad range of literacy-processing behaviors and their vast repertoires of ways to problem-solve new and unknown words. These find-ings underscore the need for a complex theory in helping at-risk children become competent and flexible.

Table 7.1 continued

STUDY/SOURCE	METHOD	BASIC FINDINGS/CONCLUSONS
E. L. Kaye *continued*	flexible control of a broad range of literacy-processing behaviors.	
E. Rodgers Understanding Teacher and Student Talk During Literacy Instruction in a One-To-One Tutoring Setting Unpublished doctoral dissertation, The Ohio State University E. Rodgers Language Matters: When is a Scaffold Really a Scaffold? In T. Shanahan & F. Rodriguez-Brown (Eds.), *Forty-Ninth Yearbook of the National Reading Conference*	In a case study of one Reading Recovery teacher and two students, examined the nature of the talk during new book reading. Data included videotaped lessons, interviews, and field notes. The analysis revealed three kinds of scaffolds: continuous, mended, and misleading (which was rarely present).	The complexity of scaffolding provided by Reading Recovery teachers is described in terms of the instructional decisions that teachers make on a moment-by-moment basis about the kind of help to provide and when to provide it in response to a child's attempts to read. These instructional decisions are not scripted or memorized; instead, the teacher is responsive to the student's attempts at difficulty, drawing from what the teacher knows about what to teach and how to teach.
M. C. Schmitt The Development of Children's Strategic Processing in Reading Recovery *Reading Psychology*	Examined and described first-grade children's development of strategic processes for problem-solving words, detecting and correcting errors, and confirming responses rather than increasing item knowledge in Reading Recovery instruction.	The study indicated that these Reading Recovery children increased their attempts to solve words and decreased unsuccessful attempts, engaged in more self-monitoring and cross-checking, self-corrected more miscues, and increased rereading behaviors as a strategy for problem solving and confirming. The article suggests the children were developing active construction processes that signal self-regulation.
S. D. Wong, L. A. Groth, & J. F. O'Flahavan Characterizing Teacher-Student Interaction in Reading Recovery Lessons Universities of Georgia and Maryland, National Reading Research Center Reading Research Report	Using a sociocultural framework, analyzed five Reading Recovery teachers' interactions with children in two contexts, familiar reading of known stories and reading new stories. Used five categories to classify behavior: telling, modeling, prompting, coaching, and discussing (talking about the text).	Researchers found that teachers were less directive when students reread familiar texts and tended to behave as coaches to support children's attempts. During reading of new texts, however, there was an increase in teacher behaviors such as modeling, prompting, and discussing comments that fostered efficient processing of continuous texts.

Writing Materials

Writing is an important component of the daily Reading Recovery lesson. The children learn how to compose and construct a message, with stronger teacher support in early lessons and less support as they take control of the writing process. The writing in the lesson is accomplished on unlined paper bound together in a book. The top part of the page is used for working out the construction of words, developing fluency in letter and word writing, and practicing efficient letter formation. The bottom part is for the final written message. The teacher copies the sentences on sentence strips and cuts them into phrases, words, or word parts. The child reassembles the message and rereads the story.

Magnetic Letters and White Board

Each individualized lesson includes work with phonological awareness and phonics skills within text and in isolation. In several parts of the lesson, children learn letter-sound relationships in reading and writing, and they learn how letters and words work in regular and irregular ways. Bright, various colored plastic magnetic letters are an important part of the lesson. The teacher uses the letters and a white board to help children extend letter knowledge, to develop fast visual discrimination of letters, and to learn how words work so they can use this knowledge while reading and writing texts. The goal is fast, flexible use of the print information.

A Final Thought

While many questions remain about the complexity of children's learning and contingent teaching, the following characteristics of the Reading Recovery lesson appear to be critical to the success of the intervention (Clay, 2001, pp. 221–222):

- one-to-one teaching
- teaching activities selected to meet the needs of individuals
- individual pacing and sequencing
- delivery by a well-trained teacher who keeps good records, knows all aspects of the child's learning history, and adapts daily to ensure the construction of an effective processing system

Each activity within a Reading Recovery lesson is determined by the specific needs of the learner at that time. The Reading Recovery teacher does not use the framework prescriptively, but rather designs the tasks to provide for an individual learner to act and move forward on a path to a changed future.

CHAPTER 8

Training and Professional Development: An Investment in Teachers

Improvements in student achievement require improvements in teacher performance. Teachers are prepared to enter the profession by limited preservice preparation programs that can only introduce them to the complexities of their roles. Development of their skills over time depends on the professional culture within which they do their work (Hargreaves, 1994). Teachers' skills may matter more than any educational approach or the accompanying materials (Darling-Hammond, 1996). If professional development is the key to student success, then attention to teacher learning is an obligatory component of every educational reform effort. The key delivery system for Reading Recovery is the training and professional development of teachers.

The current national goal of having highly qualified teachers for every child implies that teaching is a singularly important factor in a child's education, and for at-risk children, likely the most important factor. If that is true for all children, it is especially critical for children having learning difficulties. Informed and skilled teaching is essential and will not be available without high-quality, intensive, and continuous professional development. As reported in Chapter 1, the results of a large-scale study indicated that money spent on improving teacher performance netted greater student achievement gains than did any other use of school resources (Darling-Hammond, 1996). The researcher suggested that we could make an enormous contribution to America's future if we could provide the current generation of teachers with the knowledge and skills they need to help students learn. In this chapter, we describe the Reading Recovery professional development model and relevant research that has been conducted to support teacher learning and efficacy.

Reading Recovery: An Investment in Teachers' Futures

Reading Recovery represents an investment in the professional skills of teachers as it operates within an educational system through four key programs: (a) intensive, daily, one-to-one, 30-minute lessons for children; (b) a professional development program through which educators learn to teach children who have extreme difficulty learning to read and write; (c) a network of professional support for teachers and administrators involved in Reading Recovery; and (d) a research program to continuously monitor results and provide information for problem solving related to implementation (Clay & Watson, 1982; Gaffney & Anderson, 1991).

A Three-Tiered System for Training and Professional Development

Professional development is delivered through a three-tiered system (Gaffney & Anderson, 1991). Training for Reading Recovery professionals is differentiated to meet the needs of each group of professionals. Table 8.1 delineates the roles of teachers, teacher leaders, and university trainers.

Table 8.1 Reading Recovery Professional Development

PROFESSIONAL DEVELOPMENT FOR TEACHERS	PROFESSIONAL DEVELOPMENT FOR TEACHER LEADERS	PROFESSIONAL DEVELOPMENT FOR TRAINERS
• enables teachers to learn to design a series of lessons tailored to the specific needs of an individual child while they simultaneously serve children in daily lessons • teaches professionals to make effective, moment-by-moment decisions while teaching and to analyze their teaching afterwards • supports effective teaching of the hardest-to-teach children • provides a way for teachers to continue to study and learn about children whose learning is puzzling	• provides for expert professionals called teacher leaders to train and support Reading Recovery teachers • advises on all aspects of delivery of the program in a school, a district, or a consortium of districts • enables teacher leaders to create understanding of the potential, the focus, and the limits of Reading Recovery • creates teacher leaders who carry out local training programs, support a local implementation of quality, and guide the instruction of the most difficult children	• provides a third level of leadership through university-based professors who serve as trainers of teacher leaders at established centers • enables university trainers to advise all professionals about new developments based on research • helps trainers provide guidance to teachers and administrators on issues that may facilitate or impede the delivery of effective programs • creates and maintains a trainer network that actively guides all Reading Recovery programs through any necessary adaptations and adjustments to aspects of teaching and implementation that are needed over time as knowledge and society change

These three groups of personnel have clearly defined roles; they work together to make the Reading Recovery delivery system work efficiently. Reading Recovery teacher leaders, who provide training for teachers in school districts, are prepared through a yearlong residential program at a recognized university training center. Teachers participate in training for an academic year while they work with children and also fulfill other professional responsibilities. Trainers of teacher leaders spend a year in residence doing postdoctoral work while they learn the practical, theoretical, and implementation factors necessary to run a university training center.

Becoming a Reading Recovery Professional

Teachers are selected by their schools and school districts to work within one school with struggling first graders for at least 2 to 2½ hours each day. For the rest of the day, they serve in other capacities.

Teacher leaders are selected by their school districts and accepted at a university center pending an interview with faculty members. They agree to a full year of training. They sometimes serve a consortium of districts or work at a regional center. Teacher leaders teach children for part of the day and provide onsite assistance to teachers the remainder of the day.

A university applies to become a Reading Recovery university training center through a process of application to the consortium of universities involved (the North American Trainers Group). Trainers are selected by their universities and are accepted by a university training center for trainers of teacher leaders for the initial year of training.

For all three groups of Reading Recovery educators, training continues after the initial year with a built-in renewal system to update them on new ways to be effective in their work.

University Training Centers

University training centers are directed by faculty who have multifaceted roles in that they train teacher leaders and also provide leadership for a large number of connected school districts. There are more than 20 university training centers in North America, each maintaining a network of support and means for updating practice for a large number of teacher training sites. The universities provide the yearly graduate program to train Reading Recovery teacher leaders. University trainers hold faculty or administrative positions and also teach children, engage in research, support implementation at affiliated teacher training sites, and provide ongoing professional development for Reading Recovery personnel at all levels. They also may contribute to teacher education programs or have administrative responsibilities at their particular institutions.

Teacher Training Sites

In local areas, teacher leaders provide yearlong initial training for Reading Recovery teachers who receive university credit at U.S. sites. Teachers not only attend weekly classes to discuss theory and practice, but they also apply their learning every day through teaching Reading Recovery children.

Reading Recovery teachers at elementary schools are supported by their teacher leaders who visit schools to observe lessons and consult on hard-to-teach children. They also provide ongoing professional development for trained Reading Recovery teachers to continue building teaching skills and to provide information about changes in Reading Recovery—in the lesson framework, in teaching approaches, and in implementation.

The Reading Recovery Training Model

Research has revealed salient characteristics of effective models that should be considered in the design of professional development programs for teachers. Research supports teacher reflection (Bos & Anders, 1994) and conversation among colleagues (Combs, 1994).

Reading Recovery has been described (Alverman, 1990; Pinnell, 1994) as an inquiry-oriented model for professional development. The model requires teachers to systematically and regularly assess and analyze the child's current understandings, closely observe behavior for evidence of progress, self-analyze teaching behavior to determine effect on the child's learning, and tailor specifically planned interactions to extend children's understandings.

An integral component of Reading Recovery training is the opportunity for extensive conversation with colleagues. Sessions for all three groups of educators involve extensive use of a one-way glass behind which one member of a class teaches a child. Together, the class members observe two lessons in most sessions. Freed from teaching, they are able to talk while observing, a process that allows them to put their observations and analyses into words—almost a think-aloud process. In their conversations, they articulate their questions and dilemmas; they describe reading behavior and teaching moves in great detail. This process builds case knowledge over many observations of different children at different points in time. The experience helps teachers think critically about the art of teaching. They can "become more flexible and tentative, to observe constantly and alter their assumptions in line with what they record as children work. They need to challenge their own thinking continually" (Clay, 1997, p. 663).

Research suggests that intensive and extensive levels of support, monitoring, and coaching help in increasing skills (Anders & Evens, 1994; Moore, 1997). Many districts are employing coaches in schools to provide the ongoing, sustained support that it takes to make teaching more effective (Neufeld & Roper, 2003). It makes sense that coaching teachers in their practice is the most powerful means to increase their knowledge and improve their practice (Costa & Garmston, 1994). Teacher leaders provide coaching to teachers to help them solve problems close to their practice and learn to make teaching decisions on the run while teaching.

Using a sociocultural framework, a group of researchers (Wong, Groth, & O'Flahavan, 1994) analyzed Reading Recovery teachers' interactions with children in two lesson components: familiar rereading and reading novel texts. They found that teachers were adjusting their interactional patterns according to the difficulty level of the text; they were being less directive and acting more as coaches while children reread familiar material, but increasing behaviors such as modeling, prompting, and discussing the text during the reading of new material in order to foster efficient processing. The researchers stated that "teachers trained in Reading Recovery seem to know from moment to moment what text to focus on, when and how to prompt, when to tell, when to coach, and when to allow readers to direct their own reading" (p. 23). This same study revealed that teachers' scaffolding comments occurred not in isolation but "dynamically as the teachers attempted to find the appropriate support for the student at the right time" (p. 21).

No packaged teaching materials can substitute for an informed teacher's design and adjustment of lessons for an individual child, tailoring moment-to-moment interactions to help that one child use present knowledge to extend understanding. This skillful teaching is no easy task. One-to-one tutoring makes tailoring possible but does not guarantee student success as shown in a large-scale experimental study summarized in Chapter 10 (Pinnell et al., 1994). Instead, tutoring creates a context within which the teacher can concentrate on one learner (who deserves this level of focus because confusions must be untangled immediately so that he or she can profit from classroom instruction).

The spontaneous nature of teacher-child interactions is difficult for research to capture and to press into a formula that may be directly taught to teachers and transferred to other situations. Research has shown that teachers can learn to interact with students to promote learning, and this skill can be refined and extended over time, given a high-quality, systematically applied, and continuous professional development program.

Studies of the Reading Recovery Model

Studies of the initial course in Reading Recovery (see Pinnell, 1994; Power & Sawkins, 1991) indicate that training has a powerful effect on the individuals involved. An early U.S. study by Shannon (1990) indicated changes in focus and knowledge across 8 months of professional development. Teachers grew in their ability to evaluate, describe, and explain behavior. A key to learning was observation of real-life lessons and the chance to talk with peers during observation. In a case study, Woolsey (1991) found evidence that theoretical concepts deepen and become more generalizable after the initial training. Other researchers have explored the continuous learning that is expected of Reading Recovery teachers. A summary of studies is shown in Table 8.2.

The studies detailed in Table 8.2 support the Reading Recovery model for training and also provide evidence that professional development makes a difference. Professional development is the best dollar spent if we are serious about

Table 8.2 Studies of Teacher Learning Within the Reading Recovery Professional Development Model

STUDY/SOURCE	METHOD	BASIC FINDINGS/CONCLUSONS
B. J. Askew, T. Fulenwider, R. Kordick, S. Scheuermann, P. Vollenweider, N. Anderson, & Y. Rodriguez Constructing a Model of Professional Development to Support Early Literacy Classrooms In E. M. Rodgers & G. S. Pinnell (Eds.), *Learning From Teaching in Literacy Education: New Perspectives on Professional Development*	The researchers designed and implemented a professional development program for teachers based on the Reading Recovery model. Six staff developers participated in the project and provided ongoing feedback in the process of developing, testing, and refining the model.	Results of this qualitative study confirmed that teaching, assessment, and observation led to better understandings about learning and development. Teachers appeared to form theories through engaging in these processes. The results also confirmed the importance of grounding professional development in participants' questions, inquiry, and experimentation; forming collaborative groups; staying close to the work with children; and being characterized as sustained and intensive.
C. A. Lyons A Comparative Study of the Teaching Effectiveness of Teachers Participating in a Yearlong and Two-Week Inservice Program *Learning Factors/Teacher Factors: Issues in Literacy Research and Instruction. Fortieth Yearbook of the National Reading Conference*	As part of a larger field study of student outcomes, the researchers studied 24 teachers who had been trained in the regular Reading Recovery model, as well as 12 teachers trained in an alternative model that involved a shorter sequence of sessions with no behind-the-glass experience.	Training emerged as a critical factor in student achievement and a strong contributor to teachers' use of effective behaviors. Lyons concluded that the model enables teachers to internalize and transform psychological processes. This study supported the idea that social construction of knowledge applies to teachers' learning. Those teachers who were trained in the extensive Reading Recovery model (two treatment groups) also had the highest student outcomes in the study.
C. A. Lyons Constructing Chains of Reasoning in Reading Recovery Demonstration Lessons *Multidimensional Aspects of Literacy Research Theory and Practice. Forty-Third Yearbook of the National Reading Conference*	Researchers collected observation data from and interviewed 13 Reading Recovery teachers-in-training at two points in time: at 3 months and 6 months.	Data indicated that teachers learned to assist each other in thinking about instructional decision making, with the group cooperatively constructing *chains of reasoning*, a process that teachers reported as increasing their decision-making power. This cooperative consultation enabled teachers to challenge each other, providing alternative explanations for students' behavior and specifying evidence to support hypotheses.
C. A. Lyons The Use of Questions in the Teaching of High Risk Beginning Readers: A Profile of a Developing Reading Recovery Teacher	Researchers used a 3-year interpretive case study to examine the development of one Reading Recovery teacher's understanding and questioning practices over time. Data were videotaped lessons, which were first ana-	This study provided evidence that over 3 years the teacher continued to grow in her understanding of how to prompt and ask questions in a way that supported learning. Over 3 years, instruction became more skillful and complex, moving from trying out prompts and questions to using them skillfully to take into

Table 8.2 continued

STUDY/SOURCE	METHOD	BASIC FINDINGS/CONCLUSONS
Reading and Writing Quarterly	lyzed by experts and then discussed with the case study teacher while viewing the tape.	account the child's perspective.
C. A. Lyons, G. S. Pinnell, & D. E. DeFord *Partners in Learning: Teachers and Children in Reading Recovery*	Researchers studied six teacher leaders in training for one year. Data included observational notes of student behavior, running records of oral reading, writing samples to determine shifts in student learning, teachers' journals to record personal reflections about the effects of teaching decisions, audiotapes of lessons, and records of weekly meetings between teachers and one researcher with the purpose of evaluating instruction.	Researchers found that as teachers became more sensitive to emerging behaviors signaling student change, they began to tailor their own behaviors to meet the developing abilities. They concluded that this model incorporated a way of learning how to learn into their instructional repertoires.
J. Power & S. Sawkins *Changing Lives: Report of the Implementation of the Reading Recovery Program on the North Coast*	Researchers conducted a qualitative study of a group of teachers who participated in a year of initial training in Reading Recovery.	They found an initial desire on the part of teachers to be told the answers, as well as frustration when points were turned back to the group for decision making. Sessions were described as "intense" and "exhausting." The results confirmed the potential of the program for teacher change.
E. Rodgers, S. Fullerton, & D. E. DeFord Making a Difference with Professional Development In E. M. Rodgers & G. S. Pinnell (Eds.), *Learning From Teaching in Literacy Education: New Perspectives on Professional Development*	The researchers implemented a systematic professional development program for 23 experienced Reading Recovery teachers. Teachers participated in all-day group meetings to view videotapes of their lessons in addition to behind-the-glass experiences; these meetings were followed by individual school visits with feedback. Teachers were asked to rate their own effectiveness prior to and after the experience on 21 teaching practices using a five-point scale.	There was an overall rise of +.31 on the five-point scale across items. Self-ratings decreased on using records to inform instruction and analyzing running records to inform instruction. Items increased on teaching the hardest-to-teach students and on planning and executing effective experiences with linking sound sequence with letter sequence. Students in the first-grade cohort made better gains than the previous year's cohort of students taught by the same teachers. Examination of videotape indicated that changes in practice were detectable.
D. Shannon A Descriptive Study of Verbal Challenge and Teacher Response to Verbal Challenge in Reading Recovery Teacher Training Unpublished doctoral dissertation, Texas Woman's University	The researcher conducted a yearlong participant-observer investigation of a 12-member Reading Recovery teacher class. She examined the role of verbal challenge and teacher response during live demonstrations.	The researcher identified 19 categories of verbal challenge and 21 categories of response. She noted the role of explanatory questions and noted changes in focus. Teachers' acquisition of knowledge was evident in their ability to evaluate, describe, and explain behavior. She concluded that the opportunity to observe authentic lessons is a key factor in teachers' ability to interpret and transfer learning to their own teaching.

improving students' achievement in literacy. No kits, scripts, or other sets of materials can guarantee student progress. A research-based technique is only as good as the person who analyzes students' strengths and needs, selects the approach, applies it in a particular way, assesses the results to inform further teaching moves, and at the same time maintains a warm and trusting relationship with children while engaging their interest. The demands on teachers are high, and they are even higher if they are working with vulnerable children who have already begun to fail in reading. Reading Recovery teachers use a dynamic and integrated combination of teaching actions, all supported by research. Research-based methods are important, but teacher training is the key to success, a principle that is supported by evidence from empirical research (Pinnell et al., 1994, summarized in Chapter 10).

Teacher training is the key to student success. According to Rumbaugh (2002), Reading Recovery requires that teachers possess a solid foundation of reading knowledge, theory, and skills, and they need to learn to use data to inform their work with children. He argues that principals and supervisors could benefit from similar rigor in their own training. Another factor, often unrecognized, is teachers' motivation to teach. The National Reading Panel (NICHD, 2000b) claims that:

> Few if any studies have investigated the contribution of motivation to the effectiveness of phonics programs, not only the learner's motivation to learn but also the teacher's motivation to teach. The lack of attention to motivational factors by researchers in the design of phonics programs is potentially very serious....Future research should be...designed to determine which approaches teachers prefer to use and are most likely to use effectively in their classroom instruction. (p. 2-97)

Reading Recovery professional development has a number of characteristics that work together to support teacher learning. Participants observe phenomena that are important to them—those directly related to the problems of teaching—while at the same time they receive guidance from an expert. They read and discuss material, applying theory to real examples to build content knowledge. Daily they are expected to closely observe and analyze children's behavior, making careful records and investigating hypotheses. They present case examples (through written records and live demonstrations) for their peers to consider and discuss, and they see themselves as a group of professional colleagues who learn together over time and who recognize the central role of language in learning. According to Gaffney and Askew (1999), certain characteristics of the teacher development model closely match those that were proposed by Darling-Hammond and McLaughlin (1995). Gaffney and Askew list several characteristics:

- teachers engaged in concrete tasks of teaching, assessment, observation, and reflection that illuminate learning
- grounded in participants' inquiry, reflection, and experimentation
- collaborative, involving a sharing of knowledge
- connected to and derived from teachers' work with children
- sustained, ongoing, intensive, and supported by coaching, modeling, and collaborative problem solving on specific problems of practice
- connected to other aspects of school change (p. 87)

Reading Recovery has institutionalized these characteristics across all three levels of training that occur (Gaffney & Askew, 1999). Teachers, teacher leaders, and university faculty work together on their practice, gathering and analyzing data at the individual child level, the school level, the district and state levels, as well as nationally and internationally (see Chapter 9). They confront research and theory directly, seek colleague support, apply concepts to real teaching, and evaluate their own teaching actions.

Reading Recovery Programmatic Evaluation: Accountability for Student Outcomes

The goal of Reading Recovery is to dramatically reduce the number of first-grade students who have extreme difficulty learning to read and write and to reduce the cost of educating these learners to educational systems. This goal requires Reading Recovery children to make faster-than-average progress so that they can independently work within an average group setting in their respective first-grade classrooms.

In order to achieve this goal, children meet individually with a Reading Recovery teacher for 30 minutes each day for an average of 12 to 20 weeks. As soon as they develop effective reading and writing processing strategies that enable them to work within an average range of classroom performance and demonstrate they can continue to achieve, their lessons are discontinued, and new students begin individual instruction.

Reading Recovery teachers have taught more than 1.4 million children in the United States since the intervention was first introduced in North America in 1984. The expansion of Reading Recovery and the continued success of the students can be attributed to the program's strong scientific research base and annual ongoing program evaluation. Evaluating the effectiveness of Reading Recovery on student learning was an integral part of the original design of the intervention (Clay, 1979), and it continues today.

In this chapter we take a closer look at the Reading Recovery evaluation process and student outcomes. The chapter is organized into six parts:

1. Clay's basic research that contributed to the knowledge base and development of Reading Recovery

2. the Reading Recovery program evaluation process

3. national data documenting student outcomes

4. unique features of Reading Recovery

5. evaluation data that support Reading Recovery's concept of early intervention

6. subsequent progress of Reading Recovery children

The Knowledge Base of Reading Recovery

Reading Recovery is based on substantial research relative to how children learn to read and write. Marie Clay's basic research on young children's reading and writing behaviors conducted in the 1960s combined quantitative and qualitative methodologies (Jones & Smith-Burke, 1999). Her quantitative research used appropriate techniques for sampling, data collection, and analysis. The observational measures she developed (see Chapter 5) were subjected to appropriate statistical analysis to ensure their reliability and validity (Clay, 1985, 1991, 1993, 2002).

Clay's design and methods were also consistent with conditions of qualitative research. She collected observation data systematically at frequent intervals and used reliable and standard measures of observing and recording children's behaviors. In her dissertation study (Clay, 1966) and subsequent observation studies (Clay, 1972, 1991, 2001), samples of high-, average-, and low-progress groups of children's reading and writing behaviors were collected and analyzed. The qualitative and quantitative research guided her development of a theory of literacy acquisition that informed her thinking about how best to teach low-progress children to read and write and how to prepare teachers to teach them (see Chapter 4). Three strands of research contribute to Reading Recovery's knowledge base:

1. assessment of literacy learning

2. design and delivery of instruction

3. data collection and evaluation

Assessment of Literacy Learning

Assessment of children's reading and writing achievement is based on observational techniques published in *An Observation Survey of Early Literacy Achievement* developed by Clay (2002). Clay's observation assessments have been developed through rigorous research studies and are widely used by classroom teachers, reading teachers, evaluators, and researchers because of their sound measurement qualities. The survey tasks have high reliability and validity. A unique feature of Reading Recovery is that every day, every teacher collects data while teaching daily lessons to track the progress of Reading Recovery children. These data include running records, book graphs, vocabulary charts, and writing samples (see Chapter 5). Teachers also record on lesson records their observations of children's behaviors as they attempt to read and write. The lesson records and other sources of information collected daily for every child help Reading Recovery teachers monitor children's progress. The data are also used to analyze changes that occur over time as children work through their lessons.

Design and Delivery of Instruction

Clay undertook a research program that consisted of eight studies to determine if it was possible to change the design and delivery of traditional literacy education to meet the needs of children having the most difficulty learning to read and write. A number of studies explored this question, beginning with the original design studies in 1976 and 1977, and they were followed by field trials, monitoring studies, analyses of content studies, replication studies, and subgroup studies (Clay, 1993). Differences in subsequent editions of the published Reading Recovery training manuals continue to reveal refinements in the procedures as more research information becomes available (Clay, 1979, 1985, 1993, 2002). Changes in Reading Recovery involve a deliberate, careful, ongoing process based on continuous research. Over the years, refinements in practices have been based on current research in language and literacy learning and teaching, as well as on research and evaluation directly related to the intervention.

Researchers in the United States and other countries continue to conduct studies that inform the design and implementation of Reading Recovery. Additionally, researchers have conducted empirical studies comparing Reading Recovery with other approaches designed to help struggling students learn to read, as well as qualitative studies probing aspects of teaching, learning, and implementation (see Chapter 10).

Data Collection and Evaluation

Since first implemented in New Zealand in 1978, Reading Recovery has been subjected to ongoing evaluation through annual collection of data on every child who enters and leaves the intervention to determine what progress the child has made. Reading Recovery teacher leaders and administrators at every U.S. site systematically collect and report pretest and posttest data from the Observation Survey to the National Data Evaluation Center (NDEC), located at The Ohio State University, for analysis and dissemination. Numerous follow-up studies have documented Reading Recovery's impact on children's literacy progress for several years beyond the intervention using standardized assessments and state-mandated assessments (see Chapter 10). In the following section we take a closer look at the evaluation process.

Reading Recovery Evaluation Process

Evaluating Reading Recovery is a deliberate, careful, systematic, ongoing process based on continuous research. Refinements in practice are based on current research in language, developmental psychology, and literacy learning and teaching, as well as on research and evaluation directly related to the implementation of Reading Recovery. Procedures for data collection, analysis, assessment, and reporting are standardized nationally and required for every U.S. school district implementing the program (www.ndec.us/). Data are also collected on a random sample of grade-level peers to provide a comparison group.

General Procedures for Data Collection

The following 10 steps are required to evaluate the intervention in the United States.

1. At the beginning of the year, Reading Recovery university trainers send NDEC an updated roster of Reading Recovery teacher training sites (approximately 500 as of 2004) and affiliated teacher leaders (approximately 640 as of 2004). This registration process ensures that data entry is enabled for the more than 15,500 teachers, 2,800 school districts, and 8,700 schools affiliated with Reading Recovery in 2004.

2. In consultation with the classroom teacher and teacher leader, the Reading Recovery teacher identifies individual children having the most difficulty with literacy learning, administers the six assessments of the Observation Survey, and, in consultation with the classroom teacher and school team, selects the lowest-achieving readers and writers.

3. Using the NDEC Web site, the Reading Recovery teachers fill out demographic data; fall, entry, exit, and end-of-year Observation Survey scores; end-of-program status; reading group placement; basal program level; and background information on the children's intervention and other academic programs. Student data entry is ongoing throughout the school year as Reading Recovery slots become available and children enter the intervention.

4. The NDEC Web site uses validations to verify the data for accuracy and completeness. Upon completion a form is made available for review via the Web to a Reading Recovery teacher's teacher leader.

5. The Reading Recovery teacher provides daily lessons to each child selected.

6. As children exit Reading Recovery, regardless of status outcomes, the Reading Recovery teacher records exit scores on the NDEC Web site.

7. End-of-program scores on each of the six assessments are recorded as children's lessons are discontinued or they have completed at least 20 weeks of Reading Recovery.

8. The main goal of the intervention is to bring children served to an average reading level. Data collected at year-end on a random sample comparison group provide data to see if this objective is met.

9. Teacher leaders verify that all necessary entry, exit, and end-of-year data for children served by Reading Recovery, comparison group students, teachers, and schools are complete. They then submit their data to NDEC.

10. Annual entry, exit, and end-of-year data for each child served for every status category are analyzed, aggregated, and reported by NDEC to Reading Recovery trainers at university training centers. University trainers prepare university training center reports and state reports, and teacher leaders prepare site reports. Teacher leaders share district reports with district-level administrators and school-level data with school literacy teams. The director of NDEC prepares a national annual report that is disseminated widely throughout the United States.

Monitoring and Data Evaluation

The teacher leader at every U.S. teacher training site sends data annually to NDEC. Data submission is one of the standards required to implement the program. This permits an ongoing evaluation and monitoring of the intervention.

Evaluation data collected on the implementation of Reading Recovery from 1984 to 1998 are reported in *Reading Recovery Review: Understandings, Outcomes, and Implications* (Askew et al., 1998). End-of-year data for these years of implementation reveal that 79% of the 953,046 children who had sufficient time to experience a complete Reading Recovery intervention (defined as 60 lessons before 1998 and 20 weeks after 1998) reached criteria for successful release from the program; that is, they were performing within the average reading group of their classroom. A historical overview and discussion of data evaluation that document Reading Recovery's effectiveness from 1984 to 1998 is available in an article titled "Reading Recovery in the United States: More Than a Decade of Data" (Lyons, 1998).

In the 1998–1999 school year, Reading Recovery leadership in the United States decided to report more descriptive data to show the action taken for every child who enters Reading Recovery regardless of the outcome of the intervention. Five possible status categories for student outcomes are reported:

1. *Discontinued*: A child who has successfully met the rigorous criteria to be released from Reading Recovery during the school year or at the time of year-end testing. A child whose series of lessons has been discontinued because he or she no longer needs the support and

- has acquired a system of strategies that work in such a way that the child continues to learn from his or her own attempts to read and write,

- reads a text that the average child in first grade at school can read, and

- writes several sentences independently requiring only one or two words from the teacher.

2. *Recommended action after a full program of 20 or more weeks*: A child who is recommended by Reading Recovery professionals for assessment or consideration of other instructional support at point of departure from Reading Recovery after receiving a full series of lessons of at least 20 weeks. Actions may include referral for a longer-term intervention, classroom or small-group support, or referral to special education. Although the child did not meet criteria for discontinuing status, this category represents a positive action on behalf of the future support of the child.

3. *Incomplete program at year-end*: A child who remains in Reading Recovery at the end of the school year with insufficient time (usually less than 20 weeks) to exit the intervention. This category includes children who may continue service in summer or extended-year programs if they are available.

4. *Moved while being served*: A child who has moved while still being served, regardless of the length of the child's intervention to date.

5. *None of the above*: A child who is removed from Reading Recovery services under unusual circumstances with fewer than 20 weeks of instruction. This could include, for example, a first grader who was withdrawn from the program because school officials placed the child in kindergarten or a child whose lessons could not continue because the teacher could not complete the intervention. This is an infrequently used category, and each case is carefully documented with a narrative explanation reported to the university training center by the teacher leader.

The national database has influenced Reading Recovery research and practice; made Reading Recovery accountable to schools, school boards, and funding sources; and informed teaching, management decisions, and implementation. A technical report of Reading Recovery results in the United States is available annually through NDEC (www.ndec.us/).

Reporting and Dissemination

NDEC generates a student data summary (a roster), a site report that responds to eight research questions, supplemental tables that contain process evaluation data, alternate disaggregated data tables that disaggregate data by 10 different categories, and a spreadsheet containing all of the site's data.

Teacher leaders prepare training site-level reports based on NDEC data and then distribute them to stakeholders such as teachers, principals, or school district administrators. Teacher leaders are required to submit these site reports to their university training center.

Many teachers prepare school- and district-level reports. These reports can be edited to report data that meet needs locally and add text that addresses their situation. Teachers may share the data from school reports with school literacy teams. New system summary reports and school data summaries are intended to facilitate this process.

Universities write either university-level or state-level reports, or both, depending on their needs. NDEC processes about 15,000 reports per year. The cost to school districts is about one-third the cost of administering, processing, and reporting standardized tests and about one-tenth the cost of commercial Web-based assessment systems.

As a result of changes in technology, the time for processing data into reports has been reduced from weeks or months to hours or even minutes. Also, in 2003 for the first time, the technology developed at NDEC allowed for the virtually instantaneous creation of student, school, school district, teacher training site, university training center, and state reports for all such entities served by Reading Recovery in the United States. Those reports are always available on password-protected Web pages for Reading Recovery's teacher leaders and university trainers.

By providing so much detailed information to so many people so quickly, the functionality of these reports has shifted away from merely outcome and summative evaluation to process and formative evaluation. Stakeholders immediately receive the information they need when they need it in a user-friendly format and at the level needed to effect changes—that is, to engage in data-driven decision making.

Reading Recovery Student Outcomes

When comparing the national results from 1998 through 2004, years for which the new outcome status data are comparable, one finds small differences from year to year in the percentage of children who fell into the five status categories (see Table 9.1). Patterns were similar for the percentage of children who received a full series of lessons (i.e., lessons were discontinued or child was recommended for additional assessment or consideration for other additional support or services).

Table 9.1 End-of-Program Status of Reading Recovery Children in Each Category by Year, 1998–2004

	END-OF-YEAR PROGRAM STATUS												
	Discontinued		Recommended		Incomplete		Moved		None of Above		TOTAL
SCHOOL YEAR	n	row %	n	row %	n	row %	n	row %	n	row %	n
1998–1999	77,882	57%	21,192	16%	25,782	18%	6,473	5%	4,836	4%	136,165
1999–2000	84,734	58%	23,989	16%	25,605	17%	7,224	5%	5,373	4%	146,925
2000–2001	87,506	59%	25,502	17%	24,266	16%	6,799	5%	4,846	3%	148,919
2001–2002	86,855	60%	24,916	17%	22,469	15%	6,267	4%	5,197	4%	145,704
2002–2003	82,639	59%	25,5898	18%	20,247	14%	6,318	5%	4,856	3%	139,649
2003–2004	73,487	59%	22,745	18%	18,177	15%	5,730	5%	4,468	4%	124,607
TOTAL	494,750	59%	144,345	17%	137,252	16%	38,814	5%	29,707	3%	844,868

Remarkably similar patterns can be found when viewing data reporting the percentage of children whose interventions were discontinued or who were recommended for further action at the state level or the teacher training site level.

Figure 9.1 graphically depicts the percentage of children in each status category at the end of the year during the same 6-year period (1998–2004).

As revealed in Figure 9.2, 77% of the children had their series of lessons discontinued and 23% of the children were recommended for additional assessment

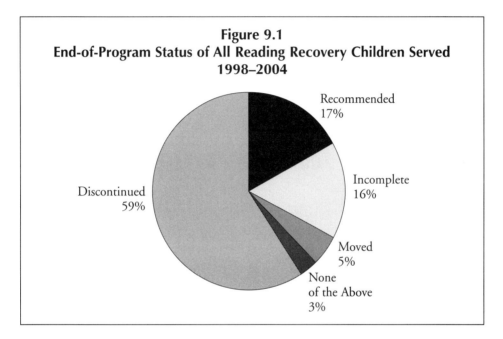

Figure 9.1
End-of-Program Status of All Reading Recovery Children Served
1998–2004

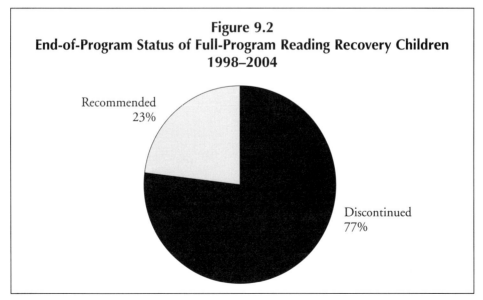

Figure 9.2
End-of-Program Status of Full-Program Reading Recovery Children
1998–2004

after they had an opportunity of at least 20 weeks of Reading Recovery. Appropriate school staff members collaborate to plan future learning opportunities for each recommended child. These evaluation data reveal that the large majority of children served in Reading Recovery experience the first outcome, while a smaller proportion of children are in the second outcome category; both outcomes represent positive actions for the child.

Unique Features of Reading Recovery

Six features of Reading Recovery make it unique when compared to other interventions designed for low-progress readers:

1. scientifically based reading research
2. national recognition and U.S. Office of Education Research and Improvement financial support
3. annual submission of data
4. replication of results
5. intervention evaluation data to inform implementation
6. Reading Recovery standards and trademark

Scientifically Based Reading Research

Reading Recovery has a strong scientific research foundation based on more than 35 years of the founder's work (Clay, 1966, 1979, 1985, 1991, 1993, 2002). The research methodology includes rigorous, systematic, and objective procedures to obtain qualitative and quantitative data to annually test three hypotheses:

1. Reading Recovery children will increase their skills in the following areas necessary for reading: letter identification, reading vocabulary, concepts about print, writing vocabulary, hearing and recording sounds (phonemic awareness and letter-sound relationships), and text reading.

2. Children who successfully complete Reading Recovery will perform on literacy measures within an average band of their classmates who did not need the intervention.

3. Children who successfully complete Reading Recovery will continue to make gains in text reading and writing vocabulary after leaving the intervention. Because these children were the lowest in first grade prior to Reading Recovery, we can verify the reduction in the number of children with extreme literacy difficulties.

National Recognition and U.S. Office of Educational Research and Improvement Financial Support

In 1987, Reading Recovery was one of 12 educational programs recognized by the National Diffusion Network (NDN), a division of the U.S. Office of Educational Research and Improvement (OERI), for its contribution to excellence in education. The U.S. Department of Education's Program Effectiveness Panel singled out Reading Recovery as exemplary and worthy of dissemination for three key reasons:

1. careful and rigorous design, methodology, data analyses, and reporting procedures

2. sufficient and adequate data to test the hypotheses

3. substantial research data to support its claims to teach the lowest-achieving children in first grade to read within an average band of children in the classroom within 12–20 weeks of one-to-one instruction

As a result of this initial recognition, NDN made funds available to U.S. universities and school districts that agreed to meet the Reading Recovery standards and guidelines to implement the intervention. From 1988 through 1997, Ohio State faculty submitted annual national research reports to the U.S. Office of Education and NDN to document the program's effectiveness, which resulted in additional funding. In 1996, due to rescission cuts by Congress, OERI's NDN was dissolved.

Annual Submission of Data

In order to implement the program, school district administrators must agree to submit data annually to NDEC. The data collection, examination, and reporting process began in the United States in 1984 and has continued for the last 20 years. No other early intervention has systematically collected, analyzed, and reported information on every child served, and no other early intervention has reported student outcomes every year for 20 consecutive years.

Replication of Results

Reading Recovery replicates its effect at the level of individual children, and the same results are achieved time and time again with different children, different teachers, and in different geographic locations. Replication of results is a vital component of scientific research and an important concept in the history and theory of research design because it allows scientists to verify research results (Campbell & Stanley, 1963; Kratochwill, 1978). Simultaneous replication has been used effectively to assess students' academic achievement in widely separated and diverse geographic settings (Frymier et al., 1989).

Replicating across time and space are the most common ways in which replication research is conducted. Table 9.1 above is an example of replication across time. Year after year, results replicate in remarkably similar fashion in key areas such as percentage successfully discontinued, exit scores, classroom teacher assessments of students served, placement rates in special education, and retention rates. More detailed replication data are available in the yearly national reports prepared by NDEC.

Replication across space is evident in the many reports produced by university training centers and teacher training sites. Most university training centers produce annual or biennial reports (see, for example, reports from Lesley University, Texas Woman's University, Purdue University, Georgia State University). Ohio, Indiana, and California produce yearly state-level reports. All of these reports show substantially similar results with minor variations on key indicators. The same is true for reports produced by individual teacher training sites.

The successful replication of Reading Recovery results across time and space is due in large part to program fidelity, which is institutionalized through the professional development model and the standards and guidelines of Reading Recovery in the United States.

Program Evaluation Data to Inform Implementation

Reading Recovery data provide a wide range of information about the performance of individual children and the implementation of the program. In addition to reporting the number of children discontinued, recommended, incomplete, moved, or none of the above, the outcome data reveal

- number of lessons for individual children,
- number of weeks of Reading Recovery lessons for children in the school,
- number of days of instruction for individual children,
- number of missed lessons for individual children and reasons,
- number of years experience for teachers,
- number of retentions in first grade,
- number of special education referrals and placements in first grade,
- level of Reading Recovery coverage in the school, and
- trends over time (by comparing successive years' data).

Careful examination of the data provides valuable insights into how Reading Recovery is working and direction to improve the implementation of the intervention. For example, if children are missing lessons because the teacher or child is in school and not available, recommendations to improve the delivery of the program can be made. If the child and teacher are available and children are not making good progress in Reading Recovery, explicit directions and suggestions for teachers can be found in *Reading Recovery: A Guidebook for Teachers in Training* (Clay, 1993).

Outcome and implementation data are used to improve the results of the intervention. For example, if a school district has a large number of children with incomplete series of lessons, administrators will be able to investigate why. It may be that children are frequently absent or that the population is highly mobile. The teachers may be missing instruction time because their lessons are too long or they are pulled out for other duties. If children who enter in the fall take too long, the result may be that there is too little time for the children who enter later to make adequate progress. In addition, start-up time in the fall and when the second group of children enter the program may affect the intervention's effectiveness.

Although the Reading Recovery intervention meets the needs of individual students on a one-to-one basis, and no two interventions are alike, sufficient commonalities exist that allow for quantitative evaluations of the quality of the implementation in any given school, school district, or teacher training site. Reading Recovery professionals and administrators who support the intervention assume that something positive is going to happen for every child entering Reading Recovery, and they share responsibility for the success of each child served. In order to accomplish this goal, they provide structures for successful implementation within the system.

Implementation data submitted to NDEC can be analyzed to determine the level of coverage at the school and district levels. A school or system has reached full coverage or full implementation when there is sufficient Reading Recovery teacher time to serve all children defined as needing the service in the school. School systems move to full coverage over several years. It is at this stage of full coverage that a dramatic decrease in the number of children with literacy difficulties will be realized.

Partial implementation should be a temporary condition, and school districts should work toward full coverage. Implementation data can be used to inform the administration about the level of coverage and to design a flexible staffing plan to support full implementation or provide training for additional Reading Recovery teachers to meet school- and district-level needs.

Because economy is an important factor in the implementation of any intervention, the length of the interventions is examined. In most cases, a child should be brought up to an average reading level in less than 20 weeks. Missed sessions for whatever reason should be few. The ongoing monitoring allows both university-based and local decision makers to identify areas for improvement and strengthen ongoing implementation.

The program evaluation data document that Reading Recovery is effective when it is implemented as originally designed and further refined by Marie Clay. When Reading Recovery is not implemented as designed, or it is changed or watered down so that the system is accommodated, it will fail to achieve its goals.

Reading Recovery Standards and Trademark

Reading Recovery is a not-for-profit partnership of universities and local school districts. In order to protect the integrity of Reading Recovery in the United States, standards governing how teachers are trained and students are taught were developed in 1989. All schools must adhere to these standards in order to be in compliance with the royalty-free trademark granted annually by The Ohio State University. This trademark helps to assure quality and consistency in Reading Recovery throughout the United States.

Reading Recovery standards and trademark are directly tied to submission of data. These data are specific to each school in every district that is implementing Reading Recovery. The data collection, reporting, and evaluation processes provide assurance that the conditions required to receive the annual trademark have been met.

Anyone associated with Reading Recovery must meet the standards as published in the *Standards and Guidelines of Reading Recovery in the United States* (2004). The university trainer must verify that this is the case. All entities associated with Reading Recovery in the United States—university training centers, teacher training sites, school districts, and schools as well as individuals such as university trainers, teacher leaders, site coordinators, and teachers—must be registered annually through NDEC.

The national data evaluation research reveals that a local implementation following Reading Recovery standards and guidelines will have better outcomes. Annual reports from NDEC also indicate consistently that Reading Recovery teacher training sites that are fully implemented (serve all students in need) are likely to experience better outcomes. The same is true of implementations that have more experienced teachers (Gómez-Bellengé, 2002a; Gómez-Bellengé, Rodgers, & Fullerton, 2003b),

One case study of two teacher training site implementations found considerably better results in the local implementation that followed the Reading Recovery standards and guidelines than in the one that lacked the support to do so (Chappell, 2001). In fact, the standards and guidelines list in great detail the conditions needed for the successful implementation of Reading Recovery. In a sense, the reason Reading Recovery is protected by a trademark, with annual data reporting required of all licensees, is precisely the belief that known factors can be used to monitor the quality of hundreds of different implementations across the United States.

116

Evaluation Data That Support Reading Recovery's Concept of Early Intervention

Prevention is a central tenet of Reading Recovery. The intervention is designed to reduce the incidence of literacy learning problems among the lowest-performing first-grade children, and it is supplemental to classroom instruction. Guided by a model of prevention (Caplan, 1964; Pianta, 1990), Reading Recovery helps the lowest-achieving children after they have been exposed to literacy learning opportunities and before the onset of serious difficulties. According to Clay (2001):

> The lowest achievers in any school will be at risk because by definition there are great distances between them and the main thrust of instruction in that school. Reading Recovery must take children from any classroom programme and return them to effective functioning in that classroom programme. Such flexibility is surprising, but essential and not usually acknowledged. (pp. 248–249)

Evaluation data collected over the last 20 years in the United States reveal that Reading Recovery can prevent a lifetime of reading difficulties if the intervention is delivered early during the first year of schooling. National data reported by NDEC makes a strong case for implementing Reading Recovery as an early intervention to prevent reading difficulties.

General Student Outcomes

Evaluation data collected and reported over the last 20 years reveal that approximately 59% of all children served in Reading Recovery have their series of lessons discontinued successfully, with about 79% of those having the opportunity to receive a full series of lessons doing the same. As a group, children served by Reading Recovery tend to enter first grade reading below Text Level 1, compared to Text Level 4 for the overall first-grade population; those children whose lessons are discontinued successfully end first grade with average text levels around 19, compared to approximately 20 for the general population.

Reduction in Special Education Identification and Retention

The percentage of children clinically evaluated by Reading Recovery teachers as having reached sustainable patterns of reading development (i.e., those whose lessons were discontinued successfully) and who are placed in special education services for learning disability consistently averages near zero percent, or about 140 for every 85,000 children on a national basis every year. This is a considerably lower placement level than for the general population, even though these children were considered at risk at the beginning of first grade. Similarly, these successful children are extremely unlikely to be retained in first grade because of reading difficulties, also occurring at a lower rate than in the general population.

Closing the Achievement Gap

Because students at risk often come from poverty or minority status populations, an important issue is whether Reading Recovery can close the reading achievement gap for poverty- or minority-status children identified at risk in fall of first grade. The important question is not so much if they close the gap relative to peers in communities with high poverty and high proportions of non-White students; it is more important to ascertain whether they close the achievement gap relative to White non-poor students. This is because high-stakes achievement tests have criteria or norms that are based on the achievement of non-poor White children.

If children are to pass these high-stakes tests in third or fourth grade and compete successfully with non-poor White students, they should be at least trending towards closing that gap following an intervention such as Reading Recovery. Using stanines as a basis of comparison, one study (Rodgers & Gómez-Bellengé, 2003) has shown that for students not served by Reading Recovery (that is, non-low readers), an initially small gap in reading achievement opens between fall and spring of first grade when data are disaggregated by race/ethnicity or by poverty status. However, for Reading Recovery students in the treatment group (i.e., those receiving the full series of lessons), data disaggregated by race/ethnicity or by poverty status illustrate that an initially larger gap closes on most measures and trends towards closing on the Text Reading Level measure.

Changing Classroom Teachers' Perceptions of Low-Performing Students

Every year, classroom teachers of Reading Recovery students are asked in the fall and again at year-end to determine in which of four reading groups they would place their students. In the fall of 2002, classroom teachers reported that 99% of the 67,791 Reading Recovery students whose lessons were later discontinued and 100% of the children who received a full series of lessons would have been placed in the low or lower-middle group by their classroom teachers. At year-end, 59% of the children whose lessons were discontinued and 46% of the children who received the full series would have been placed in the upper-middle or high reading group level by their classroom teachers. Only 7% of the children whose lessons were discontinued successfully would have been placed in the low reading group (Gómez-Bellengé, 2002a).

These data indicate that the ability to keep up with peers on literacy tasks is a critical outcome expected of successful Reading Recovery students. Furthermore, classroom teachers' responses to reading group placement provide additional informal evaluations to demonstrate that Reading Recovery children have developed effective strategies that help them learn from their own attempts to read and write and that they read at text levels comparable to the average or high readers in their classrooms.

Longitudinal Progress of Reading Recovery Children in Subsequent Years

Studies have shown that low-progress students who receive remedial reading do not maintain their gains once support has been removed (Allington & Walmsley, 1995; Johnston & Allington, 1991). In a review of Reading Recovery, Shanahan and Barr (1995) questioned whether Reading Recovery students continued to make appropriate gains or whether they returned to slow progress as demonstrated prior to Reading Recovery intervention.

In a large well-designed longitudinal study, Askew, Kaye, et al. (2002) answered this question. Data were gathered on 116 Reading Recovery students and 129 random sample children in first grade and fourth grade in 45 schools. Prior to Reading Recovery there were significant differences between Reading Recovery and random sample children in first-grade entry scores on the Observation Survey and a standardized test. At the end of fourth grade, both groups of students read above-grade-level materials with 90% accuracy or higher. Scores on the reading subtest of the state-mandated achievement test revealed that at the end of fourth grade, 85% of the Reading Recovery children passed and 90% of the random group passed. On the writing sample, 90% of the Reading Recovery group and 97% of the random sample group had passing scores. Scores on the vocabulary and comprehension subtests of Gates-MacGinitie Reading Test revealed that Reading Recovery students' gains surpassed those of their classroom peers between Grades 2 and 3 and closely matched gains between Grades 3 and 4. The authors reported, "This finding provided compelling evidence of continuing annual literacy gains for former Reading Recovery children—gains that closely matched those of their classmates" (p. 59).

Additional follow-up studies (see Chapter 10) reveal that Reading Recovery students continue to make reading and writing progress after they are no longer receiving the intervention. Furthermore, a variety of standardized and state-mandated achievement tests have been administered to document continued student literacy growth and achievement.

Summary

Reading Recovery's systematic and simultaneous replication studies document program outcomes for all children served, adhering to duplication of methods, instruments, and timelines across many sites. These studies have enabled researchers from urban, rural, and suburban school districts to verify results by focusing on local analyses of data collected at the school level while still contributing to large-scale studies to determine program effectiveness at a national level.

The most notable aspect of Reading Recovery data in the United States context is the extent to which results replicate over time and space. A close examination of NDEC's national research reports as well as an examination of state and local research reports reveals remarkably consistent patterns in student outcomes as measured by the six tasks of the Observation Survey, by success rates as measured by end-of-program status outcomes, and by non–Reading Recovery–based indicators such as placement rates in special education and grade retention rates. No other intervention in the United States can provide such documentation to support its effectiveness.

CHAPTER 10

Research That Documents the Effectiveness of Reading Recovery

Research on interventions can be classified into three categories: efficacy, effectiveness, and efficiency (Feinstein, 1977). Efficacy studies are used to determine if the intervention works under optimal conditions. While they are informative, they do not address the application in naturalistic settings without external controls. Effectiveness studies assess whether the intervention works in the field and can be integrated into existing systems. Efficiency refers to analysis of costs and benefits of the intervention. This chapter focuses on *effectiveness*, examining whether the intervention works in schools and if the effectiveness extends beyond the end of the intervention or treatment (Black & Holden, 1995).

Substantial evidence documents Reading Recovery's success with the lowest-performing first-grade students in a wide range of educational settings. This evidence is provided by a variety of study designs, including experimental and control group studies by independent researchers as well as researchers associated with Reading Recovery. A large number of these studies have been published in peer-reviewed journals.

The procedures for collecting Reading Recovery evaluation data are described in detail in Chapter 9, where effectiveness and efficiency outcome data for more than a million children in the United States are reported.

The current chapter focuses on studies designed to test effectiveness of the intervention as well as factors that may be related to outcomes. The chapter is organized in six sections:

- Reading Recovery as a research-based intervention
- reviews of research about Reading Recovery
- studies that have explored the effectiveness of Reading Recovery
- studies that examined the subsequent literacy performance of Reading Recovery children
- suggestions for consideration when reading or conducting Reading Recovery studies
- tables that summarize the studies on efffectiveness

Reading Recovery as a Research-Based Intervention

Opinions differ with regard to what is meant by a research-based program, and there is considerable debate about how it should be determined. Yet the scientific nature of intervention research is generally based on the theoretical base, evidence of effects, and evidence of replicability.

- Reading Recovery's *theoretical base* is primarily represented in the decades of research by Marie Clay. (See Chapter 4 for information about the theoretical base.) Reading Recovery is based on a complex theory of literacy learning as reflected in the components of the lesson. (See Chapter 7 for an explanation of the content of Reading Recovery lessons.)

  The development of Reading Recovery was subjected to a series of research projects across several years, including the development project, field trials, follow-up studies, replication studies, analyses of lesson content, and subgroup studies (Clay, 1993). In addition, New Zealand national monitoring evaluation studies have been conducted annually since 1984.

  Ongoing research across several disciplines continues to inform Reading Recovery professionals. A system is in place for practices to evolve in response to new learnings. (See Chapter 14 for information about a system for change in Reading Recovery.)

- *Evidence of effects* derives from high-quality experimental studies, several of which are highlighted in the following sections. Well-designed qualitative studies are also included in the review of studies about Reading Recovery effectiveness and long-term impact of the intervention.

- *Evidence of replicability* is provided in the reports of the National Data Evaluation Center that document more than 20 years of data in more than 10,000 schools across the United States (see Chapter 9). Reading Recovery uses systematic and simultaneous replication studies to document program outcomes for all children served, adhering to duplication of methods, instruments, and timelines across many sites. Replication data are available for more than one million children in the United States alone. Since all countries implementing Reading Recovery collect and report data on all children served each year, replicability extends across countries, cultures, and languages.

Published Reviews of Reading Recovery

Seven published reviews of Reading Recovery are summarized in Table 10.1 (see pp. 128–133). Six of the reviews were authored by researchers external to the

Reading Recovery community; one was prepared by a Reading Recovery researcher at The Ohio State University.

Reading Recovery Effectiveness Studies

Questions concerning the effectiveness of educational interventions have always been difficult to answer. The characteristics of the interventions, the kinds of populations to which they are applied, the meaning of effectiveness and the designs available to assess it, all create many problems for research in this field. (Plewis, 2000, p. 83)

Many interesting issues influence the study of interventions (Plewis, 2000; Plewis & Hurry, 1998). For example, the level (child, classroom, or school) at which the intervention is assigned affects the kinds of questions to be asked and the methods for answering the questions. There are also many practical issues such as integrity of delivery, cost, and leakage (ways in which the control group children could be influenced by the intervention). Plewis and Hurry (1998) further argue that a single piece of research may not be conclusive, but when added to the results from other studies, the weight of evidence may furnish a clearer picture.

In spite of the difficulties associated with the study of interventions, a large number of published studies document the effectiveness of Reading Recovery. Some are carefully designed empirical studies while others are well-designed qualitative studies. All studies reported in Table 10.2 (see pp. 134–151) focus on the intervention year and include explorations of

- intervention outcomes of participating students,
- comparisons of Reading Recovery outcomes with other interventions or with modifications,
- the influence of Reading Recovery on a variety of aspects of literacy learning, and
- studies that document support for Reading Recovery standards.

Peter Johnston (2002) expressed optimism that the work of other researchers (Vellutino & Scanlon, 2002) has reinforced and extended Marie Clay's argument that early intervention can distinguish between children who are learning disabled and children whose difficulties are related to experience and instruction (Clay, 1987). Johnston notes that Vellutino and his colleagues have approached the problem of reading difficulty as experimental psychologists studying problems in learning to read, particularly relating to word analysis and recognition, and Clay has approached the problem as a developmental psychologist interested in literacy acquisition and preventing difficulties. Johnston suggests that the convergence of research from multiple disciplines and with different perspectives may lead to considerable agreement and additional confidence in approaching the problems of reading difficulties.

Studies Exploring Subsequent Literacy Performance

Evidence of children's accelerated progress during the period of support is documented in Table 10.2. But educators call for information about the subsequent performance of Reading Recovery children—after the intervention has ended. Does their rate of learning continue at the accelerated rate, or at an average rate, or does it return to performance shown prior to the intervention? Historically, studies have shown diminished levels of learning once support has been removed (Bronfenbrenner, 1974; Page & Grandon, 1981).

There are inherent problems in the assessment of stability of effects over a period of years. For example, researchers acknowledge problem issues with longitudinal studies including sampling procedures, attrition of subjects, cohort differences, and testing effects (Nesselroade & Baltes, 1974). Another issue is the quality of the postprogram environment and its effect on the long-term effects of the program (Wahlberg & Reynolds, 1997).

Shanahan and Barr (1995) question the appropriateness of stability of learning gains for evaluating the quality of early intervention programs, suggesting that stability may be affected by responsive classroom instruction. They further suggest that while there may not be statistical significance in comparison studies, there may well be some practical significance. Yet they issued a challenge for more carefully designed studies that explore the maintenance of program gains:

> If it can be shown that children participating in the Reading Recovery program are not only brought up to the average of their classmates but that they then continue to progress at an average rate, these findings would have major implications for the timing of special support and the allocation of resources. (Shanahan & Barr, 1995, p. 978)

Researchers argue that only findings that emerge strongly and repeatedly across multiple studies employing different methods can be trusted (Walberg & Reynolds, 1997). Numerous research and evaluation studies demonstrate that Reading Recovery children continue to improve their literacy performance after the intervention has ended. Table 10.3 (see pp. 152–159) is a review of 10 published studies that examined subsequent performance of former Reading Recovery children in a variety of ways. The studies reported here used widely accepted standardized measures or state assessment measures, or both, and offer a promising response to Shanahan and Barr's challenge.

In addition to the studies reported in Table 10.3, many school districts and teacher training sites conduct their own independent analyses through their research departments. Typically these analyses use the standardized measures used by the district with all children.

Of course, many factors can affect a child's continuing performance on literacy tasks as time passes following an intervention, such as subsequent instructional experiences. Shanahan and Barr (1995) suggest that while an intervention may accelerate children's progress, instruction that is responsive to the higher achievement is needed for the promise of the intervention to be realized.

The Office for Standards in Education (1994) reported that in one New Zealand Reading Recovery Centre, the vast majority of children maintained and improved their reading ability after discontinuing from the program. The small percentage who had slipped were offered "refresher" tuition. They attributed the slippages to illness, absenteeism, home and community factors, and to unsatisfactory subsequent teaching.

Considerations When Reviewing or Conducting Research on Reading Recovery

Interpreting Reading Recovery evaluation or research studies requires an understanding of the characteristics of the implementation. The following implementation factors may influence results and should be reported:

- the age of the implementation
- the level of Reading Recovery teacher coverage in the schools studied
- the quality of Reading Recovery training and teaching
- the integrity of the implementation in meeting design standards
- the efficiency of the intervention (e.g., daily lessons)
- the level of administrative and faculty knowledge and support
- the quality of classroom programs
- other relevant factors

In studies comparing Reading Recovery to other interventions, additional factors must be considered:

- a clear explanation of all interventions studied, including theoretical framework, lesson design, method of delivery
- a clear description of the research design, including sample size and method of selection

- entry data for all children
- duration of the intervention (length of lessons and length of intervention)
- information about teachers (preparation, expertise, experience)
- appropriateness of measures used
- appropriateness of analyses
- conclusions based on the data presented

It is beyond the scope of this chapter to explore all the factors to be considered when conducting or reviewing research and program evaluations. However, it is suggested that all studies related to Reading Recovery should be examined with attention to their accuracy in reporting the original studies, issues relating to features and design and methodology, and possible biases and limitations of the findings. It is also important that evaluators become familiar with the complexity of Reading Recovery in order to ensure appropriate interpretations of data.

A Brief Summary

Studies and research reviews in peer-reviewed journals document the effectiveness of Reading Recovery and Descubriendo la Lectura for the lowest-performing first graders, including children who are English language learners. Evidence of subsequent gains in the years following the intervention is substantial. In addition to outcome data, researchers have explored factors related to the intervention and concluded that Reading Recovery

- promotes phonological awareness,
- improves the self-efficacy scores of children,
- promotes self-regulated behaviors,
- contributes to closing the gap between White and African-American children,
- promotes writing strategies,
- reduces the need for special education services and the costs of those services,
- yields positive outcomes for English language learners,
- requires one-to-one teaching,
- is dependent on highly trained teachers, and
- represents a comprehensive model of reading reflected in the lesson framework.

We know of no other intervention with the volume of published research and evaluation studies. Adopters and implementers of Reading Recovery can be confident of the rigor with which outcomes are reported and the integrity of ongoing research to learn more from and about Reading Recovery.

Numerous studies exploring Reading Recovery are currently underway because there is much to be learned about the effects of the intervention. And there is much to learn about children's learning, about teaching the lowest-achieving children, and about implementation factors that contribute to successful outcomes.

Table 10.1 Published Reviews of Reading Recovery

STUDY/SOURCE	PURPOSE	SCOPE OF REVIEW
J. V. D'Agostino & J. A. Murphy A Meta-Analysis of Reading Recovery in United States Schools *Educational Evaluation and Policy Analysis*	To provide a more comprehensive evaluation of Reading Recovery in U.S. schools by using meta-analytic procedures that allow the inclusion of many studies not considered in previous Reading Recovery reviews because of narrower guidelines	Specific meta-analytic strategies were used to study overall program effects of Reading Recovery (36 studies). Two major analyses were conducted. • Analysis I included all 36 studies regardless of apparent quality. • Analysis II examined the 11 more rigorous studies that provided pretest and posttest scores from treatment and comparison groups. Results of the two separate analyses were compared to determine if study quality influenced the overall conclusions regarding the impact of Reading Recovery. By developing norm-referenced means and standard deviations for two distinct comparison groups, authors were able to assess discontinued and nondiscontinued Reading Recovery students' test scores on multiple measures and at multiple points in time.
R. Herman & S. Stringfield *Ten Promising Programs for Educating All Children: Evidence of Impact*	To report information collected in a 3-year study conducted by the Johns Hopkins University Center for the Social Organization of Schools designed to answer two questions: • Are there specific programs or restructuring designs that can enhance the learning of students who are at risk of school failure? • What are their key characteristics and what local conditions and actions are required to replicate those promising programs?	Authors examined 10 different nationally known programs identified as holding promise for educating disadvantaged children. They reviewed 13 studies of Reading Recovery effectiveness and collected observational evidence at exemplar sites.
E. Hiebert Reading Recovery in the United States: What Difference Does It Make to an Age Cohort? *Educational Researcher*	To review and examine available data on Reading Recovery's effectiveness in American contexts, specifically as it influences an age cohort	The author examined three types of data on Reading Recovery: • the longitudinal study in Columbus, Ohio (DeFord, Pinnell, Lyons, & Place, 1990); • the comparison study of early interventions (Pinnell, Lyons, DeFord, Bryk, & Seltzer, 1994); • regional training center reports from The Ohio State University, University of Illinois, and Texas Woman's University

CONCLUSIONS AND RECOMMENDATIONS	COMMENTS
The researchers found positive program effects for both discontinued and not-discontinued students on outcomes tailored to the program and outcomes on standardized achievement measures. Effects among discontinued children were greater. They did not find large discrepancies in results between the less and more selective analyses; results on more rigorously designed studies seemed to converge with the bulk of available evidence. They found no evidence that methodological flaws or weaknesses in individual studies were responsible for previously identified effects. Analyses of follow-up studies showed that when compared to similar needy students, discontinued children widened the gap from posttest to second grade on standardized measures, and they closed the gap with average students.	Results of this meta-analysis indicated a lasting program effect, at least by end of Grade 2, on broad reading skills. Contrary to conventional belief, the researchers found no evidence that prior observed effects could be explained completely by factors resulting from methodological flaws (e.g., regression artifacts).
Expectations for Reading Recovery are high, in part because the intervention focuses on a small number of children. Reading Recovery has a reputation for producing strong, quantifiable reading gains. A potential problem noted in some sites was a tendency to blame or label the child when the strategy was not effective for the student. Districts should be prepared to address some unintended consequences of the program including staff jealousies over resources, lack of coordination, and unrealistically high expectations for the program. The consistently high fidelity of program implementation across sites was an important aspect of Reading Recovery. The high-quality staff development model for Reading Recovery is one of the most important aspects of Reading Recovery.	Authors commended the staff development model: "The intensity and the methods utilized by Reading Recovery in training and the insistence on high level of Reading Recovery performance provided an almost singularly attractive model for future staff development efforts, regardless of program type. As schools systematize and create more opportunities for serious staff development, the thoroughness of the Reading Recovery model seems to be well worth emulating" (p. 86).
A high percentage of Reading Recovery children can orally read at least first-grade text at the end of Grade 1. Once a program is in place, there is considerable fidelity in the results. Prominent elements of the Reading Recovery program are identified as characteristics of successful beginning reading instruction. Weekly training sessions give teachers an unprecedented amount of guided observation of students.	The author stated that data on many aspects of Reading Recovery implementation are inaccessible or incomplete. She cited limitations of existing data. The author recommended • studies with more comprehensive tasks that fully define the sample • exploration of effects in low-income schools and with second-language children • exploration of the underlying principles of Reading Recovery with consideration to

Table 10.1 Published Reviews continued

STUDY/SOURCE	PURPOSE	SCOPE OF REVIEW
E. Hiebert *continued*		
J. Pikulski Preventing Reading Failure: A Review of Five Effective Programs *The Reading Teacher*	To review five reading prevention programs used throughout the United States, comparing them on a number of dimensions and identifying common features of successful interventions	The five reviewed programs were Success for All, The Winston-Salem Project, Early Intervention in Reading (EIR), The Boulder Project, and Reading Recovery. Program comparisons were made in these areas: relationship between classroom and intervention; organization; length; instructional time, texts, and materials; text level strategies; word level strategies; writing; assessment; home connections; and teacher training.
G. S. Pinnell Reading Recovery: A Summary of Research In J. Flood, S. B. Heath, & D. Lapp (Eds.), *Research on Teaching Literacy Through the Communicative and Visual Arts*	To summarize what is known about Reading Recovery and what has been learned through research connected with the intervention	The author briefly describes Reading Recovery and then reviews research on program success, on teaching and learning, on teacher development, and on program implementation. Where they are available, sound critical reviews are noted.
T. Shanahan & R. Barr Reading Recovery: An Independent Evaluation of the Effects of an Early Instructional Intervention for "At Risk" Learners *Reading Research Quarterly*	To analyze the effectiveness of Reading Recovery in four dimensions: • Reading Recovery students' gains relative to gains of average- and low-achieving students • maintenance of learning gains after special instruction has ended • cost and benefits of the program • Reading Recovery's influence on other instructional changes in schools	The authors' goal was to offer a thorough, systematic analysis of all available empirical work on Reading Recovery. They reviewed all published evaluations of Reading Recovery as well as any available unpublished ones that included sufficient basic information to allow meaningful analysis. When possible to analyze data in a more precise and direct manner, data were combined across studies. Overall, consideration of existing research evaluation studies was largely qualitative.

CONCLUSIONS AND RECOMMENDATIONS	COMMENTS
Reviewed data led the author to conclude that the effects of Reading Recovery on an age cohort are unconvincing. When cost figures are calculated on the basis of success levels of students remaining in schools at Grade 4, the cost per successful student is higher.	applicability in student-teacher contexts other than tutoring A response to Hiebert's review was published in *Educational Researcher*, 25(7), pp. 23–25 (Pinnell, Lyons, & Jones, 1996). Hiebert's response to the response was printed on pp. 26–28 in the same publication.
The author concludes that attention should be given to the following issues to increase the likelihood of intervention success: • the total program of reading instruction • more time in high-quality reading instruction • individual (essential for some children) or very small group instruction • focus on first graders • texts that ensure success • multiple readings of the same text with an emphasis on meaning • inclusion of phonemic awareness and phonics instruction • daily writing activities • ongoing assessment • home-school communication • professionally prepared, accomplished teachers who have continuous support	The author argued that successful prevention programs may seem expensive, but are actually cost effective when compared with the costs of remedial efforts, retention, and special education services. In addition, the author noted that savings in human suffering and frustration cannot be calculated.
The review of research on Reading Recovery effectiveness includes studies from New Zealand, empirical studies in the United States, replication studies, results in diverse settings, the impact of contextual factors, and studies from Descubriendo la Lectura (Reading Recovery in Spanish). The review of research on teaching and learning includes areas such as studies of teacher behavior and student outcomes, teacher-student interactions, and the impact of Reading Recovery on teacher learning. A brief review of limited implementation studies is also included.	This is perhaps the most complete published summary of Reading Recovery research to date. The review includes more than Reading Recovery outcome studies and reflects the influence of Reading Recovery on insights about teaching, learning, and implementation.
Reading Recovery brings the learning of many of the lowest-achieving students up to average-achieving peers. Reading Recovery is a robust intervention in terms of consequences for student learning and replicability across sites. Reading Recovery has become a significant force in shaping the way we view early literacy development. After savings from lower retention rates and special education services, per-pupil annual expenditure is approximately $3,200 to $4,000, with variation among districts due to teacher salaries and benefits. More research is needed on Reading Recovery's impact	This review provided a comprehensive independent evaluation of Reading Recovery. Authors cited both caveats and challenges for consideration related to research and to practice. Authors of a statewide study by Pinnell, Lyons, DeFord, Bryk, and Seltzer (1994) responded to Shanahan and Barr's claim that half of the data from that study had been lost. Pinnell explained in a letter to the editor of *Reading Research Quarterly*, [32(1), 1997, p. 114] that only 5 of the 40 schools were excluded and provided the rationale. Shanahan and Barr responded to Pinnell in the same publication.

Table 10.1 Published Reviews continued

STUDY/SOURCE	PURPOSE	SCOPE OF REVIEW
T. Shanahan & R. Barr *continued*		
B. Wasik & R. E. Slavin Preventing Early Reading Failure with One-to-One Tutoring: A Review of Five Programs *Reading Research Quarterly*	To consider the effectiveness of five tutorial programs from two perspectives: empirical and pragmatic	The authors reviewed quantitative and qualitative research on five tutoring programs: Reading Recovery, Success for All, Prevention of Learning Disabilities, Wallach Tutoring Program, and Programmed Tutorial Reading.

CONCLUSIONS AND RECOMMENDATIONS	COMMENTS
on students' classroom experiences and ways to reduce costs. More rigorous research on the effects of Reading Recovery is needed as well as studies related to program refinements to enhance learning or efficiency.	
General Conclusions Across Programs: • Programs with the most comprehensive models of reading (the most complete instructional interventions) have larger impact than programs addressing only a few components of the reading process. Reading Recovery and Success for All include several reading components. • Using tutors is not enough. The content of the program and the instructional delivery may be important variables. • Using certified teachers obtains substantially larger impact than using paraprofessionals. Conclusions about Reading Recovery: • Reading Recovery brings the learning of many of the lowest-achieving students up to average-achieving peers. • Effects of Reading Recovery are impressive at the end of the implementation year, and effects are maintained for at least 2 years. • Results on evaluations of lasting effects are positive but complex. • Only Reading Recovery has attempted to assess implementation and its effect on outcome data.	Authors raised some methodological issues about Reading Recovery research and about students served. They concluded that the rapidly expanding use of Reading Recovery throughout the United States shows that the program is practical to use.

Table 10.2 Effectiveness Studies

STUDY/SOURCE	PURPOSE	SAMPLE
J. Ashdown & O. Simic Is Early Literacy Intervention Effective for English Language Learners? Evidence from Reading Recovery *Literacy Teaching and Learning: An International Journal of Early Reading and Writing*	To compare native-English speakers and English-language learners in Reading Recovery outcomes, rates of completion, and program delivery To determine whether Reading Recovery narrows the gap in reading achievement between native-English speakers and English-language learners	• 25,601 Reading Recovery children • 11,267 children in a comparison group who were in need of Reading Recovery but not served because of limited resources • 18,363 random sample children who were not identified as needing assistance Of these children, 82% were native-English speakers, 12% fluent, nonnative-English speakers, and 6% limited English proficiency (LEP). The majority of nonnative speakers spoke Spanish (54%) and Chinese (26%).
B. J. Askew The Effect of Multiple Readings on the Behaviors of Children and Teachers in an Early Intervention Program *Reading and Writing Quarterly*	To explore the impact of multiple readings of a text on the reading behaviors of Reading Recovery children and their teachers	15 first graders from five districts served by Reading Recovery during the spring Six Reading Recovery teacher leaders-in-training
B. J. Askew & D. F. Frasier Early Writing: An Exploration of Literacy Opportunities *Literacy Teaching and Learning: An International Journal of Early Reading and Writing*	To explore outcomes of the daily writing portion of the Reading Recovery lesson	82 Reading Recovery children from eight states who began their lessons at the start of school and whose lessons were successfully discontinued

MEASURES	FINDINGS/CONCLUSIONS	COMMENTS
Four tasks of Observation Survey: • Text Reading • Writing Vocabulary • Ohio Word Test • Hearing and Recording Sounds in Words	No statistically significant differences were found in success rates of LEP students and their native-English-speaking peers. Fluent ELL and LEP students were not as likely to be offered the intervention as their native-English-speaking counterparts, even though they had similar literacy abilities as measured by the Observation Survey. Students had an equal opportunity to complete a full series of lessons regardless of language background and English proficiency. Reading Recovery closed the achievement gap between native and non-native speakers, while the gap remained among the three language groups in both the comparison group and the random sample.	The study accounted for variation across sites (characteristics of students other than language and their educational environment). The authors concluded districts can be assured that Reading Recovery is an appropriate intervention for LEP children. Authors also expressed the need for more information on how students are chosen to participate in Reading Recovery. Authors called for longitudinal studies that follow these children beyond first grade.
Verbatim transcripts of four oral readings of the same text (first reading as a novel text and three familiar re-readings), along with teacher interventions and prompts Transcripts were coded according to emerging categories in order to examine children's reading behaviors and teachers' intervention behaviors (interrater agreement of .94).	Repeated readings in Reading Recovery led to increased child-initiated self-corrections and reduced teacher interventions, demonstrating a shift in the locus of control from teacher to child. The same shift in control was observed as children encountered problems or challenges in text and took action. Although not formally studied, there was observable evidence of improved oral reading fluency across multiple readings of the same text. Teacher interventions not only decreased across readings, they also shifted to confirmations, words of praise, and prompts for fluent reading.	Findings supported Clay's assertion that frequent rereading of familiar texts provides two opportunities for children: "firstly, to orchestrate the complex patterns of responding to print just as the expert musician practices the things he knows; and secondly, to read those texts with increasing levels of independence" (Clay, 1991, p. 184).
• writing books from Reading Recovery lessons • writing vocabulary charts • teacher lesson records • records of text reading	Children had different profiles of writing vocabulary acquisition (learning high-frequency and unique words). There were massive opportunities for learning to hear and record sounds in words, including regular, exception, and ambiguous words. Children learned to control many words that provided opportunities to use analogy in writing new words.	Findings led authors to conclude that through daily message writing in Reading Recovery, the lowest achievers in Grade 1 learn a great deal about print in a short period of time. The children also move toward self-regulated behaviors in writing across the Reading Recovery intervention. The study offered support for the notion of individual paths of progress rather than identified prescribed sequences.

Table 10.2 Effectiveness Studies continued

STUDY/SOURCE	PURPOSE	SAMPLE
P. Batten Investing Equity Funding in Early Literacy *ERS Spectrum*	To determine the effectiveness of Reading Recovery as an appropriate literacy intervention for children in schools receiving equity funding To see if Reading Recovery closes the literacy gap for poor minority children To determine whether the intervention is a worthwhile expenditure	Two groups of children from 15 schools in three districts received a full Reading Recovery program: • 43 low-SES African American • 52 low-SES Hispanic students
Y. Center, K. Wheldall, L. Freeman, L. Outhred, & M. McNaught An Evaluation of Reading Recovery *Reading Research Quarterly*	To evaluate the effectiveness of Reading Recovery in primary schools in New South Wales	Low-achieving children were randomly assigned to two groups: • 31 Reading Recovery children • 39 control (low-progress students who had not entered Reading Recovery by November) A third group (n=39) consisted of students from five matched schools. By the end of the study, sample sizes were (1) 23, (2) 16, (3) 32.
M. M. Clay & B. Tuck A Study of Reading Recovery Subgroups: Including Outcomes for Children Who Did Not Satisfy Discontinuing Criteria Funded by the Ministry of Education in New Zealand Shorter version found in M. M. Clay, *Reading Recovery, A Guidebook for Teachers in Training*	To examine whether outcome status could be predicted from entry scores To examine how schools were providing for three Reading Recovery subgroups after Reading Recovery lessons had been discontinued	Subgroup 1: 140 Reading Recovery children who reached average-band performance for their class (randomly selecting 24.3% of the total national group) Subgroup 2: 140 Reading Recovery children who made progress but did not reach this criterion level and were recommended to receive specialist reports (100% of the total national group) Subgroup 3: 140 Reading Recovery children who entered Reading Recovery late in the school year and were continued in their second year (randomly selecting 21.6% of total national group)

MEASURES	FINDINGS/CONCLUSIONS	COMMENTS
Two Observation Survey tasks (fall and spring measures): • Text Reading Level • Hearing and Recording Sounds in Words	Both African-American and Hispanic students began Reading Recovery lessons with below-level performance (Stanine 3 on Hearing and Recording Sounds in Words and Stanine 1 on Text Reading). At the end of Grade 1, both groups scored well within the average range on both tasks at Stanine 7.	The author concluded that Reading Recovery does demonstrate an investment that reduces the achievement gap of disadvantaged urban children.
• The Diagnostic Survey • Burt Word Reading Test • Neale Analysis of Reading Ability • Passage Reading Test • Waddington Diagnostic Spelling Test • Phonemic Awareness Test • Cloze Test • Word Attack Skills Test • Woodcock Reading Mastery Test	At short-term evaluation (15 weeks), Reading Recovery scores were superior to control students on all tests measuring reading achievement but not on two of three tests of metalinguistic skills. At medium-term evaluation (30 weeks), there were no longer significant differences between Reading Recovery and control children on seven of eight measures. However, the book level test was significantly higher for the Reading Recovery group.	The authors suggested considerable caution when examining medium-term results because so few children from the original control group cohort were remaining (N=16). Authors claimed that Clay's studies had excluded about 30% of children who were either removed or not discontinued from the program. Clay's 1979 data negate this claim. No children were dropped from her analyses. Clay responds to this claim in a letter to Reading Research Quarterly, 32(1), 1997, p. 114. This independent evaluation using an experimental design with random assignment demonstrated highly significant and lasting effects of the intervention.
• all six tasks of the Diagnostic Survey • Burt Oral Reading Test (nationally standardized test published by the New Zealand Council for Educational Research) • detailed records of text reading and writing vocabulary • follow-up testing for referred children - text reading of	Most children's lesson series were successful and were discontinued. Both discontinued and referred groups made important gains in test scores, with the majority of the discontinued children performing at or above the national Stanine 5 at exit. Individual variations were seen in (a) test score pattern, (b) progress made during Reading Recovery, and (c) the level of congruency of progress when reading is compared with writing. Predictions of outcome status based on entry scores for either high or low scorers were	Authors cautioned against using entry characteristics and progress in program in a deterministic fashion. A full program of instruction (12–20 weeks) provides the best practical estimate of which children will require further assistance. Authors also cited the need to continue and complete all lesson series (i.e., minimize the numbers of incomplete programs).

Table 10.2 Effectiveness Studies continued

STUDY/SOURCE	PURPOSE	SAMPLE
M. M. Clay & B. Tuck *continued*		Note: Random sampling was controlled for school and teacher difference.
S. G. Cohen, G. McDonnell, & B. Osborn Self-Perceptions of "At Risk" and High Achieving Readers: Beyond Reading Recovery Achievement Data In *Cognitive and Social Perspectives for Literacy Research and Instruction: Thirty-eighth Yearbook of the National Reading Conference*	To study the impact of Reading Recovery on children's perceptions of their own competence to succeed in school-related work and to direct their own learning To compare Reading Recovery self-appraisals with those of other at-risk students in remedial programs and with high-achieving students	138 first graders in a predominantly upper middle-class school district • 50 in Reading Recovery • 48 in other remedial programs • 40 high-achieving students
B. E. Cox, Z. Fang, & M. C. Schmitt At Risk Children's Metacognitive Growth During Reading Recovery Experience: A Vygotskian Interpretation *Literacy Teaching and Learning: An International Journal of Early Reading and Writing*	To determine whether participation in Reading Recovery led to a concomitant increase in metacognitive knowledge and regulation	17 Reading Recovery first graders in four elementary schools • six girls and 11 boys • seven African-American and 10 White children • five children from low-income families
C. A. Crevola & P. W. Hill Initial Evaluation of a Whole-School Approach to Prevention and Intervention in	To examine the effectiveness of a whole-school approach to prevention and intervention in early literacy (ELRP) implemented in 27 schools in Victoria, Australia after one year of implementation	27 government primary schools that demonstrated • a systemwide index of educational disadvantage • a need in the literacy area • literacy as a priority • access to a Reading Recovery program

MEASURES	FINDINGS/CONCLUSIONS	COMMENTS
graded paragraphs - Burt Oral Reading Test - spelling test • questionnaire survey and interviews for referred children	likely to be wrong in a significant number of cases. Predictions of outcome status after 10 weeks of Reading Recovery were likely to be wrong in 15–30% of the cases. From follow-up data on referred children, the authors called for systemic improvements relating to (a) providing more effective delivery of subsequent services for the referred children and (b) a research program directed to developing more effective ways to work with these children.	
• attribution scale (Cohen, 1983) • self-efficacy measure similar to one described by Schunk (1985)	A MANOVA revealed significant differences between groups. Reading Recovery students exhibited similar patterns in attributions as the high-achieving students. Reading Recovery children were significantly different from other at-risk students in attributing their success to ability, effort, and mood. The self-efficacy scale indicated that Reading Recovery students view themselves as more competent on school-related tasks than the other at-risk students in remedial programs.	Authors concluded that after Reading Recovery, students appeared more like their high-achieving peers in their attributions to success in school (ability, effort, mood, task difficulty, and teacher help). Reading Recovery students seem to view themselves as more competent in literacy tasks than do other at-risk students. Results corroborated Clay's claims (1987) that Reading Recovery students become self-regulated learners.
A dictated oral tale provided by the children for others to read. Analyzed using Cox's (1994) linguistic procedures for evidence of metacognitive utterances.	At the entry Reading Recovery session, 15 of the 17 children used some type of metacognitive speech that indicated a regulatory function. At the exit session, all 17 participants produced metacognitive speech directed at controlling their literacy products and processes. Repeated measures MANOVA revealed statistically significant growth in metacognition during their Reading Recovery experience. There were distinctive differences in quality between entry and exit metacognitive utterances. At entry, most utterances indicated general planning, whereas at exit they showed marked growth in self-appraisal and regulatory capacities.	This study suggested that during the Reading Recovery experience, children develop a much clearer sense of themselves as readers and writers; become more cognizant of the literacy task in which they were engaging; and are more proficient in using language to regulate strategic control over text content, structure, and audience needs.
• three subtests of the Woodcock Language Proficiency Battery • six measures of the Observation Survey • *The Record of Oral Language: Biks and*	Data from the 1996 school year provided the schools with information concerning areas needing further attention for the 1997 school year. Authors stated that it was premature to draw firm conclusions before 3 years of implementation and data analysis. However, progress in the trial schools	There were five components in the comprehensive design: high expectations for all students; detailed, systematic, ongoing profiles of literacy progress; good teaching targeted to the learning needs

Table 10.2 Effectiveness Studies continued

STUDY/SOURCE	PURPOSE	SAMPLE
C. A. Crevola & P. W. Hill *continued* Early Literacy *Journal of Education for Students Placed at Risk*		• the support and commitment of the entire school 25 matched site control schools with the same index of educational disadvantage Data were available for 3,605 students in 200 classes and 51 schools.
L. Dorn & A. Allen Helping Low-Achieving First Grade Readers: A Program Combining Reading Recovery Tutoring and Small-Group Instruction *ERS Spectrum* *Literacy, Teaching and Learning: An International Journal of Early Literacy*	To describe and evaluate an approach that supplemented Reading Recovery with small-group early literacy instruction	231 students from nine schools: • 95 Reading Recovery only • 93 small group only • 43 small group followed by Reading Recovery
B. Elbaum, S. Vaughn, M. T. Hughes, & S. W. Moody How Effective are One-to-One Tutoring Programs in Reading for Elementary Students At Risk for Reading Failure? A Meta-Analysis of the Intervention Research *Journal of Educational Psychology*	To review the research on adult conducted one-to-one reading interventions for elementary students at risk of reading failure and to compare the effectiveness of different intervention factors	The review included 42 samples of students from 29 research studies conducted between 1975 and 1998 that included tutoring and comparison elementary students. Both published and unpublished studies were included in the research sample.

MEASURES	FINDINGS/CONCLUSIONS	COMMENTS
Gutches (Clay, Gill, Glenn, McNaughton, & Salmon, 1983) Measures were administered in a pretest and posttest design. The 10 separate measures were compiled into a composite score.	indicated large effects from the design with a high degree of confidence for both the individual measures and the composite score.	of each student; an intervention for students who fail to make progress in the classroom (Reading Recovery); and supportive links between home, school, and community. Data from the 3-year implementation will be necessary before firm conclusions can be drawn about the effectiveness of the model. Preliminary findings indicated that a comprehensive design that includes Reading Recovery as a safety net will have large and positive effects.
The Observation Survey	Of the children in the small-group-only treatment, 30% reached successful levels of reading achievement. (These children had higher entry scores than the Reading Recovery children.) Of the group of Reading Recovery–only children (the lowest achievers), 76% met the rigorous discontinuing criteria. Of the children who had small-group intervention before Reading Recovery intervention, 56% reached successful achievement levels. The combined average number of lessons (for the small group plus Reading Recovery treatment) was about the same as it was for the Reading Recovery–only group whose programs were successfully discontinued.	Findings supported the powerful effects of one-to-one teaching as compared to group instruction for low achievers, and results matched those of Pinnell et al. (1994) indicating that Reading Recovery is the most effective intervention for the lowest-achieving children.
The unit of analysis in this study was effect size computed as the difference between the mean posttest score for the intervention group minus the mean posttest score of the comparison group divided by the standard deviation of the comparison group. Effect sizes were calculated for a range of outcome measures reported in the research studies.	The mean weighted effect size for the Reading Recovery interventions (d = 0.66) was significantly higher than that for the other matched interventions (d = 0.29; p. 615). For Reading Recovery samples, the mean weighted effect size for standardized measures was less than that for nonstandardized measures (d = 0.60 vs. 0.80, respectively), but the difference was not statistically reliable (p. 613). The authors concluded that "the findings of this meta-analysis support the argument that well-designed, reliably implemented, one-to-one interventions can make a significant contribution to improved reading outcomes for many students whose poor reading skills place them at risk for academic failure." (p. 617)	In their conclusions the authors ignore the major findings of their meta-analysis related to Reading Recovery and instead recommend that schools consider small-group interventions conducted by college students or volunteers. There is no support for this recommendation in their analysis of research on first-grade at-risk students. See the RRCNA Web site for a more detailed review of this study.

Table 10.2 Effectiveness Studies continued

STUDY/SOURCE	PURPOSE	SAMPLE
K. Escamilla Descubriendo la Lectura: An Early Intervention Literacy Program in Spanish *Literacy, Teaching and Learning: An International Journal of Early Literacy*	To determine if Descubriendo la Lectura (DLL) achieved results with Spanish-speaking first graders equivalent to Reading Recovery programs in English	All Spanish-speaking first graders who were receiving literacy instruction in Spanish in six elementary schools in an urban Arizona city (N=180). Four schools had DLL and two did not. Subjects fell into three groups: 1. 23 DLL children 2. 23 children needing DLL and not receiving it (control group) 3. all 134 children remaining in the sample (comparison group)
A. Hobsbaum, S. Peters, & K. Sylva Scaffolding in Reading Recovery *Oxford Review of Education*	To explore the writing episode in the Reading Recovery lesson for aspects of scaffolding Specific explorations: • the structure of interaction • whether interactions can be conceptualized as scaffolding procedures • whether patterns of interactions change over time	Data were drawn from a longitudinal study of 17 Reading Recovery children and seven teachers in different schools in London and the South of England.
S. Iversen & W. Tunmer Phonological Processing Skills and the Reading Recovery Program *Journal of Educational Psychology*	To determine whether the Reading Recovery program would be more effective if systematic instruction in phonological recoding skills were incorporated in the program	Three matched groups of 32 at-risk readers each were formed: • standard Reading Recovery (children taught by teachers who received Reading Recovery training) • modified Reading Recovery (children taught by teacher who received Reading Recovery training that included phonological recoding skills as part of lesson) • another standard intervention

MEASURES	FINDINGS/CONCLUSIONS	COMMENTS
• Spanish Observation Survey (fall and spring) • Aprenda Reading Achievement Test (fall and spring)	At the end of Grade 1, DLL children had not only caught up to the comparison group on the Spanish Observation Survey, but surpassed them. Differences were statistically significant on all tasks except text reading. DLL students also significantly outperformed the control group (p<.05) on all measures. On Aprenda, when standard scores were connected to percentiles, only the DLL and control groups made gains. In May, the DLL group was at the 41st percentile, the comparison group at the 31st percentile, and the control group at the 28th percentile. Progress of the comparison and control groups lagged statistically behind that of the DLL group. While findings were encouraging for DLL students, the study raised some concerns regarding quality of Spanish reading instruction within regular bilingual classrooms.	This study provided positive evidence for the potential of the DLL program (Reading Recovery in Spanish). Results demonstrated that the program has a great deal of promise in assisting children who are struggling to become literate in Spanish. The author cautioned that the study was limited by sample size and encouraged additional studies. She also called for studies to explore the sustaining of initial gains across grade levels and as children transition from Spanish to English instruction. Annual national data on DLL outcomes support Escamilla's early findings.
Sources of data • detailed field notes • transcribed audiotapes of lessons • writing books for each child	Researchers found that the scaffolding process does underpin teaching in the Reading Recovery intervention. They identified three phases within the program showing change across time: • teachers monitor and structure the learning within the task • children independently identify their needs and teachers prompt to retrieve and make connections • children exercise increasing control over cognitive processes through the use of regulatory language The phases indicate that the interactive framework within the writing portion of a Reading Recovery lesson is a process of scaffolding learning.	This study is an example of theoretical and pedagogical investigations within the Reading Recovery context. Researchers in this study contributed to the theory of why Reading Recovery succeeds and how writing fits into the success story. Distinctions were drawn between research on scaffolding within short-term experimental tasks where the goal is to solve a unique problem and long-term, instructional contexts where the curricular goals are ever-increasing (p. 17).
• Diagnostic Survey (all 6 tasks) • Dolch Word Recognition Test • Yopp-Singer Phoneme Segmentation Test • Phoneme Deletion Test • Pseudoword Decoding Task	The two Reading Recovery treatment groups performed at very similar levels at discontinuing. Both groups performed much better on all measures than children in the standard intervention group. Both Reading Recovery groups often performed significantly better than classroom controls (especially on phonological segmentation and phoneme deletion). Results revealed that the modified Reading Recovery group reached levels of performance required for discontinuing faster than the standard Reading Recovery group.	Authors acknowledged that both the standard and modified Reading Recovery programs included explicit instruction in phonological awareness. This experimental study revealed considerable advantages for Reading Recovery procedures.

Table 10.2 Effectiveness Studies continued

STUDY/SOURCE	PURPOSE	SAMPLE
P. R. Kelly Working with English Language Learners: The Case of Danya *The Journal of Reading Recovery*	To explore Reading Recovery outcomes and subsequent literacy performance of an English-language learner in a case study format	One student, who was initially one of the lowest-performing students in her English-only classroom and whose first language was Spanish, received Reading Recovery tutoring from January through August of her first-grade year.
C. A. Lyons & J. Beaver Reducing Retention and Learning Disability Placement through Reading Recovery: An Educationally Sound Cost Effective Choice In R. L. Allington & S. A. Walmsley (Eds.), *No Quick Fix: Rethinking Literacy Programs in America's Elementary Schools*	To describe the impact of Reading Recovery on retention and learning disability referrals across a 5-year period in two Ohio school districts	Study 1: 207 students served by Reading Recovery Study 2: all first graders in a school district Study 3: all first graders in a school district
C. A. Marvin & J. S. Gaffney The Effects of Reading Recovery on Children's Home Literacy Experiences *Literacy Teaching and Learning: An International Journal of Early Reading and Writing*	To examine the change in home literacy activities and behaviors of children who participated in Reading Recovery	130 families of first graders • 40 with a child served by Reading Recovery • 30 with a child who was a poor reader in the fall but not served • 60 with a child on grade level in the fall

MEASURES	FINDINGS/CONCLUSIONS	COMMENTS
• Observation Survey • ScottForesman Test Packet for Text Reading • Developmental Reading Assessment	Danya reached average proficiency levels in reading on Observation Survey measures through a full program of Reading Recovery. In subsequent reading assessments during second and third grade, Danya continued to perform at grade-appropriate reading levels on the Developmental Reading Assessment. She also performed well on measures of comprehension.	The author concluded that Reading Recovery was effective in promoting Danya's accelerated literacy development during first grade, putting her on a path of success that continued to build in second and third grades after Reading Recovery was concluded. Her ability to sustain progress well beyond Reading Recovery tutoring supports the success of this intervention with English language learners.
Study 1: Comparison over a 5-year period of the number of Reading Recovery students retained or referred to LD after a full program Study 2: Comparison of number of children retained 3 years prior to and 4 years after Reading Recovery implementation Study 3: Comparison of number of children placed in LD classrooms 3 years prior to and 3 years after Reading Recovery implementation	Study 1: The percentage of Reading Recovery students classified as LD after Reading Recovery implementation was reduced from 36% in 1986–1987 to 9% in 1990–1991. Prior to Reading Recovery, 2.5% of the first graders were retained compared to .7% after Reading Recovery was implemented. Study 2: Three years prior to Reading Recovery implementation, 4.3% of all first graders were retained. Three years after Reading Recovery was partially implemented (four of nine schools), 2.9% were retained. Study 3: Three years prior to Reading Recovery implementation, 1.8% of all first graders were placed in LD classrooms. Three years after Reading Recovery was partially implemented, .63% were placed in LD classes.	Data from two Ohio school districts demonstrated that considerable savings are realized through the use of Reading Recovery by • reducing the number of first-grade retentions, • avoiding unnecessary special education evaluation and placement, and • reducing the number of students assigned to longer-term remedial reading programs.
A 32-question survey (multiple choice and checklist format)	Reading Recovery children had more deficiencies in home literacy experiences at the beginning of the year than the other two groups, and they were still different from on-level children at year-end. There were significant improvements for Reading Recovery children in their home literacy behaviors: • frequency of independent reading and reading aloud to adults • independent writing of words, sentences, and stories There were slightly downward changes in Reading Recovery parents' long-term expectations of their children's future academic accomplishments, focusing instead on Grade 1. There were changes in the ways Reading Recovery parents read to their children	The authors suggested that participation in Reading Recovery may have influenced both the children's role as reader at home (as active and capable) and the parent's perceptions and support of the children's reading and writing abilities. The authors also stated that while Reading Recovery does not purport to influence home literacy activities, the positive effects are welcomed indirect outcomes. They called for further study in the area.

Table 10.2 Effectiveness Studies continued

STUDY/SOURCE	PURPOSE	SAMPLE
C. A. Marvin & J. S. Gaffney *continued*		
J. C. Neal & P. R. Kelly The Success of Reading Recovery for English Language Learners and Descubriendo la Lectura for Bilingual Students in California *Literacy Teaching and Learning: An International Journal of Early Reading and Writing*	To determine if Reading Recovery and DLL interventions resulted in reading and writing success for two groups of bilingual children: English language learners (ELL) receiving Reading Recovery instruction Spanish-speaking children in bilingual classrooms receiving DLL instruction	Children who had received Reading Recovery or DLL in California from 1993-1996: • 2,359 Spanish-speaking children in DLL • 3,992 English language learners in Reading Recovery • 17,787 Reading Recovery children as a comparison group
E. A. O'Connor & O. Simic The Effect of Reading Recovery on Special Education Referrals and Placements *Psychology in the Schools*	To examine the effects of Reading Recovery on special education referral and placement rates To compare referral and placement rates of Reading Recovery children with a comparison group of children who did not receive Reading Recovery services	• 2,354 children with a complete Reading Recovery program (1,862 discontinued, 492 recommended) • 1,770 comparison group children (children identified as at-risk in the fall, but not served in Reading Recovery because of limited resources or because they no longer needed the intervention)
G. S. Pinnell Reading Recovery *Elementary School Journal* (report of a study by Pinnell, Lyons, & DeFord)	To explore whether Reading Recovery could succeed with low-achieving children To determine whether those children maintained their gains (Summary of pilot-year data and first-year data in Columbus, Ohio)	The lowest-achieving first-grade children were randomly assigned either to Reading Recovery (n=55) or to a control group (n=55) served daily in individual lessons taught by a trained paraprofessional. Both groups were compared with a random sample of average and high-progress first graders (n=102) as an indication of average progress.
G. S. Pinnell, C. A. Lyons, D. E. DeFord, A. Byrk, & M. Seltzer Comparing Instructional Models for the Literacy Education	To compare the effectiveness of Reading Recovery with three other instructional models for early intervention	Lowest-achieving first-grade readers (N=324) were randomly assigned, within schools, to one of five groups: • Reading Recovery • Reading Recovery–like intervention with partially trained teachers • skills-based individual intervention

MEASURES	FINDINGS/CONCLUSIONS	COMMENTS
	between fall and spring. By the spring parents of Reading Recovery children were significantly more likely to encourage children to self-corrrect and sound out words than they were in the fall.	
Observation Survey tasks: • Text Reading • Writing Vocabulary • Hearing and Recording Sounds in Words	Statistically significant progress was made by both target populations; Reading Recovery and DLL enabled low-performing ELL and Spanish-speaking children to improve their performance on text reading and writing measures. The success rates of these children compared favorably with the total population of Reading Recovery children served in California. Additionally, the target populations of children achieved scores within the average range of a cohort of their peers drawn from a random sample of first graders.	Findings demonstrated that Reading Recovery is an effective intervention for low-performing ELL students receiving literacy instruction in English, and that DLL is an effective intervention for low-performing Spanish-speaking children receiving literacy instruction in Spanish. These interventions reduced reading failure for these populations by helping children to catch up with their peers in a relatively short period of time.
Observation Survey NYU scan form that provided information about retention and special services received by both groups of subjects	Children with a complete Reading Recovery program were referred for testing and placed in special education at significantly lower rates than the comparison group. Reading Recovery served as a successful short-term intervention for the majority of low-achieving students. Only three of the discontinued children were classified as learning disabled.	Authors concluded that their findings demonstrate that the majority of initially poor achievers can avoid special education with early intervention and confirm the diagnostic value of Reading Recovery for the recommended children. They further suggested that with more available resources, many of the children in the comparison group may not have been referred or classified as learning disabled.
• The Diagnostic Survey (all 6 tasks) • writing sample • Comprehensive Test of Basic Skills (2 subtests)	Reading Recovery children performed better than control children (p<.05) on seven of the nine measures at the end of first grade. They compared well with the random sample group. In subsequent years, Reading Recovery children continued to perform well on text reading. Effect sizes were reduced over the years.	This study provided early evidence in the United States of Reading Recovery's immediate and long-term positive effects. Results of this experimental design were audited by a team of renowned researchers.
• Gates-MacGinitie Reading Test • Woodcock Reading Mastery Test Two tasks of the Observation Survey: • Dictation • Text Reading Level	Reading Recovery subjects performed significantly better than any other treatment and comparison groups on all measures. Essential differences were related to • individual instruction • the lesson framework (combination of techniques) • teacher training	Reading Recovery emerged as most powerful of the tested interventions at the conclusion of the experiment and at the beginning of Grade 2. This large-scale experimental design with random assign-

Table 10.2 Effectiveness Studies continued

STUDY/SOURCE	PURPOSE	SAMPLE
Pinnell et al. *continued* of High-Risk First Graders *Reading Research Quarterly*		• group instruction by a Reading Recovery teacher • control group
L. C. Quay, D. C. Steele, C. I. Johnson, & W. Hortman Children's Achievement and Personal and Social Development in a First-Year Reading Recovery Program with Teachers in Training *Literacy Teaching and Learning: An International Journal of Early Reading and Writing*	To determine whether a group of children in the first year of Reading Recovery implementation in a district differed from an equivalent control group of children on standardized measures of achievement, teacher ratings of academic progress, promotion rates, and teacher perceptions of personal and social development at the end of Grade 1	• 107 Reading Recovery children • 107 control group children 34 elementary schools Groups were equivalent on • gender • ethnicity • scores on the Observation Survey 70% in each group were African-American and most were in free or reduced-price lunch programs
M. C. Schmitt The Development of Children's Strategic Processing in Reading Recovery *Reading Psychology*	To examine and describe first-grade children's development of strategic processes for problem-solving words, detecting and correcting errors, and confirming responses rather than increasing item knowledge To investigate an evaluation rubric for analyzing strategic processing	27 Reading Recovery children in four schools being taught by six experienced teachers • 7 African-American children • 20 White children 5 low-SES children
M. C. Schmitt Metacognitive Strategy Knowledge: Comparison of Former Reading Recovery Children and Their Classmates *Literacy Teaching and Learning: An International Journal of Early Reading and Writing*	To explore elementary school children's metacognitive knowledge of strategies appropriate for use before, during, and after reading To determine whether children who had participated in Reading Recovery in first grade had similar understandings as their current grade-level classmates	486 randomly selected third- and fourth-grade children in 253 schools that had been involved in Reading Recovery for more than 2 years • 214 males • 272 females

MEASURES	FINDINGS/CONCLUSIONS	COMMENTS
		ment was independently analyzed by a team of researchers.
• Iowa Test of Basic Skills • Gates-MacGinitie Reading Test • Observation Survey • classroom assessment of student progress	At the beginning of the year, the two groups were equivalent on gender, ethnicity, and achievement. At the end of the school year, multivariate and univariate analyses of variance indicated that the Reading Recovery children were significantly superior to the control group children on • ITBS Language Tests • Gates-MacGinitie Reading Test • all tasks of the Observation Survey • classroom teachers' assessments of achievement • classroom teachers' ratings of personal and social growth • promotion rates	This experimental study using multivariate analyses showed a clear advantage for Reading Recovery children on multiple measures.
• Running records of text reading taken at three points during the study • strategic processing analysis (developed by author for the study)	ANOVAs indicated that these Reading Recovery children increased their attempts to solve words and decreased unsuccessful attempts, engaged in more self-monitoring and cross-checking, self-corrected more miscues, and increased rereading behaviors as a strategy for problem solving and confirming responses.	This study suggested that active construction and a sense of responsibility on the part of the learner are signals for self-regulation.
Metacomprehension Strategy Index	Previewing and predicting were common activities recognized by third and fourth graders as effective strategies for comprehension. Summarizing and using fix-up strategies became more salient in fourth grade. ANOVAs indicated there were no differences between children who had participated in Reading Recovery and their classmates with regard to declarative and conditional knowledge of metacomprehension strategies. Significant growth was found between third and fourth grades, suggesting that growth of metacognitive knowledge is a developmental characteristic.	This large-scale study of randomly selected children provided information regarding the strategies elementary school children recognize as valuable and clearly indicated that the formerly lowest-achieving first graders (former Reading Recovery children) were on equal footing with their classmates 2 and 3 years after the intervention with regard to metacognitive knowledge.

Table 10.2 Effectiveness Studies continued

STUDY/SOURCE	PURPOSE	SAMPLE
R. M. Schwartz Literacy Learning of At-Risk First Grade Students in the Reading Recovery Early Intervention *Journal of Educational Psychology*	To investigate the effectiveness and efficiency of Reading Recovery in closing the performance gap between average and at-risk readers across first grade	37 Reading Recovery teachers submitted the names of two at-risk students for random assignment to first- or second-round Reading Recovery service • 37 first-round Reading Recovery children • 37 second-round Reading Recovery children Reading Recovery teachers submitted data on a low-average and high-average student in the same classroom as the first- and second-round Reading Recovery children • 37 low-average classroom children • 37 high-average classroom children
K. A. D. Stahl, S. A. Stahl, & M. C. McKenna The Development of Phonological Awareness and Orthographic Processing in Reading Recovery *Literacy Teaching and Learning: An International Journal of Early Reading and Writing*	To determine whether techniques used in Reading Recovery lessons promote progress in the metalinguistic areas of phonemic awareness and phonological recoding	A total of 30 at-risk first-grade students were rank ordered. The lowest-achieving children (n=11) were entered into Reading Recovery; a control group of 19 subjects eligible for Reading Recovery was formed.

MEASURES	FINDINGS/CONCLUSIONS	COMMENTS
Observation Survey at the beginning of the year, at mid-year transition, and at year-end Tasks administered at midyear transition and year-end: • Yopp-Singer Phoneme • Segmentation Task • Sound Deletion Task (adapted from Rosner) • Slosson Oral Reading Test (revised) • Degrees of Reading Power Test (Form JO and K0)	The at-risk students who received the intensive one-to-one Reading Recovery intervention during the first half of the school year performed considerably better at midyear than similar students randomly assigned to receive the intervention during the second half of the year. Without intervention, the at-risk students identified for second-round service made slow progress in classroom settings. There were no significant differences between the first-round Reading Recovery group and the high-average group, and the Reading Recovery group scores were higher than the low-average group. Both Reading Recovery intervention groups closed the performance gap with their average peers.	This experimental study with random assignment demonstrated that Reading Recovery is effective in reducing the gap between first-round at-risk children and their average peers by raising their literacy levels to a point where they can benefit from classroom and other literacy experiences. Without the intervention, at-risk children do not make the accelerated progress to catch up with their peers. Measures of intervention efficiency showed that early intervention is an efficient investment due to reduction of students needing long-term literacy support.

• Observation Survey
  - Letter ID
  - Dictation Task
• Pseudoword test (Stahl & Stahl)
• Yopp-Singer Test of Phoneme Segmentation
	Reading Recovery students made significantly greater improvement than the control group on measures of phonological processing. Discontinued Reading Recovery students demonstrated strategies similar to children in the alphabetic stage by the 16th week of Grade 1.	This study suggested that Reading Recovery children acquire phonological awareness and phonological recoding within Reading Recovery lessons. The inclusion of all Reading Recovery participants and the utilization of measures other than Clay's responded to methodological concerns stated in other reports.

Table 10.3 Subsequent Performance of Reading Recovery Children

STUDY/SOURCE	PURPOSE	SAMPLE
B. J. Askew & D. F. Frasier Sustained Effects of Reading Recovery Intervention on the Cognitive Behaviors of Second Grade Children and the Perceptions of Their Teachers *Literacy Teaching and Learning: An International Journal of Early Reading and Writing*	To examine the literacy performance of former Reading Recovery children at the end of second grade and to compare that performance with a random sample of their peers To explore comprehending behaviors of both groups of children To explore classroom teachers' perceptions of the literacy performance of both groups	54 second graders from nine Texas school districts that successfully completed Reading Recovery sessions in Grade 1 53 random sample children (excluding Reading Recovery children) from the same schools The sample represented ethnic diversity and both urban and suburban districts.
B. J. Askew, E. Kaye, D. F. Frasier, M. Mobasher, N. Anderson, & Y. G. Rodríguez Making a Case for Prevention in Education *Literacy Teaching and Learning: An International Journal of Early Reading and Writing*	To determine if prevention, rather than remediation, works in the education field by assessing the reading performance of a group of discontinued Reading Recovery children through fourth grade	218 discontinued Reading Recovery first graders and 244 random sample first graders from 45 schools were identified in the first year of the study. By the end of fourth grade, 116 discontinued Reading Recovery children and 129 random sample children remained. The sample represented ethnic diversity.

MEASURES	FINDINGS/CONCLUSIONS	COMMENTS
Three literacy tasks • text reading • dictation • spelling Three indicators of comprehending behaviors • running records • retellings • fluency ratings classroom teacher questionnaire	Reading Recovery children scored at slightly lower, but within average, levels of their second-grade peers on all three literacy tasks. MANOVAs showed no significant difference (p<.05) between Reading Recovery and random sample children on the three retelling indices or when the indices were considered together. MANOVAs showed no significant difference (p<.05) between groups when fluency was considered as a single factor or when considering phrasing or smoothness as factors. There was a significant difference on the pacing factor, with the random sample group demonstrating a faster pace on oral text reading. In general, classroom teachers perceived former Reading Recovery children as average. In some areas, however, teacher perceptions did not match up with student performance.	The authors called for the use of additional tasks in following the literacy behaviors of former Reading Recovery children, specifically standardized measures. They also called for more exploration of the mismatch between teacher perceptions and student performance. The study offered support for running records as a way to make inferences about processing the meaning of text. Difficulties encountered with retelling and fluency measures were discussed.
• Gates-MacGinitie Reading Test at beginning of Grade 1 and end of Grades 1–4 • Observation Survey at beginning and end of Grade 1 • Test of Oral Text Reading at beginning of Grade 1 and at end of Grades 1–4 • Texas Assessment of Academic Skills (TAAS) at the end of Grades 3 and 4 • classroom teacher questionnaire at end of Grades 1–4 • school information questionnaire at beginning and end of study	There were significant differences between the Reading Recovery sample and the random sample at the beginning of Grade 1. Scores at the end of Grade 1 provided a dramatic demonstration of accelerated progress of Reading Recovery children. After first grade, literacy gains on the Gates-MacGinitie for the Reading Recovery sample closely matched those of their classmates. Reading Recovery children remained within the average band of classroom performance at each testing point after the intervention. At the end of fourth grade, 95% of the Reading Recovery children were able to orally read grade-level text at an instructional level. On the TAAS measure, 85% of the Reading Recovery sample passed the reading test compared to 90% of the random sample. Classroom teachers reported that most Reading Recovery children were performing within expected ranges of their classrooms and that relatively few of these initially low-performing children were receiving literacy services outside the classroom.	Findings led authors to suggest that secondary prevention should play a larger role in schools by intervening when children are first identified as having literacy difficulties and lessening the need for more extreme, tertiary interventions. Reading Recovery children subsequently benefited from primary prevention (classroom programs) and continued to make literacy gains. Results match Juel's (1988) finding that average readers in first grade are likely to remain average in later years.

Table 10.3 Subsequent Performance continued

STUDY/SOURCE	PURPOSE	SAMPLE
C. Briggs & B. K. Young Does Reading Recovery Work in Kansas? A Retrospective Longitudinal Study of Sustained Effects *Journal of Reading Recovery*	To determine the long-term impact of Reading Recovery by determining whether children who successfully complete the program in first grade sustain their gains in reading at the end of fourth grade when compared to a grade-level stratified random sample of their peers in matched schools	Treatment group: 56 students randomly selected from the available pool of 295 Reading Recovery students served in 1998–1999 (across eight districts) Comparison group: 79 fourth-grade students from three schools with matched socioeconomic levels and minority percentages that did not have Reading Recovery in 1998
W. Brown, E. Denton, P. R. Kelly, & J. C. Neal Reading Recovery Effectiveness: A Five-Year Success Story in San Luis Coastal Unified School District *ERS Spectrum*	To determine the long-term impact of Reading Recovery on reading achievement for five cohorts of students who received a Reading Recovery intervention in Grade 1	760 students in San Luis Coastal Unified School District, CA who were initially the lowest-performing students in first grade and were served by Reading Recovery between 1993 and 1998
K. Escamilla, M. Loera, O. Ruiz, & Y. Rodríguez An Examination of Sustaining Effects in Descubriendo la Lectura Programs *Literacy Teaching and Learning: An International Journal of Early Reading and Writing*	To examine the long-term impact of Descubriendo la Lectura (DLL), or Reading Recovery in Spanish, on second- and third-grade Spanish- speaking students	Participants were second and third graders in bilingual Spanish classrooms in 39 schools in the southwestern United States: • 89 second graders discontinued from DLL in Grade 1 • 95 random sample second graders (Spanish readers in bilingual classrooms representing average readers) • 42 third graders discontinued from DLL in Grade 1 • 38 random sample third graders
G. S. Pinnell Reading Recovery: Helplng At Risk Children Learn to Read *Elementary School Journal* (report of a study by Pinnell, Lyons, & DeFord)	To explore whether Reading Recovery could succeed with low-achieving children To determine whether those children maintained their gains (summary of pilot-year data and first full-year data in Columbus, Ohio)	The lowest-achieving first-grade children were randomly assigned either to Reading Recovery (n=55) or to a control group (n=55) served daily in individual lessons taught by a trained paraprofessional. Both groups were compared with a random sample of average and high-progress first graders (n=102) as an indication of average progress.

MEASURES	FINDINGS/CONCLUSIONS	COMMENTS
• Gates MacGinitie Reading Test (Level 4, Form K)	In Grade 4, students who had discontinued from Reading Recovery in first grade had scores similar to the comparison group on vocabulary, comprehension, and overall reading tests. No statistical differences in mean scores were observed between the discontinued and incomplete groups and the comparison group on Gates-MacGinitie subtests (vocabulary and comprehension) and the total score.	This longitudinal study of a relatively small but statistically significant number of students found that students who successfully finished their Reading Recovery programs had literacy scores similar to the comparison group 3 years later. This outcome suggests that the gains made in first grade continued after the intervention.
• Observation Survey • Iowa Test of Basic Skills (ITBS) • Stanford Achievement Test, 9th Edition (SAT-9)	81–85% of children who had a full Reading Recovery intervention reached average proficiency levels in reading by the end of first grade on Reading Recovery measures and the ITBS. High proportions (65–85%) of children continued to perform at average reading levels on both ITBS and SAT-9 in Grades 2, 3, 4, and 5.	Authors concluded that most children who successfully completed a full program of Reading Recovery continued to perform at average reading levels several years after the intervention. Considering these were initially the lowest-performing children, their continued progress through fifth grade is impressive.
• Spanish Text Level Reading • SABE-2 Spanish Reading Achievement Test • student information survey (completed by classroom teachers) For children in schools that had transitioned to English: • English Text Level Reading • Gates-MacGinitie English Reading Test	There were no major differences in participation of DLL and random sample students in special programs. DLL and random sample students were comparable in reading group placement and in classroom teachers' perceptions of their literacy abilities. DLL children were reading at text levels above their peers on Spanish Text Level Reading and equivalent to their peers on SABE-2. (There was an achievement decline for both groups on SABE-2 in Grade 3.) The majority of the children were continuing to read in Spanish in Grades 2 and 3. Of the small number tested in English, DLL students were doing as well as the random sample in Grades 2 and 3, although both groups had low achievement.	The study indicates that DLL is having a positive impact on Spanish-speaking students in much the same way Reading Recovery impacts English-speaking students. Research on subsequent performance of DLL children must consider political and social realities related to instruction for bilingual children. More research is needed that relates to the implementation of bilingual education.
• Diagnostic Survey (all 6 tasks) • writing sample • Comprehensive Test of Basic Skills (2 subtests)	Reading Recovery children performed better than control children ($p<.05$) on seven of the nine measures at the end of first grade. They compared well with the random sample group. In subsequent years, Reading Recovery children continued to perform well on text reading. Effect sizes were reduced over the years.	This study provided early evidence in the United States of Reading Recovery's immediate and long-term positive effects. Results of this experimental design were audited by a team of renowned researchers.

Table 10.3 Subsequent Performance continued

STUDY/SOURCE	PURPOSE	SAMPLE
K. Rowe Factors Affecting Progress in Reading: Key Findings from a Longitudinal Study *Literacy, Teaching and Learning: An International Journal of Early Literacy*	To provide information over a 4-year period regarding factors affecting students' literacy development, with a particular focus on reading achievement, and to identify key factors affecting that development.	The sample included 5,092 students and 256 classes in 92 schools. The longitudinal design involved repeated measures nested within classes/schools and repeated measures on schools. The second design involved cross sections of students nested within schools that were changing over time.
V. Ruhe & P. Moore The Impact of Reading Recovery on Later Achievement in Reading and Writing *ERS Spectrum*	To investigate the impact of Reading Recovery on student literacy achievement in fourth grade To compare Grade 4 literacy scores of the general population with three groups of former Reading Recovery children: those whose lessons were successfully discontinued, those recommended for additional assessment and possible action, and those with an incomplete series of lessons at year-end	An SQL record linkage program was used to link microdata from two populations: • 1,260 Reading Recovery students in Maine in 1998 • 14,286 students who took the Grade 4 Maine Educational Assessment (MEA) reading and writing tests in 2001
M. C. Schmitt & A. E. Gregory The Impact of an Early Literacy Intervention: Where Are the Children Now? *Literacy Teaching and Learning: An International Journal of Early Reading and Writing*	To determine if Reading Recovery's goal of reducing the number of children at the low end of the achievement distribution in Grade 1 is maintained in subsequent years To determine how former Reading Recovery children's literacy performance compares with their peers	Participants were randomly selected from 253 Indiana schools: • Second-grade discontinued Reading Recovery = 95 • Third-grade discontinued Reading Recovery = 89 • Fourth-grade discontinued Reading Recovery = 93 • Second-grade peers = 95 • Third-grade peers = 84 • Fourth-grade peers = 92

MEASURES	FINDINGS/CONCLUSIONS	COMMENTS
Reading Achievement • Primary Reading Survey Test • Test of Reading Comprehension • English Profile • Reading Bands	Reading Recovery children benefited notably from participation. Some Reading Recovery students were achieving beyond the 80th percentile level of their non–Reading Recovery peers. Lower limits of the distribution for achievement measures were higher for Reading Recovery children. Gains of Reading Recovery children seemed to have been sustained in Grades 5 and 6.	Reading Recovery appeared to be meeting its intended purpose for those students involved.
• Maine Educational Assessment	Reading Recovery children whose lessons were successfully discontinued in Grade 1 performed at average achievement levels in reading and writing in Grade 4. Most of these children were indistinguishable from the general fourth-grade population. Children who were recommended for further assessment or service after a full Reading Recovery series of lessons in Grade 1 performed below the class achievement average in Grade 4. Yet, 63% of these children partially met or met expectations in Grade 4 reading and 37% in Grade 4 writing. Children with an incomplete series of lessons at year-end also performed below the average in Grade 4. However, 72% met or partially met expectations in Grade 4 reading and 47% in writing.	Authors concluded that most children whose Reading Recovery lessons were successfully discontinued became indistinguishable from the general Grade 4 population and ceased to be at risk. They also suggested that children in other outcome categories benefited from the intensive one-to-one teaching in Reading Recovery. For some of these children, early intervention combined with long-term actions can ensure that more of these children meet literacy expectations in later years.
• Test of Oral Reading • Gates-MacGinitie Reading Test • Indiana State Test of Educational Progress (ISTEP)	On the Test of Oral Reading, Reading Recovery children were reading texts above grade level and performing at similar levels as their peers one, two, and three years after the intervention. Frequency distributions indicated that their achievement approximated the distribution spread of their grade-level peers. On the Gates-MacGinitie Reading Test the vast majority of the former Reading Recovery children performed within an average band of the cohort sample groups at each grade level. On the ISTEP, scores for former Reading Recovery children whose lessons had been discontinued approximated a normal distribution with a mean at the 45th percentile and a standard deviation of 21.7, an unexpected pattern of progress for children who began as the lowest achievers in Grade 1.	Findings aligned with other studies that suggest continued progress (including progress on standardized measures) for children who successfully completed Reading Recovery lessons in Grade 1.

Table 10.3 Subsequent Performance continued

STUDY/SOURCE	PURPOSE	SAMPLE
K. Sylva & J. Hurry Early Intervention in Children with Reading Difficulties: An Evaluation of Reading Recovery and a Phonological Training *Literacy, Teaching and Learning: An International Journal of Early Literacy*	To evaluate the effectiveness of two different interventions (Reading Recovery and Phonological Intervention)	Almost 400 children from seven English level authorities; diverse sample with inner-city overrepresented nationally; • 22 Reading Recovery schools • 23 Phonological Intervention schools • 18 control schools

MEASURES	FINDINGS/CONCLUSIONS	COMMENTS
• British Ability Scale Word Reading • Neale Analysis of Reading • Clay's Diagnostic Survey (5 tasks) • Assessment of Phonological Awareness • British Ability Scale Spelling • background information on each child	Intervention Year: Phonological Intervention effect was more specific than Reading Recovery and not as secure. The only area where Phonological Intervention children significantly improved compared to control group was on test of phonological awareness. Reading Recovery children made significantly more progress than control group on every measure of reading. Second Year: Phonological Intervention was less effective than Reading Recovery, and the effects narrowed.	Reading Recovery was the more powerful intervention and the more expensive. However, Reading Recovery was particularly effective for socially disadvantaged children who were overrepresented in special needs programs. While cost of Reading Recovery was higher than that of other groups, the cost gap was narrowing and predicted to narrow further.

CHAPTER 11

The Economy of Prevention:
A Compelling Argument for Preventing Failure

Prevention has become a hallmark in the health sciences and has been shown to reduce the incidence of lingering problems and the costs associated with them. The health and medical fields have been forced to examine costs relative to benefits and effects due to escalating health costs, changes in fee reimbursement systems, the aging of the population, the costs of expanding technologies, and the allocation of resources for interventions for critical diseases (Hummel-Rossi & Ashdown, 2002).

Evaluating prevention costs relative to benefits and effects in education has received less attention despite the fact there are compelling reasons to consider prevention of failure a top priority for study from all angles. Indeed there are many motivators for considering education costs, including shifting demographics, increasing pressures on educational budgets, and large and increasing numbers of disadvantaged and special needs students (Hummel-Rossi & Ashdown, 2002). A notable exception in education was the evaluation of the Perry Preschool Project (Barnett, 1985; Barnett & Escobar, 1987). The researchers addressed the question, "Can early intervention be economically efficient?" They found that early intervention for disadvantaged children yields an economic return that renders it a good investment relative to other uses of society's resources.

Among the most important findings were reductions in the need for special education, reductions in crime and delinquency, increased employment and earnings, and decreased dependence on welfare. Monetary benefits were estimated for the participants, society, taxpayers, and the potential victims of crime. There were also important outcomes for which dollar values could not be estimated: increased educational attainment and decreased births to teenage mothers. The Perry Preschool Project was effective in shaping public policy that supported funding for early intervention with disadvantaged children because it was found to be effective and profitable for taxpayers.

In a comprehensive review of the literature relating to cost analysis, Hummel-Rossi and Ashdown (2002) offered some considerations related to cost analyses in education:

- There is much to learn from the cost analysis work in the fields of health and medicine; education is also a service delivery system.

- In deciding which programs to compare when analyzing costs, there should be evidence that all programs compared produce the desired outcomes.

- The analysis of costs of educational programs is more complex than it initially appears. Numerous factors influence such analyses, including the needs of the population served, the duration of the intervention, and the perspectives and scope of the intervention.

- The selection of corresponding measures of success or outcomes is critical. Measurements must be designed to assess the full range of costs and effects, including quantitative and qualitative outcomes. Indicators that are more difficult to assess such as student satisfaction, self-esteem, teacher satisfaction, and parent perceptions may be important factors in the analysis.

- In education there are many groups that have a stake in resource allocations and decision making (e.g., administrators, teachers, boards of education, students, parents, tutoring companies, textbook publishers, and taxpayers). Diverse stakeholder interests must be acknowledged when analyzing the cost of educational strategies.

Hummel-Rossi and Ashdown (2002) recommended a worthwhile protocol for cost-effectiveness studies in education that should contribute to greater understanding and rigor in the future of educational research.

In this chapter we argue that effective prevention efforts in education, in this case Reading Recovery as an early intervention to prevent literacy failure, will reduce the need for more expensive, long-term measures that will inevitably follow the occurrence of failure. As a secondary prevention effort, Reading Recovery identifies children as soon as the learning process goes wrong and offers timely, effective, short-term intervening action. The emphasis is on the *economy of prevention* because we know that the costs of literacy failure to schools and to society are exorbitant. If we can teach the lowest children to read and write successfully in Grade 1, the cost of that service "is a bargain" (Cunningham & Allington, 1994, p. 255).

Theoretical Foundations for Prevention Strategies

All too often prevention strategies and early intervention programs are adopted without consideration to their underlying theoretical assumptions. Yet all prevention strategies draw on theories related to literacy difficulty. Some are based on simple theories, others on complex theories.

The theoretical base for Reading Recovery is described in detail in Chapter 4. An underlying principle is that:

Learners would need to be able to read and write texts relatively independently in ways that could lead to the learner taking on new competencies

> through his or her own efforts in the classroom....[The early intervention] must ensure that readers and writers become competent independent processors of new information and that they have ways of going beyond the known when necessary. A treatment programme must create a broad-based foundation of cognitive competencies with the potential to be self-extending at some later time. (Clay, 2001, p. 219)

Reading Recovery takes the position that prevention of literacy difficulties requires a watchful teacher who assists the learner in developing and integrating a complex set of processes from the beginning. An understanding of this view of complexity is necessary in delivering results for interventions aiming to prevent subsequent literacy difficulties for as many children as possible (Clay, 2001).

The Notions of Prevention That Make a Difference

The notions of prevention considered throughout this chapter are based on the theoretical assumptions of Reading Recovery explained earlier. Arguments presented assume an understanding of these assumptions—and that a theory of literacy processing will help teachers of young children who are having extreme difficulties learning to read and write.

Prevention Leads to Desired Literacy Outcomes

Consider the desired outcome of Reading Recovery: to dramatically reduce the number of learners who have extreme difficulty with literacy learning and the long-term costs of these learners to educational systems. It is well-documented that this goal is best realized with prevention strategies early in a child's schooling. A longitudinal study of 54 children from first through fourth grades indicated that children who were average readers at the end of Grade 1 are likely to be average or above average in Grade 4. Conversely, the study demonstrated there is a .88 probability that a child who was a poor reader at the end of first grade would remain a poor reader at the end of fourth grade (Juel, 1988). Another study suggested that efforts to correct reading problems after Grade 3 are largely unsuccessful (Kennedy et al., 1986). There is very little evidence to suggest that remedial programs beyond Grade 2 have any level of success in correcting reading problems (Hiebert & Taylor, 1994; Slavin, Karweit, & Wasik, 1992; Taylor, Strait, & Medo, 1994). Yet, scientific research has demonstrated that intensive, early intervention programs can greatly reduce the number of children who fail to learn to read and write in first grade (e.g., Center, Wheldall, Freeman, Outhred, & McNaught, 1995; Iversen & Tunmer, 1993; Schwartz, 1996, in press). Clearly the early attention to prevention of failure can yield positive outcomes for children and cost benefits to the system. If only a portion of annual expenditures spent on remediating reading problems were spent on preventing them, children and schools would be well-served.

Consider how much children learn about reading and writing in Grade 1. Then think of how far behind their classmates students will be if they are not successful in this early process. Preventive tutoring, as a prereferral intervention, deserves an important place in discussions of reform in compensatory, remedial, and special education (Wasik & Slavin, 1993).

For the investment, Reading Recovery yields two positive outcomes for the most vulnerable children. First, it meets the stated goal of reducing the number of learners with extreme literacy difficulties. In the United States, approximately three-fourths of the children who have the opportunity for a full series of Reading Recovery lessons in Grade 1 reach grade-level expectancies in a short period of time. Second, Reading Recovery identifies a small number of children who make progress but who may need longer-term supplementary help. After about 20 weeks of intensive diagnostic teaching, the child can be referred for further evaluation and supplementary help if necessary. These outcomes have been reported for more than 1.4 million children in the United States, and in a variety of contexts including urban, suburban, and rural schools (see Chapter 9 for detailed information about evaluation studies and Tables 10.1, 10.2, and 10.3 in Chapter 10 for review of effectiveness research). Similar results are replicated in five countries around the world. An investment in Reading Recovery brings reliable results.

Educators in the United States are concerned about student outcomes for children who are English language learners. Reading Recovery offers documented evidence of success with these children who are learning to read in English while learning the language concurrently (Ashdown & Simic, 2000; Neal & Kelly, 1999). For children whose initial literacy learning is in Spanish, Descubriendo la Lectura also provides positive outcomes (Escamilla, 1994). An investment in Reading Recovery and Descubriendo la Lectura ensures the commitment to positive outcomes for all children, including those who enter our schools speaking a language other than English.

To accomplish the two intended outcomes of Reading Recovery with reliability, each school or system sets a goal of *full coverage*. Full coverage ensures that there is access to Reading Recovery and Descubriendo la Lectura for all children who need it. When that is accomplished, the school can achieve a dramatic decrease in the number of children passed on to second grade with literacy difficulties. Implementation of the intervention as designed ensures the greatest benefit from the investment (see Chapter 12).

Prereferral Intervention Is a Good Investment

Some children who have a full series of Reading Recovery lessons do not reach grade-level expectations but do make significant progress in their literacy learning.

They receive the added benefits of a sound prereferral intervention and diagnostic service. The school can reliably identify children who do need longer-term help. Compensatory programs will not be filled with children who could have benefited from an early intervention, and the system will save the high costs of long-term support. With Reading Recovery as a screening tool, the teacher documents the child's learning strengths and needs for 20 weeks and passes on a rich body of diagnostic information to the teacher who will continue to serve the few children who need longer-term support.

Prevention Yields Long-Term Benefits

Reading Recovery is an investment in the future of a child. There is strong evidence that the impact of Reading Recovery is long-lasting. With good classroom teaching, most of these initially low-achieving children who reach grade-level expectations in Grade 1 continue to progress with their peers after the intervention. Though the children may have achieved the goals of successful literacy, they remain vulnerable to life's circumstances as well as to the quality of instruction that must take them forward in the classroom literacy program grade by grade. Reading Recovery guidelines recommend that schools monitor the children through Grade 4 to ensure that children do not slip back.

Several researchers have examined the long-term effects of Reading Recovery. In a study of 5,000 children in 100 Australian schools, Rowe (1995) followed the progress of Reading Recovery students from Grade 1 to Grade 5 or 6 and found that they were distributed across the same score range as the general school population and with fewer low scores. Rowe's analysis demonstrated that Reading Recovery had removed the tail-end of the achievement distribution. Four to five years of classroom and school influence rendered children who were tail-enders no different from the normal variability. At the beginning of their years in school, they had been clustered at the low range. By Grades 5 and 6 that was no longer the case.

Several studies in the United States have confirmed Rowe's findings that in later grades, the scores of Reading Recovery children more closely approximate the spread of scores in the general population. For example, one longitudinal study found that Reading Recovery children compared favorably with their class peers at the end of Grade 4 on standardized tests and state assessment measures. Reading Recovery children who achieved average class performance in Grade 1 continued to make progress in regular classroom literacy programs (Askew, Kaye, et al., 2002). A study of Spanish-speaking children in Descubriendo la Lectura also indicated positive long-term yields for the investment (Escamilla, Loera, Ruiz, & Rodríguez, 1998). For reviews of other studies that have explored subsequent performance of Reading Recovery children, see Table 10.3 in Chapter 10.

Prevention Is a Short-Term Investment for a Long-Term Benefit

Many interventions for low-achieving children provide costly service year after year for the same children, yet few children achieve the goal of grade-level achievement in a short period of time, and most never achieve it at all. With Reading Recovery, there is a one-time cost for 12 to 20 weeks of intensive teaching before individual lessons are discontinued. The child who was given a full series of lessons is now meeting grade-level expectations or has been identified for longer-term service. The child who was identified for further service will have made considerable progress even if not yet achieving grade-level performance.

Reading Recovery is a short-term intervention because of the characteristics of the instruction and the resulting achievement outcomes. The carefully designed individual series of lessons delivered by Reading Recovery teachers helps children build an efficient learning system. Acceleration, or the enabling of a child to move faster in literacy development in order to catch up with peers, is a big factor in the economy and effectiveness of the intervention. Acceleration occurs because the Reading Recovery teacher is trained to have a deep level of understanding of reading and writing processes and of possible sequences in learning to read and write, is able to observe and analyze each child during learning episodes, can gauge appropriate learning experiences for each individual child, and can make teaching decisions based on the child's knowledge (Clay, 1993; Jones, 2001). The child is able to learn faster and catch up with his or her peers and can benefit from classroom instruction, eliminating the cost of long-term help.

Prevention Efforts Influence the Demand for Special Education Services

> To render a diagnosis of specific reading disability in the absence of early and labor-intensive remedial reading that has been tailored to the child's individual needs is, at best, a hazardous and dubious enterprise, given all of the stereotypes attached to this diagnosis. (Vellutino et al., 1996, p. 632)

Vellutino and his colleagues found that tutoring as a first intervention aided in distinguishing between reading difficulties caused by cognitive deficits and those caused by experiential deficits. Consider the cost savings when early intervention prevents inappropriate diagnoses of learning disabilities.

An examination of the effects of Reading Recovery on the rates of referral and placement in special education in New York City showed that children who received the Reading Recovery intervention were referred for testing and placed in special education at a statistically significant lower rate than children who were not served by Reading Recovery (O'Connor & Simic, 2002). Lyons and Beaver (1995) found that the percent of low-achieving children referred for special education screening was dramatically reduced in two Ohio districts after Reading Recovery was implemented. These findings represent cost savings to schools and districts and incalculable savings to children and their families.

Prevention Reduces the Incidence of Retention

Retention rarely has positive effects (Allington & McGill-Franzen, 1995; Shepard & Smith, 1990). Not only is it costly to the school system in dollars, but there is simply no evidence that it improves achievement. Moreover, it is likely to be detrimental to children's self-esteem. Instead of retaining children in kindergarten with all of its negative effects, schools can send the children to Grade 1 and offer a highly effective intervention that will afford them the opportunity to succeed on the same level as their peers. This is not only a sound economical decision, but one that considers the emotional effects on children as well. The previously cited Lyons and Beaver (1995) study found that retentions in two Ohio districts were reduced following the implementation of Reading Recovery.

Retention and transitional-grade classes are expensive and not effective. Allington and McGill-Franzen (1995) argue that the savings from eliminating retention could be used to fund educational efforts that will accelerate literacy development and ensure that children will become literate along with their peers.

Prevention Can Reduce the Literacy Achievement Gap

A recent issue of *Educational Leadership* (Scherer, 2004) was devoted to a discussion of the achievement gap in the United States from a variety of perspectives. The Association for Supervision and Curriculum Development Leadership Council took the position that

> All underserved populations—high poverty students, students with special learning needs, students from diverse cultural backgrounds, nonnative speakers of English, and urban and rural students must have access to
>
> - Innovative, engaging, and challenging coursework (with academic support) that builds on the strengths of each learner and enables students to develop their full potential.
>
> - High-quality teachers supported by ongoing professional development.
>
> - Additional resources for strengthening schools, families, and communities. (Scherer, 2004, p. 94)

Schools across the United States are working diligently to close the literacy achievement gap among all population groups. Several studies offer a promising outlook for the role of Reading Recovery in this effort. In Chapter 9, we provide convincing evidence that Reading Recovery is closing the gap between low achievers and their average classmates during the first-grade year. Batten (2004) found that an investment in Reading Recovery reduces the achievement gap of disadvantaged urban children. In a study of racial and socioeconomic literacy gaps in Ohio, Rodgers, Wang, and Gómez-Bellengé (2004) found that Reading Recovery helped reduce the achievement gap between African-American and White children and between poor and middle-class children, respectively. At the same time, the achievement gap between these same groups widened from the beginning to the end of first grade for those children who did not participate in Reading Recovery, providing compelling support for the implementation of Reading Recovery. Other studies (Ashdown & Simic, 2000; Neal & Kelly, 1999) demonstrate that Reading Recovery yields positive benefits for nonnative English speakers.

Prevention Influences a Child's Self-Efficacy and Self-Esteem

We all know the effects of failure on children. A loss of self-esteem and self-worth at any time is devastating, but consider the impact on a 6-year-old! A study by Cohen and colleagues (1989) found that after Reading Recovery lessons, children become more like high achievers in their attributions to success. They also view themselves as more competent in literacy tasks than other at-risk students. Prevention of literacy failure and its resulting impact on self-esteem is a strong investment benefit. More recent research (Rumbaugh & Brown, 2000) finds similar effects, with Reading Recovery children showing higher self-concept scores than control students at a statistically significant level. While it is difficult to attribute costs to these factors, it is well-known that the influence of self-esteem yields benefits to the child, the classroom, and the society in which the child lives.

Prevention Benefits More Than the Children Served

It is important not to limit the benefits of prevention to the outcome measures alone. We should also capture unanticipated outcomes, described by Barnett (1993) as qualitative residual. A wider range of outcomes deserves consideration, including the professional skills of teachers, the capacity of schools to solve literacy problems, and the societal benefits of the prevention efforts.

Reading Recovery is an investment in the professional skill of teachers. A trained Reading Recovery teacher offers the lowest-achieving first graders the highest-quality literacy instruction. In addition, Reading Recovery teachers bring their knowledge of how to work effectively with low-achieving students to their work with other students who are finding literacy learning difficult, and they can serve as consultants to other teachers. A testament to the level of expertise of Reading Recovery is the demand for Reading Recovery professionals to serve in leadership roles in literacy in schools and universities. (See Chapter 8 for more information on professional development in Reading Recovery.)

Classroom teachers also realize benefits from Reading Recovery implementation. Reading Recovery helps make classroom teaching more manageable by enabling children with literacy difficulties to participate in reading and writing events in the classroom. Classroom teachers also benefit from the partnership with a Reading Recovery teacher to support the learning of a struggling reader. Membership on a school team provides a vehicle for solving literacy problems within the school.

A full implementation of Reading Recovery builds the capacity of the school and the district to work successfully with the lowest-achieving students. It provides a demonstration that the lowest-achieving children can be successful and raises the expectations for achievement in the school. As part of a comprehensive literacy plan, Reading Recovery provides an early safety net to prevent failure. A team of professionals at the school and district levels collaborates to ensure high-quality literacy opportunities for every child.

Prevention efforts benefit from cost analysis using a broad societal perspective. For example, the benefits of improving a student's literacy in Grade 1 may extend beyond Grade 4, perhaps resulting in increased higher education that could result in increased contributions to the tax base (Hummel-Rossi & Ashdown, 2002). In the Perry School Project (Barnett, 1985), children in the early intervention program completed more public higher education than did the control group, costing society more. However, over time this cost was returned to society through higher wages and taxes on earnings. This visionary view of cost and benefits is often lacking from educational decision making.

The Economy of Reading Recovery

The complexity of calculating costs of interventions has been emphasized throughout this chapter. For administrators attempting to determine costs and benefits of any intervention or prevention program, multiple factors must be considered. In the appendix of this book, we are including some possible formulas for calculating per-pupil costs of Reading Recovery. In considering costs, it is important to remember that Reading Recovery is a one-time cost for 1 to 20 weeks and is most efficient when implemented as designed (see Chapter 12). It is also important to remember that simplistic formulas cannot clearly present the full array of effects and benefits.

Four possible formulas for calculating per-pupil cost of Reading Recovery located in the appendix are described below:

- Appendix A: A formula adapted from that of Gómez-Bellengé (2002b) is available for educators who wish to analyze the cost of Reading Recovery implementation in their districts. A chart is provided for entering local information about costs.

- Appendix B: A working chart is provided for calculating the costs of children whose lessons were discontinued after reaching grade-level expectations.

- Appendix C: A cost analysis study by Bueker (2004) focused on a large urban school district in the Northeast and included everything from the costs of initial teacher and teacher leader training to the cost of building the required one-way glass classroom. A working chart is provided for local data entry.

- Appendix D: This chart provides a way to compare Reading Recovery to other programs that target the same population and seek to achieve the same outcomes. With this chart format, it is important to consider the documented results of supplementary programs and the cost to the district of interventions such as Title I, special education, and small-group supplementary instruction. Costs should be compared in relation to student outcomes.

Again, analyzing costs of prevention is a complex process. The appendixes represent surface-level cost considerations. Decision makers must also consider the benefits of Reading Recovery that cannot be measured by dollars and take into account all of the information offered in this chapter. (See Table 12.2 in Chapter 12 for a list of benefits.)

Some Final Thoughts

Henry Levin (1989) challenges educators to acknowledge that some children will cost more to educate than others. He argues that we can expect to spend about 50% more to educate the at-risk child. As we consider investments in children, just as we do in our personal investment portfolios, we must consider both short-term and long-term investments. It will indeed cost the system to teach some children in the individual Reading Recovery setting for a short term, but the long-term savings will far outweigh the initial investment. Isn't 30 to 50 hours of intensive intervention—the equivalent of 2 weeks of schooling—more economical than years of special education or remedial compensatory services?

Without question the benefits of successful academic performance go beyond the dollars saved. It is important to acknowledge all of the benefits of Reading Recovery implementation to children, teachers, schools, and systems (see Chapter

12). Practitioners and administrators also acknowledge the far-reaching benefits of literate children to their parents, to the community, and ultimately to society.

Until we institutionalize Reading Recovery as a necessary preventative safety net for a few children, we will continue to pay for the consequences of literacy failure. It means setting our fiscal priorities to include this requisite part of a comprehensive literacy plan in our budgets. It also means communicating to the stakeholders and policymakers the need for Reading Recovery and all of its economical and educational benefits. Let us take a visionary view of cost—and tie our investments to what really matters in schools. The most vulnerable children are counting on us to change their futures.

> The criticism most often made of Reading Recovery is that it is too expensive and that it requires too much training. However, getting these results with the hardest to teach children leads us to conclude that the teacher training is providing the teachers with extraordinary insights and skills. It does cost money to hire and train Reading Recovery teachers but it also costs money to employ transitional grade teachers (e.g, pre-first grade classes), resource room teachers, and remedial teachers too. It costs money to retain children....When you compare the success rate of Reading Recovery with other programs that keep children for years and never get them reading on grade level, Reading Recovery is a bargain. (Cunningham & Allington, 1994, p. 255)

CHAPTER 12

Implementing Reading Recovery
in a School or a System: A Dynamic Process

Smart administrators protect their investment in Reading Recovery by ensuring a high-quality implementation. They consider the processes involved in opening up the existing system to accommodate and support this innovation.

Reading Recovery is mounted in an educational system, which may be a school, a group of schools, a district, a state, or a country. Implementation issues are often related to the age of the innovation within the system. Clay (1994) describes five challenges that emerge at different stages of implementation.

1. *Initiating Reading Recovery into the System:* At the beginning stages, systems are more concerned with getting teaching up and running in their schools, getting an informed administration and staff, and building a network within and across schools to support the goals of Reading Recovery. Often only a limited number of children are reached at this stage, and we cannot predict the full power of the intervention.

2. *Sustaining the Efforts:* When a program is up and running, there will continue to be challenges in sustaining the intervention. Teachers and administrators must know the operating rationales and be consistent in their application. The system must solve its own problems within the rationales and in consultation with the site's teacher leader. The system is now working toward a consistent turnover of children in order to serve as many children as possible.

3. *Expanding Services to Serve All the Children Defined as Needing It:* Expansion offers the challenge of reaching full implementation by allocating resources to serve all children defined as needing the intervention. This stage may call for flexible staffing and innovative ways to utilize personnel across the system and within individual campuses.

4. *Addressing Problems of Size or Scale:* Problems of scale and size emerge as the system considers challenges like statewide implementation, service to rural and sparse populations, service in large educational systems, and the expanding or shrinking need for training. This stage calls for flexibility and may require collaborative problem solving across schools, districts, regions, and even states in order to sustain the quality of the intervention.

5. *Keeping Reading Recovery Vital When It Has Been Established for a Number of Years:* There is ultimately the challenge to keep Reading Recovery vital and responsive after it has been established for several years. Problems at this stage include the possibility that the visible need for the program may disappear, leading to the misperception that there is no longer a need for the service. This is a threat to any prevention effort that is successful. Interestingly, Clay (1992) suggests that there will be a lag time before the systemic effects of the innovation are noticed—and a further period before they begin to be ignored.

Because of the complexity of systemic relationships, "an innovation likely to survive will be one which is cohesive both internally (in terms of theory, training, program design, evaluation), and with the host system (i.e., it must be workable, contributing, cost-effective, and a winner with the stakeholders)" (Clay, 1993, p. 33). Reading Recovery has systems in place to ensure internal and external cohesion (Gaffney & Askew, 1999). Support for the internal cohesion of Reading Recovery is offered by Nobel Prize winner Kenneth Wilson (Wilson & Daviss, 1994):

> The program does incorporate several key features of a successful redesign process. It has shaped its methods according to the results of its own and others' research. It has tested and honed its techniques through years of trials and refinements, analogous to industry's processes of product prototyping and test marketing. It equips its specialists with a common body of proven knowledge and skills that allow instructors to tailor each lesson to each child's needs—rather than expecting every child to adapt an identical course of lessons that moves at an inflexible pace. Equally important, the program maintains rigorous systems of self-evaluation or quality control, and offers ongoing training and support to the teachers and schools— 'dealers,' in effect—that adopt it. (pp. 50–51)

A brief explanation of the framework for Reading Recovery implementation may be helpful. As shown in Figure 12.1, each Reading Recovery teacher training site (whether it serves a single district or multiple districts) is affiliated with a university training center. Multiple district sites may be formed as consortia or as a single district that provides contracted services to other districts. Each school served by the teacher training site is affiliated with that site. In multiple district sites, an administrator from each district is generally designated to work with the designed Reading Recovery site coordinator to ensure quality district implementation.

The primary focus of this chapter is external cohesion, specifically the context of the host system in which Reading Recovery resides. Two host systems are highlighted: districts and schools. Attention is given to Reading Recovery as part of a

174

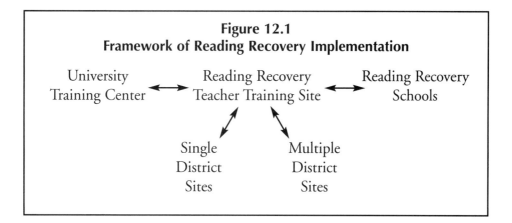

Figure 12.1
Framework of Reading Recovery Implementation

comprehensive literacy plan and to issues that influence successful implementations. We also suggest ways administrators can protect their investment and realize the benefits of institutionalizing Reading Recovery.

Reading Recovery as Part of a Comprehensive Literacy Plan

Reading Recovery as Prevention

If districts and schools make a commitment to the prevention of literacy difficulties, the stakeholders must have a clear understanding of prevention in education. Borrowing from health and medical sciences, we propose a conceptual model of prevention based on the work of Caplan (1961, 1964). The model was elaborated by Pianta (1990) as a framework for placing special education into a cycle of prevention. The framework includes three levels of prevention: primary, secondary, and tertiary.

Primary prevention is available to everyone, including groups and individuals not yet identified as having a problem to be prevented (Gaffney, 1994; Pianta, 1990). Like an inoculation against measles, primary prevention in schools attempts to inoculate against causes of subsequent problems and to reduce the rate of occurrence of a particular problem. Good classroom instruction is an example of primary prevention.

Secondary prevention is directed to a select group of the population with higher probability of problems in an area, such as providing flu shots to the elderly. It involves early identification and treatment of problems before they develop into potentially handicapping conditions. While effective primary prevention should reduce the incidence of the disorder and prevalence rates, effective secondary prevention should decrease the duration of individual cases (Lorion, 1983).

In education, even with excellent staff development and better-trained teachers, some children will need individual intervention (secondary prevention) to prevent future problems (Leslie & Allen, 1999). Reading Recovery is an example of secondary prevention in schools, providing a second chance to learn literacy behaviors. Leading to two positive outcomes, the goal of Reading Recovery is (a) to reduce the number of children who pose problems for schools because they do not reach grade-level expectations and (b) to identify a small percentage of those children who will be recommended for further assessment and possibly tertiary prevention (Jones & Smith-Burke, 1999).

Tertiary prevention refers to intervention after the occurrence of serious and enduring problems. The most common forms of tertiary prevention in public schools are special education, retention in grade level, and long-term remedial services such as Title I. Eligibility rules for tertiary prevention tend to make the task of intervention more difficult because children have to demonstrate failure before service is provided (Pianta, 1990). There is evidence that children with difficulties rarely catch up with their peers (Juel, 1988; Stanovich, 1986).

The focus changes from prevention to remediation when provided at the third (tertiary) level of prevention. To reduce the need for extensive tertiary services, money spent on early prevention is a more responsible expenditure of education funds.

As a secondary prevention option, Reading Recovery offers a safety net to prevent literacy difficulties for many children. In addition to the benefits to these children, schools and systems realize cost benefits when they accomplish the clear goal of Reading Recovery: to "dramatically reduce the number of learners who have extreme difficulty with literacy learning, and the cost of these learners to educational systems" (Clay, 1998, p. 210).

Creating a Comprehensive Literacy Plan

Each educational system has two problems to solve related to literacy: (a) how to deliver good first instruction in literacy and (b) what kind of supplementary opportunities should be provided for children who are low-achieving even in a good instructional program (Clay, 1996). A comprehensive literacy plan for a school or a system must include three essential components (see Figure 12.2), aligned with the three levels of prevention mentioned earlier:

- high-quality classroom instruction (primary prevention)
- effective early safety nets such as Reading Recovery for children who need more than good classroom teaching (secondary prevention)
- continuing extra support for a few students (tertiary prevention)

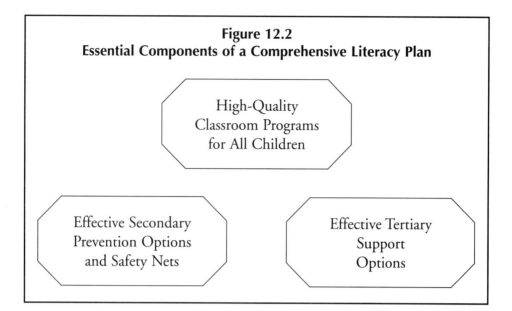

Figure 12.2
Essential Components of a Comprehensive Literacy Plan

High-Quality
Classroom Programs
for All Children

Effective Secondary
Prevention Options
and Safety Nets

Effective Tertiary
Support
Options

The comprehensive plan must also include structures that ensure success (see Figure 12.3). Districts and schools must clearly articulate their commitments to each component of the comprehensive plan and to each support system.

No classroom in the first grade will be adequate for all children. Acting as a safety net within a good literacy program, Reading Recovery can be a component of a strong, comprehensive approach to bring all students to literacy. Most children will return to average performance in regular classrooms and continue their literacy learning with their classmates. For a small number of children, Reading Recovery will serve as an intensive period of diagnostic teaching prior to referral for special education or other school services. Both outcomes are positive for children and for the system.

Classroom teaching calls for a comprehensive approach including a wide range of literacy-related activities with whole groups, small groups, and individuals in a variety of subject areas. Reading Recovery is a specific approach to prevent literacy problems and is targeted to a limited number of learners within a classroom program (Fountas & Pinnell, 1996). Reading Recovery provides supplementary instruction which is not intended to supplant the literacy program of the classroom but rather to enhance it so children can benefit from participation.

Marie Clay (1996) explained the relationship between classroom programs and Reading Recovery in this way:

> Children can enter Reading Recovery from any program and return to any program. Reading Recovery does not require classroom programs to

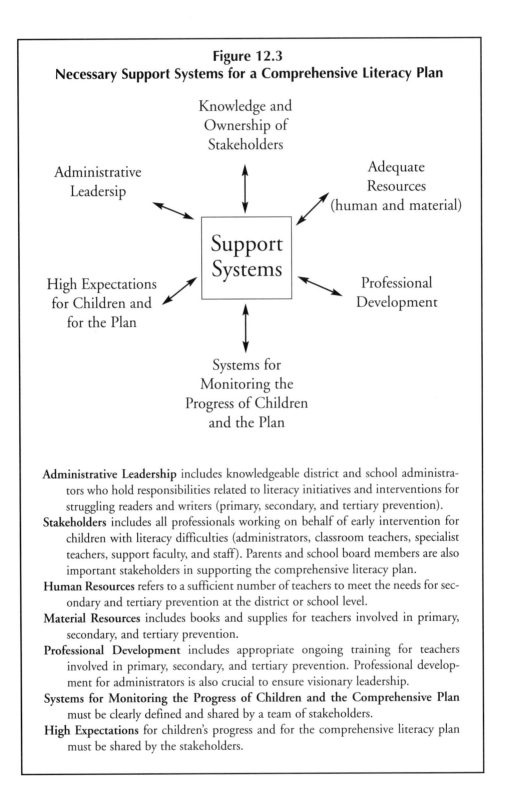

Figure 12.3
Necessary Support Systems for a Comprehensive Literacy Plan

Knowledge and Ownership of Stakeholders

Administrative Leadersip

Adequate Resources (human and material)

Support Systems

High Expectations for Children and for the Plan

Professional Development

Systems for Monitoring the Progress of Children and the Plan

Administrative Leadership includes knowledgeable district and school administrators who hold responsibilities related to literacy initiatives and interventions for struggling readers and writers (primary, secondary, and tertiary prevention).

Stakeholders includes all professionals working on behalf of early intervention for children with literacy difficulties (administrators, classroom teachers, specialist teachers, support faculty, and staff). Parents and school board members are also important stakeholders in supporting the comprehensive literacy plan.

Human Resources refers to a sufficient number of teachers to meet the needs for secondary and tertiary prevention at the district or school level.

Material Resources includes books and supplies for teachers involved in primary, secondary, and tertiary prevention.

Professional Development includes appropriate ongoing training for teachers involved in primary, secondary, and tertiary prevention. Professional development for administrators is also crucial to ensure visionary leadership.

Systems for Monitoring the Progress of Children and the Comprehensive Plan must be clearly defined and shared by a team of stakeholders.

High Expectations for children's progress and for the comprehensive literacy plan must be shared by the stakeholders.

change. However, some things make it harder for Reading Recovery children to continue to improve after discontinuing, and these things include a weak classroom program or one with low achievement outcomes.

Reading Recovery cannot be compared with any classroom program or any teaching method. It is designed to take the children who become the lowest achievers in any classroom and were taught by any teaching method and provide them with a series of lessons supplementary to that program. (p. 1)

In summary, schools must provide strong classroom programs, Reading Recovery for children identified as needing early literacy support, and effective tertiary programs for a small number of children after the intensive diagnostic teaching offered through Reading Recovery. Schools cannot afford to abandon—or weaken—any of the three offerings in working toward literacy for all children.

Initiating a Reading Recovery Implementation

Effective implementation of Reading Recovery and Descubriendo la Lectura depends on extensive support from the school district and the schools. It is an intensive intervention that requires understanding, ownership, and commitment from teachers, administrators, school boards, and area universities. Therefore, districts considering adopting Reading Recovery need an understanding of the steps toward implementation. The following steps are proposed for those considering the establishment of a site for training Reading Recovery teachers.

1. Send a representative team on a fact-finding visit to a university training center where Reading Recovery teacher leaders are trained. If possible, visit established sites in your local area. Build understanding and support for program implementation at all levels within your district.

2. Release one or more experienced and highly qualified (master's degree required) individuals to participate in the teacher leader training program for one academic year. This person will return to the district or site to train Reading Recovery teachers.

3. Establish an area with a one-way glass for teaching sessions and adequate space for follow-up class discussions.

4. Support the teacher leader in training 8 to 12 Reading Recovery teachers annually. Determine a procedure to ensure the selection of highly qualified and successful teachers.

5. Arrange for weekly training sessions for the teachers-in-training across an academic year. Secure an agreement with an area university to provide graduate credit for the courses.

6. Make the necessary staff arrangements to enable Reading Recovery teachers to spend a minimum of 2½ hours daily with at least four individual students. They will fulfill other job responsibilities for the remainder of the day (e.g., classroom teacher, Title I teacher).

7. Make the necessary staff arrangements to enable the teacher leader to teach children and to manage the Reading Recovery intervention at the district or site level.

8. Purchase books and supplies; the start-up cost for nonconsumable materials is approximately $2,500 per Reading Recovery teacher.

9. Comply with the *Standards and Guidelines of Reading Recovery in the United States* (2004) for training, data collection, and implementation. These standards protect your investment and must be followed to maintain active Reading Recovery status.

Some schools and small districts may wish to implement Reading Recovery but are too small to create a teacher training site. In this case, administrators may contact local sites about the possibility of affiliation or contact a trainer at the regional university training center for suggestions.

Creating a Development Plan for Reading Recovery Implementation

Districts and schools should have a development plan for implementing and operating their Reading Recovery intervention, and these plans should be created by teams of stakeholders at the respective levels. The Reading Recovery teacher leader and site coordinator will be critical members of these teams. Table 12.1 is a guide for preparing short-term and long-term plans to institutionalize Reading Recovery within a comprehensive literacy plan.

Issues Related to Successful Implementation

Many factors influence successful implementations. Some crucial implementation factors are highlighted in this section:

- informed leadership
- shared ownership and understandings
- adequate coverage
- quality teaching and training
- use of data to inform decisions

Informed Leadership

As with any school or system endeavor, the role of the administrator is critical. In Reading Recovery, system-level and school-based administrators must be knowledgeable and collaborative in working with all stakeholders on behalf of the children needing Reading Recovery service.

Table 12.1

Implementation Questions for Reading Recovery Stakeholders

Is there a written plan for implementing Reading Recovery and Descubriendo la Lectura
— at the site level?
— at the district level?
— at the school level?
Does the plan include long-range and short-range goals
— for placing Reading Recovery as a safety net within a comprehensive literacy program?
— for expansion of coverage in the district and school?
— for funding that is diversified?
— for selecting and training high-quality teacher leaders?
— for selecting and training successful teachers?
— for providing continuing contact and professional development for Reading Recovery personnel?
— for selection of appropriate staffing models?
— for protecting teaching time?
— for building knowledge and ownership of stakeholders?
— for sharing understandings about Reading Recovery?
— for establishing a district team?
— for establishing school teams?
— for evaluating and reporting student outcomes?
— for monitoring former Reading Recovery children and serving as their advocates?
— for institutionalizing Reading Recovery?
— for keeping Reading Recovery visible and dynamic?
— for utilizing teacher leader expertise in planning and implementing Reading Recovery?
— for protecting the investment by adhering to standards and guidelines?
— for ongoing evaluation and revision of the plan?

Site- or District-Level Leadership

At the district or site level, a leadership team will oversee the implementation and operation of Reading Recovery. The Reading Recovery site coordinator and teacher leader are essential members of this team. It is also important to include key administrators responsible for language arts, federal programs, and other appropriate departmental functions within the district. District- or site-level leaders will build an infrastructure for Reading Recovery within a comprehensive plan for literacy and will work with individual schools in adopting Reading Recovery as a school initiative. The district team will create a development plan (see previous section) to include plans for expansion.

Site coordinator. The Reading Recovery site coordinator for the district or consortium of districts is an administrator who is responsible for overseeing and managing the implementation of Reading Recovery within the site.

Major responsibilities of the Reading Recovery site coordinator include

- oversee the long-range site plan for Reading Recovery
- interface with all levels of administration within the site
- build broad-based support for Reading Recovery at the district and school levels
- work to embed Reading Recovery within larger comprehensive plans
- build understandings and ownership of Reading Recovery at the district level
- work toward full implementation of Reading Recovery in every school
- create and manage a Reading Recovery budget with guidance from the site's teacher leader
- assume responsibility for compliance with Reading Recovery standards and guidelines
- examine and use data for continuous improvement
- support the work of the site's teacher leader
- secure internal and external funding for Reading Recovery
- work toward institutionalization of Reading Recovery in schools and districts
- collaborate with university training centers on issues related to training and implementation
- communicate and disseminate information to various audiences

Teacher leader. Each site must have one or more credentialed Reading Recovery teacher leaders who may work for a single large district or across districts in a consortium arrangement. The teacher leader provides initial and ongoing training of Reading Recovery teachers as well as assistance to Reading Recovery schools.

Major responsibilities of Reading Recovery teacher leaders include

- teach children in Reading Recovery lessons
- provide initial training for new Reading Recovery teachers
- provide continuing contact sessions for previously trained teachers
- provide on-site support to Reading Recovery teachers
- problem-solve about children having unusual difficulty
- support the development of school Reading Recovery teams
- monitor progress of children
- oversee data collection and reporting
- provide information sessions for various audiences
- manage the operation of the Reading Recovery efforts at the district level
- provide the rationales for operating decisions in Reading Recovery
- problem-solve with teachers and principals about implementation issues

School Leadership

School principal. At the school level, the principal has a key role in implementing and operating Reading Recovery. Principals assist the school staff in making Reading Recovery an integral part of the vision for children's learning. The principal becomes part of a Reading Recovery team, offering skillful leadership.

Major roles of principals in Reading Recovery schools include

- know about Reading Recovery
- communicate the goals, purposes, practices, and results to various audiences
- create a plan for incorporating Reading Recovery into the school's plan for literacy
- build commitment and ownership through collaboration with the entire staff
- create a collaborative school Reading Recovery team
- work with the school Reading Recovery team and district administrators to achieve full coverage for all children in the school who need the service

- select teachers for training who have the potential for intensive, high-quality service to children with the most difficulties in literacy learning

- manage space, time, and materials to support teaching and learning

- support teachers in initial training and ongoing professional development

- monitor and evaluate results of Reading Recovery in the school and use data to problem-solve and improve results

- model high expectations for all students

A Principal's Guide to Reading Recovery (2002), available from the Reading Recovery Council of North America, provides detailed information for principals implementing and operating the intervention within their schools. School-level Reading Recovery teams have become a key component of a smooth, effective implementation; these teams are discussed later in this chapter. The principal's commitment and participation is essential to the success of the team.

Reading Recovery teacher. The Reading Recovery teacher in each school also assumes a leadership role in the implementation of Reading Recovery within the school.

Major roles of Reading Recovery teachers include

- work with a minimum of four Reading Recovery children daily

- continue professional development throughout tenure as a Reading Recovery teacher

- collaborate with classroom teachers

- communicate with parents

- serve as a member of the Reading Recovery school team

- work with the principal in implementing Reading Recovery at the school level

- serve as a resource for classroom teachers in supporting Reading Recovery children in the classroom

- collaborate with other Reading Recovery teachers in the network on issues related to teaching and implementation

University Leadership

University trainer. University trainers are faculty members working in established centers for training Reading Recovery teacher leaders.

Major responsibilities of university trainers include

- operate the university training center to support a network of affiliated sites

- train teacher leaders
- provide ongoing professional development for teacher leaders
- provide implementation support to sites and districts within the university training center network
- implement, develop, and expand Reading Recovery within the region
- conduct research and evaluate intervention outcomes
- provide leadership for Reading Recovery at local, state, national, and international levels

Trainers work closely with teacher leaders and site coordinators in implementing and operating Reading Recovery. They are available as a resource for network sites.

Shared Ownership and Understandings

In order to sustain any innovation, basic understandings about the purposes, rationales, and processes of the innovation must be shared (Fullan, 1985). In addition to shared understandings, ownership must be felt by the stakeholders who collaborate to provide the structures for successful implementation within the system. All stakeholders must be perceived to have a responsibility for the success of each child served. Fullan (1991) cautions that true ownership does not occur magically at the beginning of an implementation but that "ownership in the sense of clarity, skill, and commitment is a progressive process" (p. 92).

At the District Level

At the district level, a team of stakeholders should collaborate in the implementation and operation of Reading Recovery. The team should include the Reading Recovery site coordinator, the site's teacher leaders, the language arts or curriculum director, the federal programs director, and other key administrators who have a vested interest in the children served by Reading Recovery or Descubriendo la Lectura. This team should become very knowledgeable about Reading Recovery and about their roles in the implementation. They are also responsible for communicating about Reading Recovery to district decision makers and policymakers. University trainers are available to support site coordinators and teacher leaders in building ownership in Reading Recovery.

The Reading Recovery site coordinator and teacher leader are responsible for providing staff development for principals regarding their role in Reading Recovery. In addition to professional development at the point of adoption in the school, opportunities for principals to learn more about Reading Recovery should continue. The principal is the key to school-level implementation and should have clear understandings.

At the School Level

Each campus needs to develop a Reading Recovery team to monitor the progress of Reading Recovery children and to guide implementation in the school. An informed Reading Recovery team ensures that the intervention runs effectively to serve the children in the school and that the decisions about program operation ensure optimal results. The team provides an interface across programs serving young children—classroom programs, Reading Recovery, special education, Title I, and bilingual/ESL.

The team meets regularly to engage in problem solving regarding Reading Recovery's effectiveness and efficiency at the school. The principal's active participation is essential to the team's success. Membership on the school team depends on the composition of staff and specialists who work in the school. During the development of the team process in the school, the teacher leader's participation is very important. After the team is working successfully within the school, the teacher leader becomes a consultant to the team on problems related to staffing, training, student selection, scheduling, evaluation of the data, and any other difficult issues that may arise.

For detailed information about Reading Recovery school teams, refer to *A Principal's Guide to Reading Recovery* (2002).

Adequate Coverage

A fully implemented Reading Recovery program over several years leads to a dramatic reduction in the number of children with literacy difficulties in Grades 2–6. Clay (1994) defines *full coverage* as having sufficient Reading Recovery teacher time to serve all children defined as needing the service. She cautions that partial implementation is a temporary condition and a period that reveals all the implementation difficulties. It is a time for persistence and a focus on individual success stories. As schools move toward full coverage, most problems of implementation disappear (Clay, 1994). It is important to consider coverage needs for Descubriendo la Lectura and Reading Recovery separately.

The level of Reading Recovery coverage influences student outcomes (Gómez-Bellengé, Rodgers, & Fullerton, 2003a). National data for 2001–2002 showed that schools with full Reading Recovery support had a discontinuing rate of 65% of all children served, while schools with very low coverage had a discontinuing rate of 55%. Schools with high levels of coverage also had fewer children with incomplete programs at the end of the year.

Principals ask questions about how many Reading Recovery teachers are needed for their schools. The answer will depend on the number of children needing Reading Recovery's extra help and can be estimated by looking at reading levels and other scores of children at the end of the year. Kindergarten and first-grade teachers can also offer advice about coverage. Scores on the tasks published in *An Observation Survey of Early Literacy Achievement* (Clay, 2002) provide information about needs for the school.

Flexible staffing plans support the realization of full coverage. Schools with a significant number of trained Reading Recovery teachers have built the capacity to serve all needy children within a flexible staffing framework.

If the need for coverage in a particular school seems overwhelming, with a large percentage of the first graders needing help, the school should also be addressing other issues such as classroom programs and practices in pre-kindergarten and kindergarten classes. Reading Recovery is the safety net for a good comprehensive literacy program in a school. Within an effective program, it is possible to configure the necessary Reading Recovery support.

Coverage is an issue at all levels. Schools, districts, and sites should create a realistic plan for expanding coverage—within schools and across schools. The site's teacher leaders and site coordinator are excellent resources for producing such a plan. Trainers at university training centers are valuable resources when planning expansion at all levels, including state implementations.

Quality Teaching and Training

Reading Recovery is an investment in teachers and teacher training. Selection of the highest-quality teacher leaders and teachers is essential for a successful implementation. Initial training at both levels must be strong.

An important feature of Reading Recovery is the ongoing nature of training through continuing contact sessions for teachers and professional development sessions for teacher leaders. The quality of these sessions influences the success of Reading Recovery at the local level. Teacher leaders must have time to work with individual teachers to problem-solve about the teaching of individual children, especially those offering the greatest challenges.

Administrators are a critical factor in supporting Reading Recovery's design for training and monitoring teachers' work with children. They must protect the time of Reading Recovery teachers and teacher leaders and support their ongoing learning to improve outcomes with children.

For detailed information about Reading Recovery professional development, see *A Principal's Guide to Reading Recovery* (2002, pp. 34–38) and Chapter 8 in this volume.

Use of Data to Inform Decisions

As detailed in Chapter 9, Reading Recovery's data evaluation system is unlike any other. Because of the amount and type of data collected, information is available for evaluating student outcomes and for making implementation decisions.

Each district and each school can use data to evaluate their implementations. Sites receive a comprehensive report annually from the National Data Evaluation Center. Reading Recovery site coordinators and teacher leaders closely examine the data to inform their decisions about strengthening the local Reading Recovery implementation.

School reports are now available as well. One function of the Reading Recovery school team is to prepare a school report that will help in making recommendations for improvement. (See *A Principal's Guide to Reading Recovery* [2002] for detailed information about analyzing school data and preparing school reports.)

Protecting Your Investment in Reading Recovery

Adopters of innovations need confidence that their investments are sound. Reading Recovery provides a number of protections to schools and systems; systems and schools are obligated to adhere to these protections.

Standards and Guidelines

Huberman and Miles (1982) found that well-outlined programs with guidelines and requirements that include technical assistance and administrative support lead to less confusion and more successful outcomes. Reading Recovery operates within a set of printed *Standards and Guidelines of Reading Recovery in the United States* (2004). These standards provide the basis for problem solving at the school or system level. "The essential conditions for the success of Reading Recovery, as a system, lie in the coherence, the resourcing and the reach of the support and quality assurance structures which are put in place for its implementation" (Office for Standards in Education, 1993, p. 162).

For each of the quality assurance structures related to implementation there are operating standards built on sound rationales. Each of the operating decisions guiding Reading Recovery implementation supports the basic goal of reducing the number of children with extreme literacy difficulties during their first-grade year. Some of the operating principles in Reading Recovery are listed below:

- selection of the lowest-achieving children
- selection of exceptional teachers and teacher leaders
- intensive, long-term, and ongoing training of teachers and teacher leaders
- one-to-one instruction
- daily teaching
- supplementary to classroom instruction
- short-term (12 to 20 weeks)

- commitment to full coverage
- commitment to early intervention and prevention
- collection and reporting of data on each child served
- implementation of effective school teams

Rationales are formulated from extensive knowledge of reading difficulties and the accumulated knowledge in the research of Reading Recovery in action. Reading Recovery teacher leaders and trainers of teacher leaders know these rationales and are able to share them with local educators and decision makers. While some may challenge the rationales, we must remember that Reading Recovery solves a problem which we did not solve in the past. To do this, teaching and practices must be different from those we may be accustomed to (Clay, n.d.).

Reading Recovery Trademark

The name Reading Recovery has been a trademark of The Ohio State University since 1990 when action was taken to identify sites that meet the essential criteria for a Reading Recovery implementation. The trademark is not a guarantee of high quality, but it contributes to the consistency of implementation across sites. In order to use the name Reading Recovery, a system must follow the standards and guidelines discussed above.

On an annual basis, Reading Recovery sites are granted a royalty-free license to use the name. Each Reading Recovery implementation is reviewed annually to determine if the site has met the standards for quality. As a protection for sites meeting these standards, there are strict controls that prevent individuals and commercial organizations from using the name Reading Recovery to promote a program that does not comply with the standards and guidelines of Reading Recovery in the United States.

A Network of Support

Reading Recovery is a collaborative venture—a partnership among schools, districts, universities, and in some instances state departments of education. This partnership ensures a unified effort to change the status of low-achieving children in literacy.

Reading Recovery sites are part of a network that depends on regular contact with a university training center. Sites may access support from the university training center and from other sites within the network to strengthen their implementations and problem-solve implementation issues.

The Reading Recovery Council of North America is a membership organization that offers support to the Reading Recovery community through publications, advocacy, and events. The council supports the work of university training centers, providing valuable network services.

A National Data Evaluation Center

Local investments in Reading Recovery are also closely monitored by the National Data Evaluation Center (see Chapter 9). Local officials can examine student outcomes and implementation decisions at the site, district, and school levels. This feedback loop is a unique feature of Reading Recovery implementation.

A Built-in System for Change

The infrastructure of Reading Recovery was designed to facilitate change. As we learn from our own evaluations and from new research, there is a system for making changes. An established, organized system for communicating these changes is managed by Reading Recovery trainers and teacher leaders who are required to attend professional development meetings (Clay, 2003a). See Chapter 14 in this volume for more information on Reading Recovery's system for change.

Remember the Benefits!

In Chapter 11, the cost of Reading Recovery implementation is explored. We know that money is saved when we reduce the number of children who are retained in Grade 1, placed in special education, or placed in other long-term compensatory programs for reading and writing. But there are many benefits of Reading Recovery implementation that cannot be accurately projected in terms of dollars saved. Table 12.2 lists these benefits of a well-implemented Reading Recovery intervention to children, schools, and communities.

A Final Comment

While Reading Recovery provides many supports and safeguards for implementers, the implementation decisions made by education systems will determine the level of success in that system. If we really want to reduce the number of children having extreme difficulty in reading and writing in our schools, we must make commitments to do what it takes. And it will take a team effort—with a dynamic process of ongoing problem solving at the school and system levels. It is an exciting time in education because we know what it will take. The question now is, will we?

Table 12.2 Benefits of Reading Recovery

— a highly effective research-based literacy intervention for first graders having difficulty learning to read and write

— a cost-effective short-term early intervention that reduces the need for long-term remedial services

— a safety net within a school's comprehensive literacy plan and a supplement to any good classroom program

— an understanding of the need for early assessment and intervention

— a powerful research-based assessment system for identifying children with difficulties during the first grade

— an organized approach to early intervention

— powerful staff development for teachers of the lowest-achieving children

— a demonstration that low-achieving children can learn, changing perceptions and expectations

— a way to make classroom teaching more manageable by enabling low-achieving children to profit from classroom reading and writing instruction

— increased capacity within each school to address and analyze problems related to reading difficulty

— data to allow staff to assess reading skills and track reading progress

— school-level (Reading Recovery teachers) and district-level (Reading Recovery teacher leaders) expertise and leadership in working with struggling young readers

— a not-for-profit collaborative effort involving schools, districts, and universities

— increased self-esteem and self-efficacy for initially low-achieving children because they know they are learning to read and write

Additional Resources: Implementation

Askew, B. J., Fountas, I. C., Lyons, C. A., Pinnell, G. S., & Schmitt, M. C. (1998). *Reading Recovery review: Understandings, outcomes, and implications.* Columbus, OH: The Reading Recovery Council of North America.

Bryk, A., Rollow, S., & Pinnell, G. S. (1996). Urban school development: Literacy as a lever for change. *Educational Policy, 10,* 172–201.

Clay, M. M. (1987). Implementing Reading Recovery: Systemic adaptations to an educational innovation. *New Zealand Journal of Educational Studies, 22*(1), 35–58.

Clay, M. M. (1990). The Reading Recovery programme, 1984–1988: Coverage, outcomes and education board figures, *New Zealand Journal of Educational Studies, 25*(1), 61–70.

Clay, M. M. (1991a). *Becoming literate: The construction of inner control* (Chapters 1, 2, and 3). Portsmouth, NH: Heinemann.

Clay, M. M. (1991b). Reading Recovery surprises. In D. E. DeFord, C. A. Lyons, & G. S. Pinnell (Eds.), *Bridges to literacy: Learning from Reading Recovery* (pp. 57–76). Portsmouth, NH: Heinemann.

Clay, M. M. (1993). *Reading Recovery: A guidebook for teachers in training.* Portsmouth, NH: Heinemann. (see pp. 81–97).

Clay, M. M. (1994). An early intervention to prevent literacy learning difficulties: What is possible? *The Running Record, 6,* 4–5.

Clay, M. M. (1997). International perspectives on the Reading Recovery program. In J. Flood, S. B. Heath, & D. Lapp (Eds.), *The handbook of research on teaching literacy through the communicative and visual arts* (pp. 655–667). New York: MacMillan Library Reference USA (a project of the International Reading Association).

Clay, M. M. (1998). *By different paths to common outcomes* (Chapters 14 and 16). York, ME: Stenhouse.

Clay, M. M. (2001). *Change over time in children's literacy development* (Chapters 6 and 7). Portsmouth, NH: Heinemann.

Fullan, M. G. (1993). *Change forces: Probing the depths of educational reform.* Bristol, PA: Falmer Press.

Gaffney, J. S., & Paynter, S. Y. (1994). The role of early literacy interventions in the transformation of educational systems. *Literacy, Teaching and Learning: An International Journal of Early Literacy, 1*(1), 23–29.

Herman, R., & Stringfield, H. R. (1997). *Ten promising programs for educating all children: Evidence of impact.* Arlington, VA: Educational Research Service.

Rinehart, J. S., & Short, P. M. (1991). Viewing Reading Recovery as a restructuring phenomenon. *Journal of School Leadership, 1*(4), 379–399.

Rodgers, E. (2001, April). *What we know about educational reform: Lessons from a successful reform initiative.* Paper presented at the Annual Meeting of the American Educational Research Association, Seattle, WA.

RRCNA Publications Related to Implementation

- *Reading Recovery Review: Understandings, Outcomes, and Implications*
- *The Journal of Reading Recovery* (has an implementation strand)
- *Reading Recovery: An Analysis of a Research-Based Reading Intervention*
- *Grassroots Advocacy Handbook*
- *A Principal's Guide to Reading Recovery*
- Public Information Packet (Fact Sheets)
- *Reading Recovery in North America: An Illustrated History*
- *Standards and Guidelines of Reading Recovery in the United States*

The Reading Recovery Web site also has information about implementation: www.readingrecovery.org.

CHAPTER 13

Reading Recovery and Public Policy: Meeting the Challenges Over Time

If a state truly wants to impact student achievement, it would mandate and fund Reading Recovery programs in all its elementary schools.

— Janet L. Emerick, Superintendent,
Lake Central School Corporation, St. John, Indiana

Although Dr. Emerick was referring to state support of Reading Recovery by policymakers in Indiana, where the program has been an integral part of the state's Early Intervention Grant Program, Reading Recovery has an important role to play in the national vision to make all children successful in literacy early in their schooling. The current focus on literacy as a primary goal for elementary school students includes a great concern for closing the gap between low- and high-achieving children as local, state, and national initiatives call for assurances that all children will be readers and writers by the end of third grade.

It is true that politics and education have always been integrally entwined in the public arena, but never more than in the last few decades when education has been a high priority in political platform issues. Couched in the concept of civil rights, efforts are being made to assure there is equity in education for all children, and that includes equal access to high-quality instruction for children regardless of socio-economic status, race, or ethnicity (Starrat, 2003). Educational issues that have emerged in the public policy arena have involved the development of academic standards, school accountability (Starrat, 2003), assessment (Neill, 2003), and teacher quality (Berry, Hoke, & Hirsch, 2004)—all of which are interrelated and mutually dependent. All issues listed here are dependent on funding, which ultimately drives the success of initiatives.

No matter the issue (i.e., assessment, standards, equal access), effective advocacy is critical to achieving success. Successful advocacy requires knowledge of the issues, effective communication skills, and access to those who can have an impact on the outcomes of public policy. It requires the involvement and cooperation of parents; community organizations; business leaders; educators; educational administrators; local, state, and federal legislators; and any other stakeholders in the future of the nation.

Reading Recovery has 20 years of involvement in the United States, and despite changes in focus as different administrations have put forth their educational agendas, Reading Recovery has met and answered the various challenges of public policy over time. The reason it has maintained its relevance while the laws or emphases have changed is that it is based on such a comprehensive and well-founded theory of how children learn to read. It has always included the various factors of sound reading instruction such as the development of phonemic awareness and phonological processing, the reciprocity of reading and writing, and the development of vocabulary and comprehension, as well as the teacher professional development component that render it applicable to literacy teaching and learning during changing public policy landscapes.

The literacy intervention's successful staying power in this country rests on its view that readers must develop independent strategies across a broad front to be successful problem solvers in reading and writing. The design of the intervention calls for daily, well-organized, and explicit instruction that is individually delivered by teachers who have been trained in a dynamic professional development model of unparalleled quality that involves observation and reflection as concurrent processes. Reading Recovery was established on the philosophy that most children can learn to read and that we must find ways to make it happen.

Reading Recovery is based on outcomes of student progress that are closely monitored and used to guide daily instruction. With a built-in collaboration between classroom and specialist teachers, the children's accelerated progress affords them the opportunity to benefit from classroom instruction and to keep pace with their peers.

The following historical perspective documents Reading Recovery's resilience across different national initiatives in the United States over time. For 2 decades, Reading Recovery has been a viable component of literacy instruction and education reform supported by federal funds. Successful advocacy efforts by Reading Recovery stakeholders, supported by the leadership of the Reading Recovery Council of North America, have played a major role as well.

The Elementary and Secondary Education Act

With a few exceptions, most federal support for education generally, and Reading Recovery in particular, comes from the Elementary and Secondary Education Act (ESEA) of 1965 and subsequent updates, called reauthorizations. When this book was written, the most recent reauthorization of the ESEA was called the No Child Left Behind Act of 2001 (NCLB) and for the first time in history required programs to meet a higher level of a scientific research base. The ESEA was comprised of 10 Titles, several of which embraced Reading Recovery as appropriate. The most notable were Title I, Part A and the new Reading First Program for Title I, Part B.

Title I, Part A

The largest single source of federal funds for education derives from the ESEA Title I, Part A. It provided $12.3 billion in the first year of the reauthorization (2004) to state education agencies, districts, and schools to improve the academic achievement of disadvantaged students. Historically most schools with Reading Recovery have used funds from Title I, Part A to address the costs of implementation.

Title I, Part B: Reading First

Title I, Part B of the ESEA provided another $5 billion in funds for 5 years for the new Reading First program. Although the U.S. Department of Education implemented the Reading First program with an emphasis on classroom instruction, it permitted the use of Reading First funds for supplemental instruction and for interventions like Reading Recovery. Reading First program implementation also required that instruction include the essential components identified by the National Reading Panel as critical to success (see pp. 198-199).

Funds for English-Language Learners in the ESEA

Descubriendo la Lectura involves work with children who qualify as English-language learners in the ESEA, and there were funds allocated for instruction. For example, Title funds that covered this cohort group include Title I, Part C (Migrant Education), which received $394 million in 2004, and Title III (Language Instruction for Limited-English Proficient and Immigrant Students), which received $681 million for fiscal year 2004.

Scientifically Based Reading Research

The reauthorization of the ESEA required most programs supported by Title I, Part A funds to meet the new federal definition of research, so public attention focused on research-based practice. According to this definition, scientific research applies rigorous, systematic, and objective procedures to obtain valid knowledge relevant to reading development, reading instruction, and reading difficulties. It includes research that (a) employs systematic, empirical methods that draw on observation or experiment; (b) involves rigorous data analyses that are adequate to test the stated hypotheses and justify the general conclusions draws; (c) relies on measurements or observational methods that provide valid data across evaluators and observers and across multiple measurements and observations; and (d) has been accepted by a peer-reviewed journal or approved by a panel of independent experts through a comparably rigorous, objective, and scientific review.

Reading Recovery aptly meets this definition as outlined below:

1. The structure and design of Reading Recovery are consistent with a large body of substantial research on reading and writing behaviors that began in the 1960s and continues today.

2. Research on Reading Recovery uses systematic, empirical methods to collect data annually on all children receiving service. Data are collected systematically at three points throughout the intervention and on a random sample of children for comparison purposes.

3. The evaluation process tests at least three hypotheses:
   - Reading Recovery children will increase their skills in the following areas necessary for reading: letter identification, reading vocabulary, concepts about print, writing vocabulary, hearing and recording sounds in words (phonemic awareness), and text reading.

   - Children who successfully complete Reading Recovery will perform on literacy measures within an average band of their classmates who do not need the intervention.

   - Children who successfully complete Reading Recovery will continue to make gains in text reading and writing vocabulary after leaving the program.

4. Reading Recovery uses systematic and simultaneous replication studies to document program outcomes for all children served, adhering to standardized methods, instruments, and timelines across all schools, school districts, training sites, and states. Replication is important because it allows scientists to verify results. Assessment in Reading Recovery has been replicated across time and location with remarkable consistency.

5. Reading Recovery research is reported in numerous published peer-reviewed research articles or research reviews that offer support for various aspects of the program.

Essential Elements of Research-Based Reading Instruction

Five essential elements of reading instruction were identified by the National Reading Panel, a group of individuals who searched the literature for evidence and then summarized their findings in a major report (summarized in two shorter reports) that helped to guide changes in literacy education[1]. Their findings were based on a review of a body of research limited by the federal definition of scientific research described above. In addition to meeting the rigorous definition of scientifically based reading research, Reading Recovery also incorporates the essential components of reading instruction identified by the National Reading Panel and included in the authorizing legislation of NCLB [Title I, Part B, Sec. 1208(3)]: phonemic awareness, phonics, vocabulary development, fluency, and text comprehension. In addition to these five essential components, four additional elements of reading instruction supported by the research literature are characteristics of Reading Recovery lessons. In Table 13.1 (see pp. 201–203), these nine components of research based reading instruction are discussed relative to Reading Recovery teaching.

Comprehensive School Reform (CSR)

First established in 1998 as part of a federal appropriations bill, the Comprehensive School Reform program was authorized in Title I, Part F of the most recent ESEA reauthorization. It is helping raise student achievement by assisting public schools across the country to implement effective, comprehensive school reforms that are based upon scientifically based research and effective practices. While Reading Recovery is not a comprehensive program, it has been funded as the early intervention component of a comprehensive approach to education reform in several states.

---

[1] The three reports are

• *Report of the National Reading Panel: Teaching Children to Read: An Evidence-Based Assessment of the Scientific Research Literacy on Reading and its Implications for Reading Instruction* (NICHD, 2000a). This document is a 33-page summary of the longer document. Five essential elements of early reading instruction are presented and discussed.

• *Report of the National Reading Panel: Teaching Children to Read: An Evidence-Based Assessment of the Scientific Research Literature on Reading and Its Implications for Reading Instruction. Reports of the Subgroups.* (NICHD, 2000b). This volume contains reports of all of the subgroups, each of which addressed a different topic in their synthesis of research. The topics addressed in the volume are alphabetics, fluency, comprehension, teacher education and reading instruction, and computer technology and reading instruction. The findings of each of these subgroups were used to generate five essential elements of early reading instruction.

• *Put Reading First: The Research Building Blocks for Teaching Children to Read: Kindergarten through Grade 1* (Armbruster, Lehr, & Osborn, 2001). This publication was produced by the Center for the Improvement of Early Reading Achievement (CIERA) and was funded by the National Institute for Literacy (NIFL). The authors examine, describe, and provide examples for each of the five essential elements of early reading instruction identified by the National Reading Panel.

Reading Excellence Act

The Reading Excellence Act (REA) was passed in 1998 with the purpose of teaching every child to read by the end of third grade. Incorporated into the ESEA in 2001, the REA has been folded into the new Reading First program. However, prior to the integration of these programs, several states included Reading Recovery as a component of their comprehensive approaches to literacy instruction.

Goals 2000

Not all federal education programs are authorized or funded as part of the ESEA. For example, the Goals 2000 program was created in 1994 by the Goals 2000: Educate America Act. Goals 2000 provided federal support for local and state educational reforms, including Reading Recovery. Intended to encourage community-based actions that meet pressing education needs and help more students achieve higher standards, the Goals 2000 program was terminated after its 5-year authorization.

State-Funded Initiatives

Public policy funding for Reading Recovery extends beyond the federal level and includes state support as well. At least a dozen states appropriate their own funds for early intervention efforts including Reading Recovery. All have continued this commitment even during difficult economic times. Just a few of the ways in which states support Reading Recovery include funding for professional development of Reading Recovery teachers and teacher leaders, support for university training centers, and funding for instructional and assessment materials. State initiatives that have incorporated Reading Recovery into their plans to meet the needs of early intervention literacy programs include Arkansas, Georgia, Illinois, Indiana, Iowa, Kentucky, Ohio, Maine, Massachusetts, Missouri, New Hampshire, and South Carolina.

The Future of Reading Recovery and Public Policy

No doubt education will continue to be a high priority in the public policy arena. Reading Recovery's track record in meeting the challenges of pubic policy will continue because of the reasons explained in this chapter, but most notably because it is based on a comprehensive and well-founded theory of how children learn to read and write. Stakeholders will continue to work diligently to advocate in a proactive way for laws and policies that support children's right to literacy.

Table 13.1 Evidence of Research-Based Reading Instructional Elements in Reading Recovery Lessons

INSTRUCTIONAL ELEMENTS OF READING	EVIDENCE FROM READING RECOVERY
Phonemic Awareness* Awareness of and ability to manipulate phonemes in spoken sounds and words	In a comprehensive review of research on beginning reading instruction, Adams (1990) acknowledged that the "importance of phonological and linguistic awareness is explicitly recognized" (p. 421) in Reading Recovery lessons. Some of the daily components of the lesson framework explicitly address phonemic awareness. For example, children use Elkonin boxes to closely examine the sequence of sounds in words, and they connect letters to sounds as they build words and work with them. In addition, they are explicitly shown how to say words slowly, use their knowledge to construct words in writing, and check on the accuracy of their reading. Consistent with Adams' analysis, subsequent research by Stahl, Stahl, and McKenna (1999) reported that all students in the Reading Recovery group made gains in tests of letter identification, phonemic awareness, and dictation, although these were not stressed in Reading Recovery lessons—and all made significantly greater improvement in phonological processing tasks than unserved at-risk students (see also Iversen & Tunmer, 1993 in Table 10.2).
Phonics* Knowledge of relationships between the letters (graphemes) of written language and the individual sounds (phonemes) of spoken language	Reading Recovery encourages purposeful decoding. Children learn specific letter-sound relationships as well as how to identify useful word parts (such as word endings and rimes). They also learn to use this information as they read and write. Reading Recovery teachers understand • the alphabetic principle and orthographic knowledge are important factors in beginning reading and writing. • children need to hear phonemes in words, associate letters with sounds, recognize and use spelling patterns, apply this knowledge in writing, and expand this knowledge to all the purposes for which it can be used in all levels of literacy processing.
Vocabulary* Understanding the meaning of words in reading or writing, both in isolation and as they occur together to communicate meaning through written language	Children acquire vocabulary in Reading Recovery lessons in a variety of ways—through conversing with adults, reading texts, composing written texts, and learning how words work. The introduction to a new text each day is designed to use unfamiliar vocabulary in a conversational way so that when children meet these words in text, they have recency and familiarity to help them derive the meaning. Word meaning is also examined during the writing component of the lesson, when children consider words to use in their own written texts. Children build reading and writing vocabularies throughout the lesson that they revisit as they read familiar and new texts and write their own messages.
Fluency* The ability to read rapidly and with phrasing by orchestrating rapid word solving, attention to meaning, and knowledge of language syntax	Fluency is explicitly recognized in Reading Recovery lessons. Guided oral rereading, recommended by the National Reading Panel (NICHD, 2000a, 2000b), takes place every day in Reading Recovery lessons. Rereading several familiar texts as well as yesterday's new book provides a context within which children can process text with less effort, leaving attention for comprehension. Children also write and reread their own messages, again providing practice in fluent reading. In reading a new text, carefully selected and supported to be within readers' control, they have the opportunity to apply word-solving and comprehending strategies in an orchestrated way so that fluency and phrasing are possible. The entire lesson sequence helps children work for fluent, phrased reading.

*Essential components identified by the National Reading Panel

Table 13.1 continued

INSTRUCTIONAL ELEMENTS OF READING	EVIDENCE FROM READING RECOVERY
Comprehension* Using a system of strategic actions, smoothly and in coordination, to construct meaning while reading continuous text	Comprehension is the goal of reading and involves a highly complex set of actions in which readers simultaneously use systems of information (NICHD, 2000a, 2000b). Reading Recovery lessons not only include attention to the basic information needed to read and write (letters, relationships to sounds, word structure) but require learners to apply knowledge to the reading and writing of continuous text. By rereading several familiar texts and taking on a new text daily, children are constantly in the position of constructing meaning from text. Before reading, their thoughts and prior knowledge are activated through a carefully constructed text introduction and through discussion (one-to-one) with the teacher, they discuss the meaning of the text after reading. Comprehension is the primary emphasis of the teacher's actions during Reading Recovery lessons, and even though items may require attention, the overall goal is constructing meaning from continuous text.
Writing Using written language to convey meaning	Although the title of this early intervention is Reading Recovery, approximately one-third of the lesson time is spent in composing and writing a message. Writing contributes significantly to the development of critical reading predictors such as phonemic awareness, phonics, and word solving; it also helps children to move forward in the development of writing processes. In Reading Recovery, children engage in the process of saying words slowly and producing the letters they can, while the teacher fills in the letters they do not yet know. Children have the opportunity to link phonological awareness to orthographic awareness. Teaching sounds in connection with letters is a highly effective way to accelerate learning (NICHD, 2000b). There is no fixed sequence of sounds because the teacher knows in great detail what children already know and can work to expand their individual repertoires, thus providing the teacher the opportunity to shape learning for each student. The teacher provides explicit phonological training through writing and then teaches children to use this knowledge reciprocally in reading. Learning through the writing component of the lesson goes much further than developing letter-sound knowledge. Children learn how to compose messages of increasing complexity over time, and they build word learning while doing so. Writing allows the teacher to help children benefit from the reciprocal relationship between reading and writing. Children expand their knowledge of language structure and their vocabularies while reading and writing. Writing slows down the process so children can examine the details of written language. They gain control over written language by using it to express their own meanings.
Motivation Deriving meaning and pleasure from reading	In the debate about beginning reading, motivation and enjoyment are not usually emphasized; however, the close relationship between the Reading Recovery teacher and student is designed to promote enjoyment of reading. Children are introduced to texts that not only guarantee success (because of careful analysis of text factors), but they are introduced to the texts in a way that engages their interest and provides a foundation for comprehension. They are supported in engaging in a satisfying inquiry process as they begin to manipulate words and parts of words to make new words. In writing, they are able to express their own meanings and put them into written language. Over time, through daily

*Essential components identified by the National Reading Panel

Table 13.1 continued

INSTRUCTIONAL ELEMENTS OF READING	EVIDENCE FROM READING RECOVERY
Motivation *continued*	writing, children produce a large body of daily messages, a process that is very satisfying to children who are just learning to read. The Reading Recovery lesson is a literacy event between an adult and child who are connected in their goal. It has been described by an outside group of evaluators as "a highly organised, intensive, and, it must be stressed, enjoyable occasion. Moreover, it is not confined to reading alone—writing and a good deal of speaking and listening also feature strongly" (Office for Standards in Education, 1993, p. 5). Children are active, taking control of their own learning while the teacher demonstrates, directs, encourages, and supports in ways that help children become independent, strategic users of literacy.
Oral Language Expanding knowledge of vocabulary and increasingly complex language structures	The heart of the Reading Recovery lesson is conversation between the teacher and child. There are quick conversations during rereading of texts that are familiar to children. There are also very specific conversations directed at the development of reading strategies during all reading activities, but particularly after reading yesterday's new book and before, during, and after the reading of the new book. Oral language development is woven throughout the lesson, supporting writing, working with words, and scaffolding reading. This is particularly beneficial to English-language learners because they have the opportunity to converse individually with an adult for 30 minutes.
Independence Becoming a self-initiated and self-managed learner	The goal of Reading Recovery is to help children make accelerated progress so that they become independent readers and writers. Intentional teaching moves are directed toward helping children consider their own actions, become aware of the effective moves they are making as readers and writers, and expand their own ability to construct meaning from text. In Reading Recovery, children work from their own language but expand their knowledge of language through reading and writing. They compose their own texts with support from the teacher who reminds them of language knowledge they have encountered through reading. The true test of independence, and the way to further develop it, is through taking on a novel text and reading it. The teacher provides enough of a scaffold to support the reading, but essentially requires the reader to process a new text with accuracy, fluency, and comprehension. There is evidence from two studies, both published in refereed journals (Cohen, McDonnell, & Osborn, 1989; Rumbaugh & Brown, 2000), that Reading Recovery contributes to children's self-efficacy through contributions to children's competence in reading and perhaps through a close relationship with an adult. Fostering independence in reading means providing the opportunity for children to integrate all of the systems of information they currently have to process a novel text. For this complex transformation to occur, skillful teaching directed toward the individual is essential.

CHAPTER 14

Change, Choices, and Challenges: The Future of Reading Recovery in the United States

In this volume, we have described many aspects of Reading Recovery, including its research base and results as well as its outcomes for teachers and children in the United States. We have discussed Reading Recovery as a systemic intervention designed to reduce the incidence of reading failure and, as a result, its consequences to the system, to the individual children, and to their families. But the truth is that Reading Recovery is hard to define or categorize. At one level it is an individual tutoring program for children. At another level it is a dynamic and intensive teacher education program. At still another level it is an international network of professionals who are dedicated to ongoing learning.

Ultimately, Reading Recovery is an intervention in the system of schooling that is provided for young children. Its timing is very close to school entry (after only one year). It is designed to work by creating positive change. In describing Reading Recovery, Clay (1987) has said that the program works to achieve change along four dimensions:

- behavioural change on the part of teachers,
- child behaviour change achieved by teaching,
- organisational changes in schools achieved by teachers and administrators, and
- social/political changes in funding by controlling authorities. (p. 36)

The organizational features of Reading Recovery work together to assure these changes, and every component of the structure is important and essential. The training leaders receive at universities and the training they in turn provide for teachers make it possible to implement the dynamic combination of approaches that comprise the Reading Recovery lesson. The systems for supporting implementation assure that the lessons are daily, supported by appropriate materials, well timed, and provided by a trained (or in-training) teacher. Data collection acts as a check on the system; if results are not as expected, teacher leaders and teachers are expected to analyze the situation and intervene. Indeed, implementing Reading Recovery is not easy. It requires educators to rethink schedules, professional development, materials, and priorities. But the results are worth the effort. In this closing chapter we reiterate what Reading Recovery has accomplished, consider the challenges we face, explain how we will sustain the quality of the intervention, and describe goals for the future.

What Reading Recovery Has Accomplished

In this volume, the accomplishments to date of Reading Recovery have been described. As we look back on 20 years of implementation in the United States, much has been accomplished. Moreover, we are finding out what it is going to take if we are serious about changing the world for children who struggle in literacy learning.

Results for Children

Reading Recovery has demonstrated that struggling children can make accelerated progress. Data have demonstrated over the last 20 years that the results of early intervention tutoring can make the critical difference. Of all children served (some even for short periods), Reading Recovery has established a record of almost 60% of children reading at Grade 1 levels. For children who have had the opportunity to have a complete series of lessons, almost 80% reach grade-level expectations and can participate with their peers in classroom instruction. Moreover, follow-up studies indicate the results are lasting.

According to Rumbaugh and Brown (2000), "School districts that choose to implement and maintain a Reading Recovery program would reap considerable benefits….Not only will the Reading Recovery participants most likely become independent readers, they will also most likely become more confident, positive, self-accepting, proud, adaptable, and eager to complete tasks" (p. 28). Shanahan and Barr (1995), after completing a review of the intervention, claimed, "Evidence firmly supports the conclusion that Reading Recovery does bring the learning of many children up to that of their average-achieving peers. Thus, in answer to the question, 'Does Reading Recovery work?' we must respond in the affirmative" (p. 989). And, as Cunningham and Allington (1994) have said, "No other remedial program has ever come close to achieving the results demonstrated by Reading Recovery" (p. 254).

Reading Recovery has shown potential for reducing the achievement gap. A study of more than 9,000 first graders reports that Reading Recovery can close or narrow the literacy achievement gap that exists along racial/ethnic and economic lines (Rodgers & Gómez-Bellengé, 2003). These researchers found that students who successfully completed Reading Recovery lessons either narrowed or closed the achievement gap along race/ethnicity and income lines when compared with students in a randomly selected comparison group.

Identification of Special Needs

It is true that Reading Recovery does not bring every child into the mainstream of school learning. For a small percentage, there is a second positive outcome; that is, children make progress but do not reach grade-level expectations and need continuing support. Scanlon and Vellutino (1996, p. 62) have made the point that "labor-intensive" intervention should be provided before children are identified as "reading impaired." Only after a high-quality, well-planned intervention has failed to produce the accelerated progress needed should the child be placed in longer-term special services. Reading Recovery helps to sort out children who need more service. Early intervention can provide a first net that moves children who do not need ongoing services into the mainstream and identifies children who need more intensive work.

Johnston (2002) credits both the work of Clay and Vellutino and Scanlon's (2002) work on interactive strategies for intervention with moving in the "right direction." Scanlon and Vellutino, he says, "have been approaching the problem of reading difficulty as experimental psychologists studying problems in learning to *read* particularly relating to word analysis and recognition. Clay has been approaching the problem as a developmental psychologist interested in *literacy* acquisition and preventing difficulties therein" (Johnston, 2002, p. 646). In view of these two related but different perspectives, Johnston believes that we might ultimately have a great deal of agreement.

Johnston (2002) credits Vellutino and Scanlon with arguing effectively for early intervention and applauds their work. He argues, however, against the idea that intervention tests should be used to classify students as disabled and then have their education turned over to professionals who are not intensively trained in helping struggling students achieve literacy. Johnston advocates the idea of *adaptive teaching*. The logic says, according to Johnston, that those students who do not solve all of their problems in early intervention need continued teaching that is adapted to their strengths and skills. "The assumption that teaching must be responsive demands that teachers have a theory from which to work—a theory that gives significance to the literate behaviors they observe and ties their teaching decisions to those behaviors in productive ways" (p. 638). He ties the work of Vellutino and Scanlon closely to that of Clay.

As a prereferral intervention, Reading Recovery quickly accelerates the learning of those who need only short-term (although intensive and expertly applied) help. Reading Recovery not only helps to identify children who need further extra teaching, but it also gives direction for the adaptive teaching that will be needed. With the rich fund of information available on children who have been served in Reading Recovery, professionals in the school can work together to identify the best ongoing support for the individual.

Reading Recovery has shown that it benefits the system in general. When the lowest achievers can read, it affects the learning of all children in the age cohort because

- it is easier for teachers to adequately plan and provide for the needs of the entire class.

- the costs of remediation may be reduced.

- long-term specialist services will be reserved for those children who truly need them, making the most of scarce resources.

- children are provided with a foundation that will serve them well throughout schooling.

Professional Development for Teachers

Reading Recovery has also been successful in demonstrating that professional development for teachers makes a difference. In a major empirical study (Pinnell et al., 1994), training emerged as a major factor in students' achievement. In fact, every evaluation of Reading Recovery has revealed the profound impact that the training has on teachers. Herman and Stringfield (1997) have claimed, "As schools systematize and create more opportunities for serious staff development, the thoroughness of the Reading Recovery model seems to be well worth emulating" (p. 86).

Ongoing professional development occurs at three levels: university trainers, site-based teacher leaders, and school-based teachers. The ongoing professional development that is an integral and required part of Reading Recovery ensures incorporation of new research and understanding of its applicability to the delivery of lessons. Reading Recovery's professional development builds teacher skills and provides continuous updating so that trained Reading Recovery teachers can implement needed changes.

The Meaning of Reading Recovery's Success

Implementing a successful educational program, especially one that provides significant benefit to the most struggling children, also means responsibility. We know from the results of Reading Recovery that we can identify early those children who are going to need intensive help. While they all fall into the lowest-achieving quartiles, they are quite different from each other.

An individual lesson by an expert teacher makes the most of each child's strengths, even if they are limited, and strategically works to expand the repertoire. This kind of instruction is the most accelerative, and some children require it before it is too late, the gap widens, failure is compounded, and emotional barriers emerge in addition to academic problems. If we can help struggling children, then we must do so. Yet meeting this challenge will require enormous effort.

Challenges of the Future

In spite of past successes, Reading Recovery and other successful educational efforts face significant challenges in the current economical and political climate.

Resources

School budgets are tight; everyone is searching for the most economical and easy-to-implement solution; there are different views of the problems of schooling. Even well-conceived efforts are usually underfunded and so drastically altered that they can no longer fulfill their original promise.

Misguided Policy

Current educational policy in the United States has the regrettable tendency to seek a quick fix. Unfortunately, the complex problems of education make the quest quite impossible. In the search for cheap and easy innovations, new inventions are pared down to what the system can afford, and administrators are often persuaded by salespeople from commercial publishing companies. When innovations do not work, the quest is on for another approach. Systems try programs, one after another. A contributing factor is the frequent change of administrators, each promising to bring in new programs to fix the system. Promising innovations are pared down to what is affordable, and in the process they become less effective.

The Problem of Change

Like all humanly conceived organizations, educational institutions have forces that work to perpetuate the existing system and help it operate. They have calendars, schedules, job descriptions, rules, and even traditions. Sometimes the rules and operations become so entrenched that they become ends in themselves rather than means to accomplishing goals. A system may become locked into particular testing practices that have been used so long and so efficiently that no one questions whether the tests are really giving teachers valuable information to help in their work with children or even providing the district with good information to guide educational policy. The established reading program may become traditional; teachers move through books and exercises rather than closely observing children and designing programs that make the most of their strengths. The assumption is that children and their families, not the program, are at fault; and those having difficulty simply receive a slowed-down version of the mainstream program. The system perpetuates itself rather than changing.

When promising innovations arise, they are often not implemented as designed. Instead, they are adapted to meet local requirements, a practice that on the surface has appeal. Adapting an innovation makes it better fit the system, but changes inevitably undermine effectiveness. Reading Recovery is a good example. Some adaptations include the following:

- Systems have trained teachers and then phased out the program so that teachers can use Reading Recovery in the classroom. Teachers who are trained in Reading Recovery are more observant and skillful, so they have a definite advantage as classroom teachers. The downside is that struggling children need the detailed one-to-one attention and tailored instruction that only skilled tutoring can provide. No classroom program, however excellent, can fully provide for the needs of the children who find reading and writing most difficult.

• Systems have trained Reading Recovery teachers and then had them use their skills to work with small groups. The approaches of Reading Recovery can not be applied to small groups, although some interventions based on Reading Recovery may be effective for some children who need extra help (e.g., Dorn & Allen, 1995). Research indicates that individual teaching is essential for the lowest achievers.

Expanding With Quality

Many studies of effective instructional approaches are tested in small experiments that involve a great deal of control. Moving promising approaches to a larger scale involves a great deal of effort. This scaling-up process is one of the greatest problems of educational research. A hothouse approach may work in a controlled and limited environment, but the training required to bring it to large numbers of children is nonexistent. Training designs do not exist.

In the case of Reading Recovery, Clay designed training that closely resembled her original studies of children in this early intervention. She and her team of researchers observed from behind a one-way glass as skilled teachers worked with at-risk students. They paid close attention to details, including both student and teacher moves. From many observations, they selected the most effective combination of teaching moves. When Clay designed the training for Reading Recovery, she basically replicated this inquiry process. This design puts teachers in the position of constructing knowledge from observations, a process that builds the understandings that underlie competent teaching.

The inquiry-oriented teacher development represents a structured process that allows Reading Recovery to expand with quality. Each teacher and teacher leader class incorporates the basic design. Teachers and teacher leaders engage in and learn the process of *talking while observing* to build their underlying understandings about how to tailor individual lessons to struggling readers. The consistency of the model led to high fidelity in the implementation of Reading Recovery lessons. According to Hiebert (1994), "Once a program is in place, there appears to be considerable fidelity in the results" (p. 21).

As Reading Recovery continues to expand, however, the challenge of fidelity becomes exponential. Sustaining the professional development network in a time of short resources and across many different educational systems is a challenge. It is necessary to develop stronger networks to support ongoing learning.

An Ongoing Process of Change

Just as systems must be devised and refined to provide for successful and accelerative early intervention efforts, so too must Reading Recovery constantly change to improve its performance. Change is an integral part of the Reading Recovery design; it changes in response to ongoing research. Theoretical constructs, teaching practices, and implementation are constantly examined in search of the most effective procedures (Jones & Smith-Burke, 1999).

Built-In Mechanisms for Change

Change in Reading Recovery is not left to chance. There are systems that ensure careful and responsible responses to patterns of change. For example, Reading Recovery's central document, *Reading Recovery: A Guidebook for Teachers in Training* (Clay, 1993), contains a record of changes in instruction. Originally published as *Early Detection of Reading Difficulties* (1979/1985), it was revised and retitled in 1993. An examination of both books reveals significant additions over years of development, including:

- more intensive attention to and detailed description of the role of phonemic awareness;
- explicit directions for teachers in helping children use letter-sound relationships, more phonemic awareness training, and phonics;
- more deliberate focus on comprehending strategies during the reading of a new book;
- differentiation between the way the teacher supports children during the reading of a new text and the role of familiar reading; and
- more information on how to teach for fluency and phrasing.

This guidebook is a central resource for teachers as they do their daily teaching. Changes result from a careful examination of Reading Recovery research across a range of disciplines. The changes are not made as an instant response either to political documents or to small studies with results that must be cautiously interpreted; however, strong strands of research with replicable findings must be considered.

Changes in Reading Recovery result from a deliberate and careful consideration of research results, answering questions such as:

- Is the research of high quality?
- Are the stated conclusions warranted?
- Have the results been replicated in other studies?
- Do the results have particular implications for work with young struggling readers?
- Do results add to the underlying understanding of children's learning or do they have specific practical applications?
- Do the results suggest changes in Reading Recovery instruction?
- What specific changes or refinements are needed?
- How will these changes be communicated?

If changes are warranted, they are communicated through the system of ongoing professional development that is a hallmark of Reading Recovery. This self-renewing system accommodates changes that are the result of carefully planned, sound research. University trainers examine research and work together to determine the impact on the program; then changes are communicated through the international Reading Recovery network.

Sustaining the Quality of Reading Recovery

Several systems have been established to support the implementation of Reading Recovery with high fidelity. The United States and Canada have established the Reading Recovery Council of North America; to support Reading Recovery worldwide, an international network of trainers has been established.

A Trademark to Protect the Investment

Reading Recovery is a trademark that was given royalty-free to The Ohio State University in the United States. Use of the Reading Recovery trademark is granted royalty-free to university training centers and teacher training sites that conduct relevant activities meeting the standards and guidelines as described in this document. Use of the trademark is subject to annual renewal.

The trademark defines the quality of Reading Recovery, thus protecting the investment that schools, school districts, and states have made in the accelerated education of young, struggling readers. In the United States, innovation in education often fails—not because the approaches are not promising, but because the necessary teacher education and systemic support are short-circuited. Educators make an investment in Reading Recovery knowing that they will get a high-quality program with ongoing support systems, as assured by the fact that it is a trademarked program. Currently there are five trademark holders for five national implementations:

1. Australia: Marie Clay
2. Canada: Ontario Institute for Studies in Education/University of Toronto and the Canadian Institute of Reading Recovery
3. New Zealand: Marie Clay
4. United Kingdom: Institute of Education, London
5. United States: The Ohio State University

Reading Recovery Standards and Guidelines

Permission to use the trademark is contingent upon compliance with a set of standards and guidelines that were written in collaboration with Reading Recovery teachers, teacher leaders, trainers, and site coordinators throughout the country. As published in the *Standards and Guidelines of Reading Recovery in the United States* (2004), they are intended to be informative and supportive to the cadre of personnel who are responsible for the establishment and maintenance of effective Reading Recovery. All countries involved in Reading Recovery have established and follow a set of standards. While these standards necessarily vary by country because of differences in educational systems, all protect the quality core of Reading Recovery as tutoring for children, professional development for teachers, and system intervention.

The importance of the standards and guidelines lies in the underlying rationales that are understood and applied by trainers and by teacher leaders and site coordinators at each site. The standards are deemed essential for assuring quality services to children and effective implementation of the program, based on research of the most effective practices. The additional guidelines have also been shown to support program effectiveness significantly.

Changes in Reading Recovery are evident in the standards and guidelines, which have been carefully structured to allow for local variations but to constantly assess those variations in relation to results from the National Data Evaluation Center.

Reading Recovery Council of North America

In the United States and Canada, Reading Recovery is not a centralized government program, nor is it a commercial venture supported by a corporation. It is embedded in public and private universities and school districts, each of which is independent of the others. There was need, therefore, for a unifying group to support Reading Recovery and sustain the quality of its quality of implementation.

The Reading Recovery Council of North America (RRCNA) is a not-for-profit organization dedicated to the vision that children will be proficient readers and writers by the end of first grade. RRCNA is a professional organization with members who are teachers, teacher leaders, university trainers, site coordinators, and partners (individuals who do not work within Reading Recovery but support its goals). RRCNA provides publications and professional development opportunities for all of its members and thus acts as an educational clearinghouse to disseminate new knowledge.

Leadership for the Future of Reading Recovery

Every widely disseminated venture faces two challenges:

(1) how to sustain quality across widely varied implementations

(2) how to maintain a dynamic quality so that the program can change in response to both internal and external research

The charge to address these two goals rests with a group of worldwide university teacher educators and researchers who work in close collaboration. Because of different educational and political systems, there is great diversity in the implementation of Reading Recovery across the world. The International Reading Recovery Trainers Organization (IRRTO) is committed to maintaining the quality, upholding the integrity, improving the efficiency and effectiveness, and supporting change and growth in Reading Recovery through international collaboration, research, and resource development. The role of IRRTO is to support Reading Recovery trainers around the world to maintain the integrity of the Reading Recovery program.

IRRTO elects a five-member executive board, with equal representation from each country that is implementing a trademarked Reading Recovery intervention and a nonvoting chair. The IRRTO Executive Board has two major functions:

1. Conduct ongoing monitoring of the international implementation of Reading Recovery by requiring each national implementation to submit an annual report of their national data collection.

2. Respond to issues and challenges to the international implementation of Reading Recovery as well as to specific national issues if they have international ramifications according to an international set of standards.

The organization has four standing committees: communications, research and development, financial development, and the training of trainers. The primary functions of the committees relate to these three major questions:

1. How does the design of Reading Recovery need to change in order to continue to develop and expand as a program for children?

2. What kinds of organizational structures are necessary in order to take Reading Recovery into the future without the leadership of Marie Clay?

3. What kinds of organizational structures are necessary to further develop the research and theoretical base of Reading Recovery?

These three questions imply an ordered process of change guided by individuals who are knowledgeable about research.

Within the international group (IRRTO), university personnel in North America (the United States and Canada) are organized into the North American Trainers Group (NATG); the leadership trainer group in Australia and New Zealand is called the Australia and New Zealand Trainer Team (ANZTT); and in Europe the organizational structure is the European Trainer Group (ETG).

In the United States, all Reading Recovery trainers are based at universities. Internationally, Reading Recovery trainers may be based in professional education centers but affiliated with universities. All have high qualifications as researchers and have published research articles not only about Reading Recovery but in a wide variety of research fields.

University personnel who are involved in Reading Recovery have multifaceted roles. They not only provide training for teacher leaders and oversee implementation at affiliated sites; they are also charged with evaluating the results of teaching as well as engaging in research to improve it. Reading Recovery trainers represent the authorization body of the trademarked Reading Recovery program.

The role of Reading Recovery trainers is especially important since they work closely with Reading Recovery founder Marie Clay, but also because they bring different strengths to the analysis of the program—its processes and its results. This group of academics is charged with guiding the implementation of Reading Recovery into the future. There is a system for considering change; research is ongoing. These four organizations—ANZTT, ETG, NATG, and IRRTO—represent an organized system for carefully implemented change.

Moving Into the Future

Reading Recovery is based on a good design because the original invention has been refined over the years with the leadership of Marie Clay and the work of Reading Recovery university trainers. The process is dynamic; change is ongoing; and the individuals involved constantly learn from what they are doing.

The overall goal of our design activity in Reading Recovery is *to sustain the quality, uphold the integrity, maintain the collaboration, improve the efficiency and effectiveness, and expand the accessibility of Reading Recovery in all parts of the world.* To accomplish these goals, Reading Recovery must continue to change through an established design process (Lyons & Pinnell, 2001; Wilson & Daviss, 1994). A dynamic design

- gives *direction* and keeps efforts moving along a line of vision rather than meandering this way and that,

- requires *cooperation* among people who need to fit complex processes together into a whole,

- provides group support for individual thinking and *problem solving,*

- allows people to combine their thinking through *synergy* so that the outcome is greater than any individual could accomplish alone, and

- allows groups to *renew* their processes and build on what they know.

To achieve this goal, North American and international networks work together to

- keep all members of the Reading Recovery world community informed and up-to-date about new developments in the theory and practice;

- promote the examination of current research with an eye to what it might imply for Reading Recovery theory and practice;

- act as a forum for decision making about revisions in teaching, implementation, training, research, and publishing related to Reading Recovery around the world;

- provide a forum for discussing local adjustments of the program that do not represent major revisions but may affect international relations and issues in Reading Recovery;

- analyze political climates and trends across countries and provide support for Reading Recovery in meeting challenges;

- initiate, support, and oversee ongoing research related to children's learning, teaching, training of teachers and teacher leaders, evaluation, and implementation of Reading Recovery around the world;

- consider and reevaluate its own structure and functioning so that it continues to meet the needs of Reading Recovery worldwide; and

- create bridges between Reading Recovery and other researchers and practitioners in the field of literacy education and the broader community.

Clear Goals and Definitions

Two salient characteristics of Reading Recovery are the clarity with which it is defined and the rigor with which its results are assessed. We conclude this document with a summary of what Reading Recovery is and is not.

- Reading Recovery is not a classroom program; it works in combination with any good instructional program.

- Reading Recovery is not intended for all children; it is designed to provide intensive help to individual struggling readers.

- Reading Recovery is not a group intervention designed to accomplish a range of goals with readers of all ages; it is one-to-one tutoring designed to help children who are having difficulty early in their school careers.

Many high-quality programs may be designed by researchers and educators who have learned from Reading Recovery—the teaching procedures for children, the organizations that support implementation, or the professional development programs. Programs that address other goals can be effectively used in combination with Reading Recovery (see Dorn & Allen, 1995). But Reading Recovery has one clear goal: "to dramatically reduce the number of learners who have extreme difficulty with literacy learning and the cost of these learners to educational systems" (M. Clay as cited in Askew et al., 1998, p. 3). By maintaining a focus on that single goal, implementing cautious change in response to research, refining approaches to teaching, and working for high quality in terms of resources and organizational factors, Reading Recovery has been successful for 2 decades in the United States. In doing so, more than 1.4 million children have been helped to read and write.

Calculating the Cost of Reading Recovery in Your District

(adapted from Gómez-Bellengé, 2002b)

	Example	Local Data
1. Average Teacher Salary	$45,000	
2. Adjusted Teacher Salary (average teacher salary plus cost of fringe benefits)	$58,000	
3. General Per-Pupil Expenditure for All Children in the System	$9,000	
4. Pupil-Teacher Ratio (districtwide ratio for all students)	11:1	
5. Reading Recovery Total FTE (number of Reading Recovery teachers times their portion of their day in Reading Recovery; e.g., 24 teachers at .5 FTE equals 12 FTE) (Note: if Reading Recovery teachers work with 4-5 Reading Recovery students daily, this should be considered as a half-FTE in the calculation. It then takes two teachers to equal one FTE. Because these teachers teach at least two rounds of children during the year, one FTE would usually yield at least 16 teaching slots for the year.)	12.0 (24 teachers @ .5 FTE)	
6. Number of Reading Recovery Students Served	200	
7. Number of Reading Recovery Students Served per FTE (total number of children served divided by the total FTE)	16.7 (200 students divided by 12.0 FTE = 16.7)	
8. Cost Per Student Served (adjusted teacher salary times the number of Reading Recovery total FTE, then divided by the number of children served)	$3,480 ($58,000 adjusted teacher cost x 12.0 FTE = $696,000) ($696,000 divided by 200 students = $3,480 per student)	

Note: Read Chapter 11 for a broader view of the economy of Reading Recovery.

Calculating the Cost Per Student Whose Lessons Were Discontinued

(an extension of Appendix A)

	Example	Local Data
Number of Students Whose Lessons Were Discontinued (Reading Recovery students achieving grade-level performance)	130	
Number of Students Whose Lessons Were Discontinued Per FTE (number of students whose lessons were discontinued divided by total Reading Recovery FTE)	10.8 (130 divided by 12.0 = 10.8)	
Cost Per Student Whose Lessons Were Discontinued	$5,354 ($58,000 adjusted teacher cost x 12.0 FTE = $696,000) ($696,000 divided by 130 students whose lessons were discontinued = $5,354)	

Note: Read Chapter 11 for a broader view of the economy of Reading Recovery.

Costs Associated with Reading Recovery Implementation
(2002–2003)

Items	Costs
Cost of teacher leader salary and benefits	
Cost of teacher leader training (amortized over 5 years)	
Cost of teacher leader's ongoing professional development	
Cost of Reading Recovery teacher's salary and benefits (50% of salary)	
Cost of training Reading Recovery teacher (amortized over 5 years)	
Cost of Reading Recovery teacher's continuing contact	
Cost of Descubriendo la Lectura Bridging	
Cost of National Data Evaluation Center data entry	
Cost of attendance at annual conference	
Cost of site visits from university trainer	
Cost of building one-way glass at training site (amortized over 5 years)	
Cost of Reading Recovery site report	
Total Costs	
Per-child cost of Reading Recovery/Descubriendo la Lectura Total costs divided by the number of children served	

Note: In Bueker's (2004) analysis, training costs were multiplied by the number of teachers and teacher leaders in the district. Cost of data entry was multiplied by the number of children participating in the district. After summing all of the costs of implementation, the total was divided by the number of children served, with an average per-child cost estimated at $5,591.

Note: Read Chapter 11 for a broader view of the economy of Reading Recovery.

Relative Cost of District/School Interventions

Intervention or Supplement	Additional Per-Pupil Cost for One Year	Average Time in Program	Total Per-Pupil Cost for Five Years	Student Outcomes
Retention				
Title I				
Special Education				
Other (e.g., small-group supplementary reading instruction)				
Reading Recovery		12 to 20 weeks	(one-time cost)	

Note: Compare the costs per child for each service and consider the results. It is tempting to think about serving more children, but service must be looked at in terms of outcomes.

See the next page for a sample chart.

APPENDIX D

Example

Intervention or Supplement	Additional Per-Pupil Cost for One Year	Average Time in Program	Total Per-Pupil Cost for Five Years	Student Outcomes
Retention	$9,500	1 year	$9,500	?
Title I	$2,000	5 years	$10,000	?
Special Education	$4,500 + $1,000 initial evaluation	5 years	$23,500	?
Reading Recovery	$3,480 for all served $5,354 for discontinued	12 to 20 weeks	$3,480 $5,354	?

Take the total per-pupil cost for 5 years of any one of the interventions and subtract the one-time cost of Reading Recovery to calculate the potential savings that can be redistributed in the district. As shown in the example above, if Reading Recovery eliminates the need for retention, there will be a savings of $4,146 per child. If Special Education services are not needed because of Reading Recovery, there is a potential savings of $18,146 per child. These savings can be redirected to other needs in the district—a tangible benefit. In addition, account for the outcomes of each invention. If interventions are not effective, the cost is even greater.

Note: Read Chapter 11 for a broader view of the economy of Reading Recovery.

TABLES AND FIGURES

Adams, M. J. (1990). *Beginning to read: Thinking and learning about print.* Cambridge, MA: MIT Press.

Allington, R. L. (2001). *What really matters for struggling readers: Designing research-based programs.* New York: Longman.

Allington, R. L., & Cunningham, P. M. (2002). *Schools that work: Where all children read and write.* Boston, MA: Allyn & Bacon.

Allington, R. L., & McGill-Franzen, A. (1995). Flunking: Throwing good money after bad. In R. L. Allington & S. Walmsley (Eds.), *No quick fix: Rethinking literacy programs in America's schools* (pp. 45–60). New York: Teachers College Press.

Allington, R. L., & Walmsley, S. A. (1995). *No quick fix: Rethinking literacy programs in America's elementary schools.* New York: Teachers College Press.

Allington, R. L., & Walmsley, S. A. (1995). No quick fix: Where do we go from here? In R. A. Allington & S. A. Walmsley (Eds.), *No quick fix: Rethinking literacy programs in America's elementary schools* (pp. 253–264). New York: Teachers College Press.

Alvermann, D. E. (1990). Reading teacher education. In W. R. Houston, M. Haberman, & J. Sikula (Eds.), *Handbook of research on teacher education: A project of the Association of Teacher Educators* (pp. 687–704). New York: Macmillan.

Anania, J. (1982). The effects of quality of instruction on the cognitive and affective learning of students (Doctoral dissertation, University of Chicago, 1981). *Dissertation Abstracts International, 42,* 4269A.

Anania, J. (1983). The influence of instructional conditions on student learning and achievement. *Evaluation in Education: An International Review Series, 7*(1), 1–92.

Anders, P. L., & Evens, K. S. (1994). Relationship between teachers' beliefs and their instructional practice in reading. In R. Garner & P. Alexander (Eds.), *Beliefs about text and instruction with text* (pp. 137–154). Hillsdale, NJ: Lawrence Erlbaum.

Armbruster, B. B., Lehr, F., & Osborn, J. (2001). *Put reading first: The research building blocks for teaching children to read.* Jessup, MD: National Institute for Literacy.

Ashdown, J., & Simic, O. (2000). Is early literacy intervention effective for English language learners: Evidence from Reading Recovery. *Literacy Teaching and Learning: An International Journal of Early Reading and Writing, 5*(1), 27–42.

Askew, B. J. (1993). The effect of multiple readings on the behaviors of children and teachers in an early intervention program. *Reading and Writing Quarterly: Overcoming Learning Difficulties, 9,* 307–316.

Askew, B. J., Fountas, I. C., Lyons, C. A., Pinnell, G. S., & Schmitt, M. C. (1998). *Reading Recovery review: Understandings, outcomes, and implications*. Columbus, OH: The Reading Recovery Council of North America.

Askew, B. J., & Frasier, D. F. (1994). Sustained effects of Reading Recovery intervention on the cognitive behaviors of second grade children and the perceptions of their teachers. *Literacy, Teaching and Learning: An International Journal of Early Literacy, 1*(1), 87–107.

Askew, B. J., & Frasier, D. F. (1999). Early writing: An exploration of literacy opportunities. *Literacy Teaching and Learning: An International Journal of Early Reading and Writing, 4*(1), 43–66. Reprinted (2003) in S. Forbes & C. Briggs (Eds.), *Research in Reading Recovery, volume two* (pp. 1–24). Portsmouth, NH: Heinemann.

Askew, B. J., Fulenwider, T., Kordick, R., Scheuermann, S., Vollenweider, P., Anderson, N., & Rodríguez, Y. (2002). Constructing a model of professional development to support early literacy classrooms. In E. M. Rodgers & G. S. Pinnell (Eds.), *Learning from teaching in literacy education: New perspectives in professional development* (pp. 29–51). Portsmouth, NH: Heinemann.

Askew, B. J., Kaye, E., Frasier, D. F., Mobasher, M., Anderson, N., & Rodríguez, Y. (2002). Making a case for prevention in education. *Literacy Teaching and Learning: An International Journal of Early Reading and Writing, 6*(2), 43–73. Reprinted (2003) in S. Forbes & C. Briggs (Eds.), *Research in Reading Recovery, volume two* (pp. 133–158). Portsmouth, NH: Heinemann.

Barnett, S. W. (1985). Benefit-cost analysis of the Perry Preschool Program and its policy implications. *Educational Evaluation and Policy Analysis, 7,* 333–342.

Barnett, S. W. (1993). Economic evaluation of home visiting programs. *The Future of Children, 3,* 93–112.

Barnett, S. W., & Escobar, C. (1987). The economics of early educational intervention: A review. *Review of Educational Research, 57*(4), 387–414.

Batten, P. (2004, Winter). Investing equity funding in early literacy. *ERS Spectrum, 22*(1), 40–45.

Berry, B., Hoke, M., & Hirsch, E. (2004). The search for high quality teachers. *Phi Delta Kappan, 85,* 684–690.

Black, M. M., & Holden, E. W. (1995). Longitudinal intervention research in children's health and development. *Journal of Clinical Child Psychology, 24,* 163–172.

Blackburn, D. J. (1995). *Changes in a Chapter 1 program when Reading Recovery was implemented: Its impact on one district*. Unpublished doctoral dissertation, Texas Woman's University, Denton.

Bloom, B. (1984). The 2-sigma problem: The search for methods of group instruction as effective as one-to-one tutoring. *Educational Researcher, 13,* 4–16.

Bos, C. S., & Anders, P. L. (1994). The study of student change. In V. Richardson (Ed.), *Teacher change and the staff development process: A case in reading instruction* (pp. 181–198). New York: Teachers College Press.

Briggs, C., & Young, B. K. (2003). Does Reading Recovery work in Kansas? A retrospective longitudinal study of sustained effects. *The Journal of Reading Recovery, 3*(1), 59–64.

Bronfenbrenner, U. (1974). Is early intervention effective? In M. Guttentag & S. Struening (Eds.), *Handbook of evaluation research Vol. 2* (pp. 519–603). Beverly Hills, CA: Sage.

Brown, W., Denton, E., Kelly, P. R., & Neal, J. C. (1999). Reading Recovery effectiveness: A five-year success story in San Luis Coastal Unified School District. *ERS Spectrum, 17*(1), 3–12.

Bruner, J. S. (1957). On perceptual readiness. *Psychological Review, 64,* 123–152.

Bryk, A. S., & Raudenbush, S. W. (1992). *Hierarchical linear models: Applications and data analysis methods.* Newbury Park, CA: Sage.

Bueker, C. S. (2004). *Examining the cost-savings of Reading Recovery: A study of one urban district.* Cambridge, MA: The Center for Reading Recovery and Literacy Collaborative at Lesley University.

Burke, A. J. (1984). Students' potential for learning contrasted under tutorial and group approaches to instruction (Doctoral dissertation, University of Chicago, 1983). *Dissertation Abstracts International, 44,* 2025A.

Campbell, D. T., & Stanley, J. C. (1963). *Experimental and quasi-experimental designs for research.* Chicago, IL: Rand-McNally.

Caplan, G. (Ed.). (1961). *Prevention of mental disorders in children.* New York: Basic.

Caplan, G. (1964). *Principles of preventive psychiatry.* New York: Basic.

Cazden, C. B. (1988). *Classroom discourse: The language of teaching and learning,* Portsmouth, NH: Heinemann.

Center, Y., Wheldall, K., Freeman, L., Outhred, L., & McNaught, M. (1995). An evaluation of Reading Recovery. *Reading Research Quarterly, 30*(2), 240–263.

Chappell, J. L. (2001). *Reading Recovery in Prince George's County, Maryland: A case study.* Columbus, Ohio: The Ohio State University.

Clay, M. M. (1966). *Emergent reading behaviour.* Unpublished doctoral dissertation, University of Auckland Library, Auckland, New Zealand.

Clay, M. M. (1972). *Reading: The patterning of complex behavior.* Auckland, New Zealand: Heinemann.

Clay M. M. (1979). *The early detection of reading difficulties*. Auckland, New Zealand: Heinemann.

Clay, M. M. (1982). *Observing young readers*. Portsmouth, NH: Heinemann.

Clay, M. M. (1985). *The early detection of reading difficulties* (2nd ed.). Portsmouth, NH: Heinemann.

Clay, M. M. (1987). Implementing Reading Recovery: Systemic adaptations to an educational innovation. *New Zealand Journal of Educational Studies, 22*(1), 35–58.

Clay, M. M. (1990). The Reading Recovery programme, 1984–1988: Coverage, outcomes and Education Board district figures. *New Zealand Journal of Educational Studies, 25*(1), 61–70.

Clay, M. M. (1991). *Becoming literate: The construction of inner control*. Portsmouth, NH: Heinemann.

Clay, M. M. (1992). Reading Recovery: The wider implications of an educational innovation. In A. Watson & S. Badenhop (Eds.), *Prevention of reading failure* (pp. 22–47). New York: Ashton Scholastic.

Clay, M. M. (1993). *Reading Recovery: A guidebook for teachers in training*. Portsmouth, NH: Heinemann.

Clay, M. M. (1994). Report of meeting on Reading Recovery implementation in North Carolina.

Clay, M. M. (1996). Is Reading Recovery aligned with a specific approach? *Council Connections, 2*(1), 1.

Clay, M. M. (1997). International perspectives on the Reading Recovery program. In J. Flood, S. B. Heath, & D. Lapp (Eds.), *Handbook of research on teaching literacy through the communicative and visual arts* (pp. 655–667). New York: Macmillan Library Reference USA (a project of the International Reading Association).

Clay, M. M. (1998). *By different paths to common outcomes*. York, ME: Stenhouse.

Clay, M. M. (2000). *Running records for classroom teachers*. Auckland, New Zealand: Heinemann.

Clay, M. M. (2001). *Change over time in children's literacy achievement*. Portsmouth, NH: Heinemann.

Clay, M. M. (2002). *An observation survey of early literacy achievement* (2nd ed.). Portsmouth, NH: Heinemann.

Clay, M. M. (2003a). Afterword. In S. Forbes & C. Briggs (Eds.), *Research in Reading Recovery, volume two* (pp. 297–303). Portsmouth, NH: Heinemann.

Clay, M. M. (2003b). *Le sondage d'observation en lecture-ecriture*. Toronto, Canada: Les Editions de la Cheneliere.

Clay, M. M. (2004). Simply by sailing in a new direction you could change the world. In C. M. Fairbanks, J. Worthy, B. Maloch, J. V. Hoffman, & D. L. Schallert (Eds.), *Fifty-third yearbook of the National Reading Conference* (pp. 60–66). Oak Creek, WI: National Reading Conference.

Clay, M. M. (2005). Stirring the waters yet again. *The Journal of Reading Recovery, (4)*3, 1–10.

Clay, M. M. (n.d.). *An information paper on implementing Reading Recovery in an education system.*

Clay, M. M., Gill, M., Glenn, T., McNaughton, T., & Salmon, K. (1983). *Record of oral language: Biks and gutches.* Portsmouth, NH: Heinemann.

Clay, M. M., & Tuck, B. (1991). *A study of Reading Recovery subgroups: Including outcomes for children who did not satisfy discontinuing criteria.* Report on research funded by the Ministry of Education, Auckland, New Zealand. (Shorter version in M. M. Clay [1993] *Reading Recovery: A guidebook for teachers in training.* Portsmouth, NH: Heinemann, pp. 86–95.)

Clay, M. M., & Watson, B. (1982). An inservice program for Reading Recovery teachers. In M. M. Clay (Ed.), *Observing young readers* (pp. 192–200). Portsmouth, NH: Heinemann.

Cohen, S. G., McDonnell, G., & Osborn, B. (1989). Self-perceptions of at risk and high achieving readers: Beyond Reading Recovery achievement data. In S. McCormick & J. Zutell (Eds.), *Cognitive and social perspectives for literacy research and instruction: Thirty-eighth yearbook of the National Reading Conference* (pp. 117–122). Chicago, IL: National Reading Conference.

Coles, G. (1987). *The learning mystique: A critical look at learning disabilities.* New York: Fawcett Columbine.

Coles, G. (1998). *Reading lessons: The debate over literacy.* New York: Hill and Wang.

Combs, M. (1994). Implementing a holistic reading series in first grade: Experiences with a conversation group. *Reading Horizons, 34*(3), 196–207.

Costa, A. L., & Garmston, R. (1994). *Cognitive coaching.* Norwood, MA: Christopher-Gordon.

Cox, B. E., Fang, Z., & Schmitt, M. C. (1998). At risk children's metacognitive growth during Reading Recovery experience: A Vygotskian interpretation. *Literacy Teaching and Learning: An International Journal of Early Reading and Writing, 3*(1), 55–76.

Crevola, C. A., & Hill, P. W. (1998). Initial evaluation of a whole-school approach to prevention and intervention in early literacy. *Journal of Education for Students Placed at Risk, 3*(2), 133–157.

Cunningham, P. M., & Allington, R. L. (1994). *Classrooms that work.* New York: HarperCollins.

D'Agostino, J. V., & Murphy, J. A. (2004). A meta-analysis of Reading Recovery in United States schools. *Educational Evaluation and Policy Analysis, 26*(1), 23–38.

Darling-Hammond, L. (1996). What matters most: A competent teacher for every child. *Phi Delta Kappan, 78,* 193–200.

Darling-Hammond, L., & McLaughlin, M. W. (1995). Policies that support professional development in an era of reform. *Phi Delta Kappan, 76,* 597–604.

DeFord, D. E. (1994). Early writing: Teachers and children in Reading Recovery. *Literacy, Teaching and Learning: An International Journal of Early Literacy, 1,* 31–57.

DeFord, D. E., Pinnell, G. S., Lyons, C. A., & Place, A. W. (1990). *The Reading Recovery follow-up study* (Technical Report Vol. 111). Columbus, OH: The Ohio State Univesity.

Dorn, L. (1996). A Vygotskian perspective on literacy acquisition: Talk and action in the child's construction of literate awareness. *Literacy, Teaching and Learning: An International Journal of Early Literacy, 2*(2), 15–40.

Dorn, L., & Allen, A. (1995). Helping low-achieving first-grade readers: A program combining Reading Recovery tutoring and small-group instruction. *ERS Spectrum: Journal of School Research and Information, 13*(3), 16–24. Reprinted (1996) in *Literacy, Teaching and Learning: An International Journal of Early Literacy, 2*(1), 49–60.

Doyle, M. A. (2000). *Reading Recovery in North America: An illustrated history.* Columbus, OH: Reading Recovery Council of North America.

Duckworth, E. (1996). *The having of wonderful ideas and other essays on teaching and learning* (2nd ed.). New York: Teachers College Press.

Elbaum, B., Vaughn, S., Hughes, M. T., & Moody, S. W. (2000). How effective are one-to-one tutoring programs in reading for elementary students at risk for reading failure? A meta-analysis of the intervention research. *Journal of Educational Psychology, 92*(4), 605–619.

Elliott, C. B. (1996). Pedagogical reasoning: Understanding teacher decision making in a cognitive apprenticeship setting. *Literacy, Teaching and Learning: An International Journal of Early Literacy, 2*(2), 75–91.

Escamilla, K. (1992). *Descubriendo la Lectura: An application of Reading Recovery in Spanish.* Report for the Office of Educational Research and Improvement (OERI). Washington D.C.

Escamilla, K. (1994). Descubriendo la Lectura: An early intervention literacy program in Spanish. *Literacy, Teaching and Learning: An International Journal of Early Literacy, 1*(1), 57–70.

Escamilla, K., Andrade, A. M., Basurto, A. G. M., Ruiz, O. A., & Clay, M. M. (1996). *Instrumento de observación de los logros de la lecto-escritura inicial*. Portsmouth, NH: Heinemann.

Escamilla, K., Loera, M., Ruiz, O., & Rodríguez, Y. (1998). An examination of sustaining effects in Descubriendo la Lectura programs. *Literacy Teaching and Learning: An International Journal of Early Reading and Writing, 3*(2), 59–81.

Feinstein, A. R. (1977). *Clinical biostatistics*. St. Louis, MO: Mosby.

Ferrerio, E., & Teberosky, A. (1982). *Literacy before schooling*. Portsmouth, NH: Heinemann.

Fitzsimmons, S. J., Cheever, J., Leonard, E., & Macunovich, D. (1969). School failures: Now and tomorrow. *Developmental Psychology, 1*, 134–147.

Flood, J., Heath, S. B., & Lapp, D. (1997). *Handbook of research on teaching literacy through the communicative and visual arts*. New York: Simon and Schuster Macmillan.

Fountas, I. C., & Pinnell, G. S. (1996). *Guided reading: Good first teaching for all children*. Portsmouth, NH: Heinemann.

Frasier, D. (1991). *A study of strategy use by two emergent readers in a one-to-one tutorial setting*. Unpublished doctoral dissertation, The Ohio State University, Columbus.

Frymier, J., Barber, L., Gansneder, B., & Robertson, N. (1989). Simultaneous replication: A technique for large-scale research. *Phi Delta Kappan, 71*, 228–231.

Fullan, M. G. (1985). Change processes and strategies at the local level. *The Elementary School Journal, 85*, 391–421.

Fullan, M. G. (1991). *The new meaning of educational change*. New York: Teachers College Press.

Fullan, M. G., & Miles, M. B. (1992). Getting reform right: What works and what doesn't. *Phi Delta Kappan, 73*, 744–752.

Fullerton, S. K. (2001) Achieving motivation: Guiding Edward's journey to literacy. *Literacy Teaching and Learning: An International Journal of Early Reading and Writing, 6*, 43–71. Reprinted (2003) in S. Forbes & C. Briggs (Eds.), *Research in Reading Recovery, volume two, 6*, 43–67.

Gaffney, J. S. (1994). Reading Recovery: Widening the scope of prevention for children at risk of reading failure. In K. D. Wood & B. Algozzine (Eds.), *Teaching reading to high-risk learners* (pp. 231–246). Boston, MA: Allyn and Bacon.

Gaffney, J. S., & Anderson, R. C. (1991). Two-tiered scaffolding: Congruent processes of teaching and learning. In E. H. Hiebert (Ed.), *Literacy for a diverse society* (pp. 184–198). New York: Teachers College Press.

Gaffney, J. S., & Askew, B. J. (1999). *Stirring the waters: The influence of Marie Clay*. Portsmouth, NH: Heinemann.

Geekie, P. (1992). Reading Recovery: It's not what you do, it's the way that you do it. In M. Jones & B. Jones (Eds.), *Learning to behave: Curriculum and whole school management approaches to discipline* (pp. 170–188). London, United Kingdom: Kegan Paul.

Gómez-Bellengé, F. X. (2002a). External validation shows that Reading Recovery works. *The Journal of Reading Recovery, 2*(1), 55–56.

Gómez-Bellengé, F. (2002b). Measuring the cost of Reading Recovery: A practical approach. *The Journal of Reading Recovery, 2*(1), 47–54.

Gómez-Bellengé, F. X., Rodgers, E., & Fullerton, S. K. (2003a). *Reading Recovery and Descubriendo la Lectura national report 2001–2002*. National Data Evaluation Center Technical Report. Columbus, OH: The Ohio State University.

Gómez-Bellengé, F. X., Rodgers, E. M., & Fullerton, S. K. (2003b). *Reading Recovery in Ohio: 2001–2002 state report*. Columbus, OH: National Data Evaluation Center.

Gómez-Bellengé, F. X., Rodgers, E., & Wang, C. (2004, February). *Gauging the effectiveness of an early intervention: The case of Reading Recovery*. Paper presented at the annual meeting of the National Title I Conference, New Orleans, LA.

Gómez-Bellengé, F., & Thompson, J. (2002). Outcomes assessment for first-round Reading Recovery students. Columbus, OH: National Data Evaluation Center.

Halliday, M. A. K. (1975). *Learning how to mean: Exploration in the development of language*. London, United Kingdom: Arnold.

Hargreaves, A. (1994). *Changing teachers, changing times: Teachers' work and culture in the postmodern age*. New York: Teachers College Press.

Harrison, L. (2002). *A study on the complementary effects of Reading Recovery and small group instruction for reversing reading failure* (Research Summary No. 102–03 Research in Literacy and Teacher Development). Little Rock, AR: University of Arkansas at Little Rock.

Heath, S. B. (1983). *Ways with words: Language, life, and work in communities and classrooms*. New York: Cambridge University Press.

Herman, R., & Stringfield, S. (1997). *Ten promising programs for educating all children: Evidence of impact*. Arlington, VA: Educational Research Service.

Hiebert, E. (1994). Reading Recovery in the United States: What difference does it make to an age cohort? *Educational Researcher, 23*(9), 15–25.

Hiebert, E. H., & Taylor, B. M. (Eds.). (1994). *Getting reading right from the start: Effective early literacy intervention*. Boston, MA: Allyn and Bacon.

Hobsbaum, A., Peters, S., & Sylva, K. (1996). Scaffolding in Reading Recovery. *Oxford Review of Education, 22*(1), 17–35.

Holmes, J. A. (1960). The substrata factor theory of reading: Some experimental evidence. In the proceedings of the fifth annual conference of the international reading association new frontiers in reading. Reprinted (1970) in H. Singer & R. B. Ruddell (Eds.), *Theoretical models and processes of reading* (pp. 187–197). Newark, DE: International Reading Association.

Huberman, A. M., & Miles, M. B. (1982). *Innovations up close: A field study in twelve school settings.* Andover, MA: The Network.

Hummel-Rossi, B., & Ashdown, J. (2002). The state of cost-benefit and cost-effectiveness analyses in education. *Review of Educational Research, 72*(1), 1–30.

Hurry, J. (2000). *Intervention strategies to support pupils with difficulties in literacy during key stage 1: Review of research.* London, United Kingdom: Institute of Education, University of London.

Institute of Education Sciences (2003). *Identifying and implementing educational practices supported by rigorous evidence: A user friendly guide.* Washington, DC: U.S. Department of Education.

Invernizzi, M. A. (2001). The complex world of one-on-one tutoring. In S. B. Neuman & D. K. Dickinson, (Eds.), *Handbook of early literacy research* (pp. 459–470). New York: Guilford Press.

Iversen, S. (1997). *Reading Recovery as a small group intervention.* Unpublished doctoral dissertation, Massey University, Palmerston North, New Zealand.

Iversen, S., & Tunmer, W. (1993). Phonological processing skills and the Reading Recovery program. *Journal of Educational Psychology, 85*(1), 112–126.

Johnson, R. L., & Young-Hubbard, J. E. (2003). An evaluation of *An Observation Survey of Early Literacy Achievement. The Journal of Reading Recovery, 2*(2), 41–48.

Johnston, P. H. (1997). *Knowing literacy.* York, ME: Stenhouse Press.

Johnston, P. H. (2000). *Running records: A self-tutoring guide.* York, ME: Stenhouse.

Johnston, P. H. (2002). The interactive strategies approach to reading intervention [Commentary]. *Contemporary Educational Psychology, 27*, 636–647.

Johnston, P. H., & Allington, R. (1991). Remediation. In R. Barr, M. Kamil, P. Mosenthal, & P. D. Pearson (Eds.), *Handbook of reading research vol. 11.* (pp. 984–1012). New York: Longman.

Jones, N. (2001). A decision-making model of Reading Recovery teaching: Figuring out what to do when. *Running Record, 13*(2), 1–5.

Jones, N. K., & Smith-Burke, M. T. (1999). Forging an interactive relationship among research, theory, and practice: Clay's research design and methodology. In J. S. Gaffney & B. J. Askew (Eds.), *Stirring the waters: The influence of Marie Clay* (pp. 261–285). Portsmouth, NH: Heinemann.

Juel, C. (1988). Learning to read and write: A longitudinal study of 54 children from first through fourth grades. *Journal of Educational Psychology, 80*(4), 437–447.

Kaye, E. L. (2002). *Variety, complexity, and change in reading behaviors of second-grade students.* Unpublished doctoral dissertation, Texas Woman's University, Denton.

Kelly, P. R. (2001). Working with English language learners: The case of Danya. *The Journal of Reading Recovery, 1*(1), 1–10.

Kennedy, M. M., Birman, B. F., & Demaline, R. E. (1986). *The effectiveness of Chapter 1 services*, Washington, DC: Office of Educational Research and Improvement, U.S. Department of Education.

Kohn, A. (2004). Test today, privatize tomorrow: Using accountability to 'reform' public schools to death. *Phi Delta Kappan, 85*, 568–577.

Kratochwill, T. R. (1978). *Single subject research: Strategies for evaluating change.* New York: Academic Press.

Lederhouse, J. N. (2003). The power of one-on-one. *Educational Leadership, 60*(7), 69–71.

Leslie, L., & Allen, L. (1999). Factors that predict success in an early literacy intervention project. *Reading Research Quarterly, 34*(4), 404–424.

Levin, H. (1989). Financing the education of at-risk students. *Educational Evaluation and Policy Analysis, 11*, 47–60.

Levine, M. (2002). *A mind at a time.* New York: Simon and Schuster.

Lorion, R. P. (1983). Evaluating preventive interventions: Guidelines for the serious social change agent. In R. D. Felner, L. A. Jason, J. N. Moritsugu, & S. Farber (Eds.), *Preventive psychology: Theory, research and practice* (pp. 251–268). New York: Pergamon Press.

Lyons, C. A. (1991). A comparative study of the teaching effectiveness of teachers participating in a year-long and two-week inservice program. In J. Zutell & S. McCormick (Eds.), *Learning factors/teacher factors: Issues in literacy research and instruction. Fortieth yearbook of the National Reading Conference* (pp. 367–375). Chicago, IL: National Reading Conference.

Lyons, C. A. (1993). The use of questions in the teaching of high risk beginning readers: A profile of a developing Reading Recovery teacher. *Reading and Writing Quarterly, 29*, 1–42.

Lyons, C. A. (1994). Constructing chains of reasoning in Reading Recovery demonstration lessons. In C. K. Kinzer & D. J. Leu (Eds.), *Multidimensional aspects of literacy research, theory and practice. Forty-third yearbook of the National Reading Conference* (pp. 276–286). Chicago, IL: National Reading Conference.

Lyons, C. A. (1998). Reading Recovery in the United States: More than a decade of data. *Literacy Teaching and Learning: An International Journal of Early Reading and Writing, 3*(1), 77–92. Reprinted (2003) in S. Forbes & C. Briggs (Eds.), *Research in Reading Recovery, volume two* (pp. 215–230). Portsmouth, NH: Heinemann.

Lyons, C. A. (2003). *Teaching struggling readers: How to use brain-based research to maximize learning.* Portsmouth, NH: Heinemann.

Lyons, C. A., & Beaver, J. (1995). Reducing retention and learning disability placement through Reading Recovery: An educationally sound cost-effective choice. In R. L. Allington & S. A. Walmsley (Eds.), *No quick fix: Redesigning literacy programs in America's elementary schools* (pp. 116–136). New York: Teachers College Press and the International Reading Association.

Lyons, C. A., & Pinnell, G. S. (2001). *Systems for change in literacy education: A guide to professional development.* Portsmouth, NH: Heinemann.

Lyons, C. A., Pinnell, G. S., & DeFord, D. E. (1993). *Partners in learning: Teachers and children in Reading Recovery.* New York: Teachers College Press.

Lyons, C. A., Pinnell, G. S., McCarrier, A., Young, P., & DeFord D. E. (1988). *The Ohio Reading Recovery project: Vol. X, State of Ohio, 1987–88.* Columbus, OH: The Ohio State University.

Marvin, C. A., & Gaffney, J. S. (1999). The effects of Reading Recovery on children's home literacy experiences. *Literacy Teaching and Learning: An International Journal of Early Reading and Writing, 4*(2), 51–80. Reprinted (2003) in S. Forbes & C. Briggs (Eds.), *Research in Reading Recovery, volume two* (pp. 231–256). Portsmouth, NH: Heinemann.

McGill-Franzen, A. (1994). Compensatory and special education: Is there accountability for learning and belief in children's potential? In E. Heibert & B. Taylor (Eds.), *Getting reading right from the start: Effective early literacy interventions* (pp. 13–35). Boston, MA: Allyn and Bacon.

Moore, P. (1997, Fall). Models of teacher education: Where Reading Recovery teacher training fits. *Network News,* 1–4.

National Institute of Child Health and Human Development (2000a). *Report of the National Reading Panel. Teaching children to read: An evidence-based assessment of the scientific research literature on reading and its implications for reading instruction* (NIH Publication No. 00–4769). Washington, DC: U.S. Government Printing Office.

National Institute of Child Health and Human Development (2000b). *Report of the National Reading Panel. Teaching children to read: An evidence-based assessment of the scientific research literature on reading and its implications for reading instruction: Report of the subgroups* (NIH Publication No. 00–4754). Washington, DC: U.S. Government Printing Office.

Neal, J., & Kelly, P. (1999). The success of Reading Recovery for English language learners and Descubriendo la Lectura for bilingual students in California. *Literacy Teaching and Learning: An International Journal of Early Reading and Writing, 4*(2), 81–108. Reprinted (2003) in S. Forbes & C. Briggs (Eds.), *Research in Reading Recovery, volume two* (pp. 257–280). Portsmouth, NH: Heinemann.

Neill, D. M. (2003). Transforming student assessment. *Phi Delta Kappan, 85,* 225–228.

Nesselroade, J. R., & Baltes, P. B. (1974). Sequential strategies and the role of cohort effects in behavioral development: Adolescent personality (1970–1972) as a sample case. In S. A. Mednick, M. Harway, & K. M. Finello (Eds.), *Handbook of longitudinal research* (pp. 55–87). New York: Praeger.

Neufeld, B., & Roper, D. (2003). *Coaching: A strategy for developing instructional capacity: Promises and practicalities.* Washington, DC: The Aspen Institute.

O'Connor, E. A., & Simic, O. (2002). The effect of Reading Recovery on special education referrals and placements. *Psychology in the Schools, 39*(6), 635–646.

Office for Standards in Education. (1993). *Reading Recovery in New Zealand: A report from the Office of Her Majesty's Chief Inspector of Schools.* London: HMSO. Reprinted (1994) in *Literacy, Teaching and Learning: An International Journal of Early Literacy, 1,* 143–162.

Page, E. B., & Grandon, G. M. (1981). Massive intervention and child intelligence: The Milwaukee project in critical perspective. *Journal of Special Education, 15,* 239–256.

Piaget, J. (1973). *The language and thought of the child.* New York: World.

Pianta, R. C. (1990). Widening the debate on educational reform: Prevention as a viable alternative. *Exceptional Children, 56*(4), 306–313.

Pikulski, J. J. (1994). Preventing reading failure: A review of five effective programs. *The Reading Teacher, 48*(1), 30–39.

Pinnell, G. S. (1989). Reading Recovery: Helping at risk children learn to read. *Elementary School Journal, 90*(2), 161–184.

Pinnell, G. S. (1994). An inquiry-based model for educating teachers of literacy. *Literacy, Teaching and Learning: A International Journal of Early Literacy, 1,* 29–42.

Pinnell, G. S. (1997). Reading Recovery: A summary of research. In J. Flood, S. B. Heath, & D. Lapp (Eds.), *Research on teaching literacy through the communicative and visual arts* (pp. 638–654). New York: MacMillan Library Reference USA (a project of the International Reading Association).

Pinnell, G. S., Lyons, C. A., DeFord, D. E., Bryk, A. S., & Seltzer, M. (1994). Comparing instructional models for the literacy education of high risk first graders. *Reading Research Quarterly, 29*(1), 8–39.

Plewis, I. (2000). Evaluating educational interventions using multilevel growth curves: The case of Reading Recovery. *Educational Research and Evaluation, 6*(1), 83–101.

Plewis, I., & Hurry, J. (1998). A multilevel perspective on the design and analysis of intervention studies. *Educational Research and Evaluation, 4*(1), 13–26.

Power, J., & Sawkins, S. (1991). *Changing lives: Report of the implementation of the Reading Recovery program on the North Coast.* Lismore, New South Wales, Australia: University of New England-Northern Rivers.

Principal's guide to Reading Recovery. (2002). Columbus, OH: Reading Recovery Council of North America.

Quay, L. C., Steele, D. C., Johnson, C. I., & Hortman, W. (2001). Children's achievement and personal and social development in a first-year Reading Recovery program with teachers in training. *Literacy Teaching and Learning: An International Journal of Early Reading and Writing, 5*(2), 7–26. Reprinted (2003) in S. Forbes & C. Briggs (Eds.), *Research in Reading Recovery, volume two* (pp. 281–296). Portsmouth, NH: Heinemann.

Rasch, G. (1960). *Probabilistic models for some intelligence and attainment tests.* Copenhagen: Danish Institute for Educational Research. Chicago, IL: University of Chicago Press.

Roderick, M. (1994). Grade retention and school dropout: Investigation of the association. *American Educational Research Journal, 31*(4), 35–45.

Rodgers, E. (2000). Language matters: When is a scaffold really a scaffold? In T. Shanahan & F. Rodriguez-Brown (Eds.), *Forty-ninth yearbook of the National Reading Conference* (pp. 78–90). Chicago, IL: National Reading Conference.

Rodgers, E. M., Fullerton, S. K., & DeFord, D. E. (2002). Making a difference with professional development. In E. M. Rodgers & G. S. Pinnell (Eds.), *Learning from teaching in literacy education: New perspectives on professional development* (pp. 119–134). Portsmouth, NH: Heinemann.

Rodgers, E. M., & Gómez-Bellengé, F. X. (2003). Closing the achievement gap in Ohio with Reading Recovery. *The Journal of Reading Recovery, 3*(1), 65–74.

Rodgers, E., Wang, C., & Gómez-Bellengé, F. (2004, April). *Closing the literacy achievement gap with early literacy intervention.* Paper presented at the American Educational Research Association's meeting in San Diego, CA.

Rowe, K. J. (1995). Factors affecting students' progress in reading: Key findings from a longitudinal study. *Literacy, Teaching and Learning: An International Journal of Early Literacy, 1*(2), 57–110.

Ruhe, V., & Moore, P. (2005, Winter). The impact of Reading Recovery on later achievement in reading and writing. *ERS Spectrum, (23)*1, 20–30.

Rumbaugh, W. (2002). Teacher supervision: Lessons from Reading Recovery. *Streamlined Seminar: National Association of Elementary School Principals, 20*(3), 1–2.

Rumbaugh, W., & Brown, C. (2000). The impact of Reading Recovery participation on student's self-concepts. *Reading Psychology, 21*, 13–30.

Rumelhart, D. E. (1994). Toward an interactive model of reading. In R. B. Ruddell, M. R. Ruddell, & H. Singer (Eds.), *Theoretical models and processes of reading*, (4th ed., pp. 864–894). Newark, DE: International Reading Association.

Sarason, S. B. (1991). *The predictable failure of education reform: Can we change course before it's too late?* San Francisco, CA: Jossey-Bass.

Scanlon, D. M., & Vellutino, F. R. (1996). Prerequisite skills, early instruction, and success in first-grade reading: Selected results from a longitudinal study. *Mental Retardation and Developmental Research Reviews, 2*, 54–63.

Scherer, M. (Ed.). (2004). Closing Achievement GAPS [Special issue]. *Educational Leadership, 62*(3).

Schmitt, M. C. (2001). The development of children's strategic processing in Reading Recovery. *Reading Psychology, 22*, 129–151.

Schmitt, M. C. (2003). Metacognitive strategy knowledge: Comparison of former Reading Recovery children and their classmates. *Literacy Teaching and Learning: An International Journal of Early Reading and Writing, 7*(1–2), 57–76.

Schmitt, M. C., & Gregory, A. E. (in press). The impact of an early literacy intervention: Where are the children now? *Literacy Teaching and Learning: An International Journal of Early Reading and Writing*.

Schwartz, R. M. (in press). Literacy learning of at-risk first grade students in the Reading Recovery early intervention. *Journal of Educational Psychology*.

Shanahan, T., & Barr, R. (1995). Reading Recovery: An independent evaluation of the effects of an early instructional intervention for at-risk learners. *Reading Research Quarterly, 30*(4) 958–996.

Shanahan, T., & Neuman, S. (1997). Conversations: Literacy research that makes a difference. *Reading Research Quarterly, 33*(2), 202–210.

Shannon, D. (1990). *A descriptive study of verbal challenge and teacher response to verbal challenge in Reading Recovery teacher training*. Unpublished doctoral dissertation. Texas Woman's University, Denton.

Shepard, L. (1991). Negative policies for dealing with diversity: When does assessment and diagnosis turn into sorting and segregation? In E. Hiebert (Ed.), *Literacy for a diverse society: Perspectives, practices, and policies* (pp. 279–298). New York: Teachers College Press.

Shepard, L. A., & Smith, M. L. (1990). Synthesis of research on grade retention. *Educational Leadership, 47,* 84–88.

Singer, H. (1994). The substrata-factor theory of reading. In R. B. Ruddell, M. R. Ruddell, & H. Singer (Eds.), *Theoretical models and processes of reading* (4th ed., pp. 895–927). Newark, DE: International Reading Association.

Slavin, R. E., Karweit, N. L., & Madden, N. A. (1989). *Effective programs for students at risk.* Boston, MA: Allyn and Bacon.

Slavin, R. E., Karweit, N. L., & Wasik, B. A. (1992). Preventing early school failure: What works? *Educational Leadership, 50,* 10–19.

Slavin, R. E., Madden, N. A., Karweit, N. L., Livermon, B., & Dolan, L. (1990). Success for All: First year outcomes of a comprehensive plan for reforming urban education. *American Education Research Journal, 27,* 255–278.

Snow, C. E., Burns, M. S., & Griffin, P. (1998). *Preventing reading difficulties in young children.* Washington, DC: National Academy Press.

Stahl, K. A. D., Stahl, S., & McKenna, M. C. (1999). The development of phonological awareness and orthographic processing in Reading Recovery. *Literacy Teaching and Learning: An International Journal of Early Reading and Writing, 4*(1), 27–42.

Standards and guidelines of Reading Recovery in the United States (4th ed. rev.). (2004). Columbus, OH: Reading Recovery Council of North America.

Stanovich, K. E. (1986). Matthew effects in reading: Some consequences of individual differences in the acquisition of literacy. *Reading Research Quarterly, 21,* 360–406.

Starrat, R. J. (2003). Opportunity to learn and the accountability agenda. *Phi Delta Kappan, 85,* 298–304.

Sylva, K., & Hurry, J. (1995). Early intervention in children with reading difficulties: An evaluation of Reading Recovery and a phonological training. *Literacy, Teaching and Learning: An International Journal of Early Literacy, 2*(2), 49–68.

Taylor, B. M., Strait, J., & Medo, M. (1994). Early intervention in reading: Supplemental instruction for groups of low-achieving students provided by first-grade teachers. In E. H. Hiebert & B. M. Taylor (Eds.), *Getting reading right from the start: Effective early literacy interventions* (pp. 107–121). Boston: Allyn and Bacon.

Teale, W. H., & Sulzby, E. (1986). *Emergent literacy: Writing and reading.* Norwood, NJ: Ablex.

Thorndike, E. L. (1904). *An introduction to the theory of mental and social measurement.* New York: Teachers College, Columbia University.

Thurstone, L. L. (1925). A method of scaling psychological and educational data. *Journal of Educational Psychology, 15,* 433–451.

Vellutino F. R., & Scanlon, D. M. (2002). The interactive strategies approach to reading intervention. *Contemporary Educational Psychology, 27,* 573–635.

Vellutino, F. R., Scanlon, D. M., Sipay, E. R., Small, S. G., Chen, R., Pratt, A., & Denckla, M. B. (1996). Cognitive profiles of difficult to remediate and readily remediated poor readers: Early intervention as a vehicle for distinguishing between cognitive and experiential deficits as basic causes of specific reading disability. *Journal of Educational Psychology, 88*(4), 601–638.

Walberg, H. J., & Reynolds, A. J. (1997). Longitudinal evaluation of program effectiveness. In B. Spodek & O. N. Saracho (Eds.), *Issues in early childhood educational assessment and evaluation* (pp. 28–47). New York: Teachers College Press.

Walmsley, S. A., & Allington, R. L. (1995). Redefining and reforming instructional support programs for at-risk students. In R. L. Allington & S. A. Walmsley (Eds.), *No quick fix: Rethinking literacy programs in America's elementary schools* (pp. 19–44). New York: Teachers College Press.

Wasik, B. A., & Slavin, R. E. (1993). Preventing early reading failure with one-to-one tutoring: A review of five programs. *Reading Research Quarterly, 28*(2), 179–200.

Wells, G. (1981). *Learning through interaction: The study of language development.* Cambridge, United Kingdom: Cambridge University Press.

Wilson, K., & Daviss, B. (1994). *Redesigning education.* New York: Henry Holt.

Wong, S. D., Groth, L. A., & O'Flahavan, J. F. (1994). Characterizing teacher-student interaction in Reading Recovery lessons (National Reading Research Center Report No. 17). Universities of Georgia and Maryland.

Woolsey, D. P. (1991). Changing contexts for literacy learning: The impact of Reading Recovery on one first-grade teacher. In D. E. DeFord, C. A. Lyons, & G. S. Pinnell (Eds.), *Bridges to literacy: Learning from Reading Recovery* (pp. 189–203). Portsmouth, NH: Heinemann.

Wright, B. D., & Linacre, J. M. (1989). *Observations are always ordinal; measurements, however, must be interval.* MESA Research Memorandum Number 44, MESA Psychometric Laboratory.

Wright, B. D., Linacre, J. M., & Schulz, M. (1989). *BIGSCALE rasch analysis computer program.* Chicago, IL: MESA Press.

INDEX OF KEY TERMS